Understanding art in

The primary school curriculum now involves children in the study of art as well as in making art. Even the youngest are expected to develop understanding of the variety of art, craft and design from different times and places; to be able to recognise and respond to the ideas, methods and approaches used by artists working in different styles and traditions; and to use their knowledge and responses as sources in making their own art.

How that will be achieved is left to teachers who have, for the most part, not studied art themselves. They need, then, to develop ways of teaching for understanding, through the use of art both from their locality and from other cultures, both past and present.

This collection describes how these requirements have been tackled by teachers and responded to by pupils. It brings together the voices of young children, and the ideas and practices of their teachers. The Robert and Lisa Sainsbury collection provides the focus for their encounters with art objects; their classrooms provide the focus for practical art. Both are the subject of action research. The resulting stories offer a wealth of first-hand evidence and practical experience from which student teachers, teachers, parents, and art educators will benefit.

As an artist, teacher, curriculum developer, teacher educator and educational researcher, **Les Tickle** has devoted over thirty years to improving the quality of pupils' and teachers' experiences of schooling. He is currently a Senior Lecturer in Education at the University of East Anglia and is the author of a number of books on education.

Frontispiece Drawing of *Little Dancer* by Natasha Baker, aged 6, from Mundesley First School, Norfolk

Understanding art
art in primary schools

Cases from teachers' research

Edited by
Les Tickle

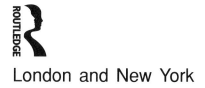

London and New York

First published 1996
by Routledge
11 New Fetter Lane, London EC4P 4EE

Simultaneously published in the USA and Canada
by Routledge
29 West 35th Street, New York, NY 10001

© 1996 Selection and editorial matter Les Tickle;
individual chapters © their contributors

Typeset in Times by Florencetype Ltd,
Stoodleigh, Devon

Printed and bound in Great Britain by
Redwood Books, Trowbridge, Wiltshire

British Library Cataloguing in Publication Data
A catalogue record for this book is available from the British Library

Library of Congress Cataloguing in Publication Data
A catalogue record for this book has been requested

ISBN 0-415-13031-X

Contents

Plates

Figures and table

Contributors

Jane Ackers was teaching part-time at Gayton First School, King's Lynn during the period of research.

Sue Allen is a teacher of children with special educational needs at The Warren School, Oulton Broad, Suffolk. The work reported in this book was carried out while teaching at a Great Yarmouth Middle School.

Rex Barker teaches at Blackdale Middle School, Norwich, where the research was also done.

Linda Cadmore is deputy headteacher at Peterhouse First School, Gorleston, Norfolk.

Maggie Croft is a teacher at Elm Tree Primary School in Lowestoft.

Sue Feather is a teacher of children with special educational needs at South Lee School in Bury St Edmunds, Suffolk.

Helen Grogutt now teaches at Alpington Primary School, Norfolk. Her research was carried out while teaching in a first school.

Alex Henderson carried out her research with her class at Hethersett Middle School, Norwich.

Jennifer Ladusans teaches at Meadow Primary School, Lowestoft.

Pauline Orsgood is deputy headteacher at Great Dunham Primary School, Norfolk.

Rachel Reed was a teacher at Halesworth Middle School, Suffolk, when she carried out the research. She now lives in South Africa.

Les Tickle is a senior lecturer at the University of East Anglia.

Jeny Walding is deputy headteacher at Mundesley First School, Norfolk.

Acknowledgements

I am deeply indebted to my colleague Dr Veronica Sekules, Education Officer of the Sainsbury Centre for Visual Arts, for the partnership which lies behind this and numerous other products of our work. In our endeavours to enhance understanding of art we have had the support of the Trustees of the Sainsbury Centre for Visual Arts, the Sainsbury Centre Board, Derek Gillman the Keeper, Kate Carreno the Centre Administrator and many other administrative, security, and support staff, the Friends Association, and the SCVA Guides. To name every-one individually would create a very long list, but all have my sincere thanks.

There would be other lists, of my colleagues at UEA Norwich, in the School of Education and Professional Development, the School of World Art Studies, and the Sainsbury Research Unit for the Arts of Africa, Oceania and the Americas. An inter-departmental and inter-disciplinary venture engages the time, expertise and skills of many, and my gratitude to them all is heartfelt. The venture has been helped by the support given across the University to the work of the Centre for Applied Research in Visual Arts Education.

All of the potentials of the University's contributions to the art educa-tion of primary school teachers and their children might have come to nothing were it not for the Norwich office of the international firm of Sedgwick, in particular its Public Relations Manager Debbie Hilton, Chief Executive Chris Williams, and directors Steve Davidson, Guy Realf and David Boag. Their enthusiasm and encouragement for a project which has so far brought over 1,500 children into the University, guided by their teachers, parents, and many other adult supporters, has been outstanding. Provision of teacher scholarships and funding to produce curriculum resource materials has created a fruitful partnership between business and education. Sedgwick is an award winner under the Business Sponsorship Incentive Scheme for its support of this work, and I am grateful to the Association of Business Sponsorship of the Arts for its b.s.i.s. award, which helped to provide curriculum resources.

The partnership has succeeded most of all because of the enthusiastic response of teachers who applied for and were granted the scholarships, and the children who have invested their energies into the study of original works of art. Some of the teachers and children are the main contributors to the book, and it is because of their commitment that some aspects of the work has been made available for others to read. These are selections from many, and everyone who has participated in the work so far is due the same level of gratitude.

I have been greatly encouraged by the support shown by Leilani Lattin Duke, Director of the Getty Center for Education in the Arts, who has kept me informed of developments in the United States. We would like to thank the Sainsbury Centre for Visual Arts at the University of East Anglia for giving its permission to reproduce much of the artwork in the book, and for providing us with James Austin's photographs for reproduction. The pieces from the Centre all come from the Robert and Lisa Sainsbury Collection. We are especially grateful to Kate Carreno and Kay Poludniowski for all their work in this respect.

We should also like to thank the following:

Alan Howard for allowing us to use the photograph on page 6.

Anthony Green RA and The Piccadilly Gallery of 16 Cork Street, London W1X 1PF, for permission to reproduce *My Mother Alone in Her Dining Room* and *The Bathroom at 29*. These appear in the colour plate section of this book.

John Davies and Marlborough Fine Art (London) Ltd for permission to reproduce *Bucket Man* 1974 in the colour plate section.

DACS for permission to reproduce *Femme* 1958 by Alberto Giacometti, © ADAGP, Paris and DACS, London 1996, on page 40.

The Henry Moore Foundation of Dane Tree House, Perry Green, Much Hadham, Hertfordshire SG10 6EE for permission to reproduce Henry Moore's *Mother and Child*, 1932 on page 41, *Draped Reclining Figure*, 1957–8 on page 91 and *Two-piece Reclining Figure No. 3*, 1961 on page 91.

Tate Publishing, Millbank, London SW1P 4RG for allowing us to use and providing us with a photograph of Henry Moore's *Two-piece Reclining Figure No. 3*, 1961 on page 91.

Eastern Counties Press and Dennis Whitehead for permission to reproduce the pictures on pages 100 and 107.

We should also like to thank all the teachers and children who have let us share their photographs and artwork in this book.

Chapter 1

Visual art and teacher research in primary schools

Les Tickle

The cases which are included in this book are from primary school teachers who responded to the challenges of the revised art curriculum. Each is characterised by three main aims: to develop the teachers' knowledge of art; to devise teaching strategies for their pupils which will help them effect the art curriculum requirements; and to research their teaching and the pupils' responses to it. Few of the teachers have an art background from school or from their teacher education courses. They responded to the new demands of the art curriculum by engaging in this triple approach to their own professional development, as part of a programme intended to bring them and their pupils into direct and prolonged contact with works of art.

Since 1993, Sedgwick, an international insurance broking and financial services group with a commitment to working in and with the community for the promotion of both education and the arts, has provided scholarships for primary school teachers to develop their knowledge and their teaching of the visual arts, with special reference to the Sainsbury Collection housed at the University of East Anglia, Norwich. It is an extensive and diverse collection of art, containing objects from many cultures and periods of time. The partnership between the commercial sector, schools, and the University has enabled the teachers to make a substantial response to the teaching of art in the national curriculum; a response which has also given them access to the expertise of art historians, anthropologists, archaeologists, artists, and art educators based in the University.

Their development of subject knowledge, use of new teaching strategies, and induction into teacher research, is usually accompanied by testimonies of excitement at the prospects, for themselves and for their pupils, of learning more about art. There is often some associated trepidation about entering the unfamiliar territory of the visual arts and of teacher research. What characterises their endeavours most notably is the commitment, determination, and willpower to improve the art experiences of both their current and future pupils. Achieving the greatest possible efficacy in the induction of every pupil, whatever the child's background, disposition and capabilities, is the main driving force. They also share a willingness to provide collaborative leadership, to share their work with other teachers.

Different aspects of knowledge and practice are deliberately sequenced in the programme they follow, at least in the emphasis given to each:

- Developing personal familiarity with art objects, and strategies for studying them, and with the lives of artists and the cultures in which art objects were created;
- Devising teaching aims and plans for pupils' projects, including preparatory work in schools; visit(s) to the gallery; and follow-up work by pupils;
- Deciding a research focus and strategy, in relation to the teaching aims and plans, and gathering data, recording and storing the evidence, and analysing and organising it into report form;
- Sharing the research and the issues it generated, among each other, with their colleagues in school, and with teachers from other schools.

Improving personal artistic knowledge and attitudes, devising art teaching projects for pupils, undertaking research into the conduct of teaching and pupils' learning, and disseminating the research, tends to happen without a neat sequence, however. From the beginning, seeking to develop some understanding and practice of educational action research is part of the learning. Thinking about what teacher research implies, and about what to research and how to do it, is a long and deliberative venture, and the seeds of thought are sown early. Equally, gaining knowledge and understanding of art continues throughout the programme, as experience in handling information about objects and artists and cultures, and experience in observing and responding to the art objects, is pursued and deepened. The focus on the potentials for pupils is a permanent and paramount concern. What might a possible project focus for pupils be? How could it be fitted into the topic for the Spring term? Which objects, artists and cultures have the greatest potential for engaging the interests of pupils? Do I know enough about this artist or that culture to enliven the pupils' learning? How will 4 year olds respond to visiting an art gallery? Will they be able to reach up to see the objects?

These kinds of self-searching, practical and thought-provoking questions show that this is new ground being broken. They are interspersed with questions about the meaning of action research in this type of curriculum development. What kinds of data might be useful? What *are* data? Where will I find them? How should I record them? Is the research topic too broad or too narrow, and how much evidence is needed to help to understand children's learning?

A central assumption of action research is that curriculum proposals and teaching practices are to be treated as problematic, as provisional, and worth testing through the collection of evidence. Its basic tenet is that teachers, seeking to extend practical knowledge and experience, constantly test out ideas. Ideas are changed according to circumstance and rethinking, which is based on experience and the analysis of evidence. These new ideas are assimilated into a repertoire of practice. A commitment to systematic questioning of teaching is characteristic of a disposition to seek an understanding of events through the mastery of investigative skills. The development of practice, it is presumed, will be most effective if it is based on the capacity to make sound judgements. In turn, such prudence will result from careful handling of evidence of professional action.

Professional development based on such assumptions involves teachers in identifying the developmental needs of themselves and their institutions, and working out their own strategies towards meeting those needs, perhaps with external support. The emphasis is on a sharing of interpretations and understanding of practical curricular concerns, and a sharing of expertise to arrive at solutions for teaching. Action research is often described and defined in the form of 'models' in which action is taken, a problem is identified, data relating to the problem are sought and analysed, actions are amended, and further evidence is sought (Elliott 1991; Hopkins 1985; Kemmis and McTaggart 1982; McKernan 1991; Winter 1989).

The motivation for carrying out action research is often a concern to improve one's practice. It is just as likely to serve teachers when changes are initiated by externally generated events, as in the cases reported later, where the need to work out one's aims and to test if they are being realised has been brought about by recent developments in the curriculum. The association of action research with 'reflective practice' is commonplace, and the work of Donald Schon (1971, 1983, 1987) has been influential in that the rhetoric of his 'reflective practitioner' has become widespread among professionals. The teachers who have written chapters in this book certainly felt a need to achieve a mastery of practice. They were in a position to initiate change in their own work, since the new requirements of the curriculum were not yet tried and tested. Their precondition for enquiry and extensive reflection was the formulation of teaching aims and the testing of practical strategies to enhance their pupils' experiences of the visual arts. The data from these teachers show that sense of inquiry and reflective thought, which pervaded their introduction of the new requirements of the art curriculum. The concern to learn from such inquiry, and to develop particular aspects of professional knowledge and practice, is very evident in their work.

However, they do not necessarily follow the procedures of 'models' of action research. Their thinking is sometimes nearer to Schon's view of reflective practice in which *reflection-in-action* is conducted on the spot, triggered by practical problems and immediately linked to action. *Reflection-on-action* is less immediate but none the less based in practice.

An example of this which these teachers reported was their initial experience of guiding a large number of young children on their first ever visit to an art gallery. Anticipation, careful planning, speculation, prediction, concern about social behaviour, and hopes about effective learning experiences were just some of the characteristics and uncertainties associated with the event. The search for evidence of pupils' responses to instructions and tasks was a high priority from the moment of arrival. Would they wander off? How long would they sustain concentration? Were there too many distractions to focus on selected objects? and so on. Readiness to act decisively in response to emerging evidence, in order to make the most of the opportunities presented, was reported widely.

There were also many immediate and spontaneous judgements to be made about how visual art projects should or could be developed in the classroom, and how school-based activities might relate to gallery visits and contact with works of art. From among these, each of the teachers chose a focus for more prolonged gathering of evidence, which formed the basis of the reports, guided by principles of action research which are included in *Understanding Design and Technology in Primary Schools* (Tickle 1996).

This meeting of innovations provides a story of not only commitment, anguish, energy, and willpower but also domestic disputes apparently! Surprise, enlightenment, confession, and other human characteristics and experiences are never far below the surface when the complexities of learning subject knowledge, teaching strategies and research methods are combined. But it is the knowledge of art, the development of teaching, and the analyses of their pupils' responses to the innovations which are the focus of each of the teacher research chapters of the book. The book is intended to serve the needs of other primary school teachers in two ways:

- By representing approaches to teaching the dimension of knowledge and understanding in primary art education;
- By providing examples of research undertaken by teachers in relation to their own developing understanding of art, teaching projects devised by them, and their own learning from researching children's responses to their teaching.

Chapter two outlines the new curriculum for primary art, and addresses what I consider to be a central and abiding problem, intrinsic to art activity and now faced by all teachers and pupils. It is the relationship between making one's art and the study of others' art. This is an interesting puzzle, which I tackle first from the point of view of the study of art. The book emphasises that dimension of the curriculum, to redress the balance from an emphasis on making art (both in school practice and in books available on teaching art). This should not be taken to imply that the study of art should come before making it. How artists relate the study of art to their making of it, how the two activities relate, is not clear cut. Understanding the process itself might lead to 'authentic' knowledge of art in classrooms. That might help to generate authentic making of art, rather than pastiche and the mimicry of techniques of other artists which seems commonplace. Those issues are part of what the later chapters explore.

Chapter three describes some research endeavours which have sought to know just how children respond to works of art. The research is both recent and fickle, the main message being an invitation to construct descriptions of teaching aims and instructional strategies, particular learning contexts, and case studies of children learning in their various circumstances. This is an appeal to test out curriculum practice. For teachers it amounts to an appeal to create their own curriculum projects, to monitor them, and to make them available for others to draw upon, emulate, amend, or vary from, in the best traditions of research.

The teachers' chapters are centred around art objects in the Robert and Lisa Sainsbury Collection. The collection holds art from all over the world, and from ancient times to the present day. It contains the work of some twentieth century European artists, such as Henry Moore, Pablo Picasso, and Hans Coper, and the kinds of art from other cultures in which they were interested. Ancient Mesoamerican (Olmec, Mayan, Aztec) sculptures, African carved heads, figurines from the Greek Cyclades Islands, are just a few sections of the collection. There are other contemporary artists represented in the collection for whom such influences are not so evident: Francis Bacon, Alberto Giacometti, John Davies, Lucie Rie, Leonora Carrington, and Anthony Green, for instance. Thus, there are some interesting cases to explore in terms of the artists' transformative uses of the ideas, images, techniques, and styles of others' art within their own work. There is also an extraordinarily wide range of objects: domestic implements of the Inuit people of the Arctic regions, ritual objects of Oceania and the American North West Coast, African masks, Indian paintings and bronzes, modern ceramics, photographs, tiny objects from ancient Egypt and classical Greece, Chinese scroll paintings, Japanese prints, large sculptures. The types of objects are sufficiently varied to promote the question of what counts as art: a native American shawl, an Inuit drill bow, an Indonesian baby carrier, Lucie Rie cups and saucers, objects of worship, objects of decoration, surrealist paintings, portraits, large bronze sculptures of reclining women, and so on.

The Sainsbury Centre for the Visual Arts is a place where many interests meet: art historians, anthropologists, archaeologists, writers, artists, art history students, student teachers, experienced teachers, teacher educators, volunteer guides, and schoolchildren. Nearby, the School of Education and Professional Development is the focus of research, scholarship and teaching in the fields of curriculum innovation, educational

Plate 1.1 Primary children studying Giacometti's *Femme* in the Sainsbury Centre (photograph: Alan Howard)

evaluation, professional learning, and the development of teaching. In establishing the Centre for Applied Research in Visual Arts Education we have tried to encourage liaison between these various disciplines and interests. Its aims are to research ways in which interpretation, knowledge and understanding of the visual arts may be promoted and developed. A particular concern is to try to make available to both teachers and children in schools some of the opportunities, including academic and scholarly expertise, which exist within a university context.

ENCOUNTERS WITH ART OBJECTS

In engaging teachers (and others) in first hand encounters with art objects and in providing information about them, the problems of enquiry faced even by experts in the fields of aesthetics, archaeology, art history, anthropology, and art production are presented as part of the experience. Some of the questions with which the encounters can begin are provided in resource materials for teachers (Sekules and Tickle 1993; Tickle and Sekules 1995). They are intended to encourage dispositions towards enquiry when confronting a specific work of art, the works of a particular artist, or objects from other artists, places, and times. Straightforward questions which can be asked of any art, artist or cultural context are used first. The aim is to stimulate a process of enquiry and response to art as a basis for developing understanding both of the art and of one's responses to it. That aim acknowledges the importance of learners constructively and actively working on the growth of their own knowledge – from the immediate aesthetic stimulus provided by artefacts; through a process of reflecting on their own responses to them; and moving on to the next stage of puzzling around the evidence of what the works represent; how were they made? from what? when? where? by whom? for whom? why? and so on. Such basic questions are not hard to formulate:

- What does it represent?
- What is/was its purpose?
- Why was it made?
- How is/was it used?
- Where and when was it made?
- Who made it?
- For whom?
- How was it made?
- How does it represent its subject?
- Does it have a story?
- Can I identify the subject?
- Is looking at it a pleasing experience?
- Is it disturbing?
- Is the object engaging?
- Is my response indifferent?
- Do the colour combinations appeal to me?
- Are the shapes/forms pleasing?
- Does the material have an interesting texture or surface quality?

In the first instance such questions are intended to uncover the nature of the encounter as one in which the previous experience of the viewer (as adult or child, teacher or student, man or woman, European or Asian, etc.) may play as much a part as the material evidence of the art objects themselves.

The personal responses, reflections, questions, and puzzles provide a basis for understanding particular art objects and the work of particular artists. They can lead to a further stage: a search for possible relationships (similarities and differences) between different objects or classes of objects, or between the work of different artists. Approaches to understanding objects in terms of similarities, differences, and relationships sometimes necessitates fitting them into a context of other objects and artists from elsewhere; their places of origin; and the social and cultural circumstances in which the artists worked. The more immediate aesthetic experience, personal interpretation, and response to individual art objects can be maintained. Different kinds of 'knowledge' complement each other.

The range of possible interpretations of the evidence available from the objects and surrounding information can be treated with an open mind. In many instances the lack of definitive answers in the visual arts is as much a characteristic of the venture of understanding them as is any gathering of firm information. A kind of flexible foraging for understanding is used, coupled with encouragement of a willingness to accept the unknown and the imponderable.

The activities of young children are self-evidently affected by a human predisposition to fit experiences into classifications of previous encounters, and sometimes to build new classifications of experience. Some evidence of that is included in the case studies. Teachers are invited to walk those same boundaries, with the confidence (as I like to put it) that for all of us ignorance may be celebrated rather than condemned, because it leaves a great deal of exploring to be enjoyed. The range and types of questions with which the exploring might begin (see p. 7) is soon extended, for example, by deepening the basic questions about representation, aesthetic characteristics, technical production, the artist responsible, and so on.

Representation

- Does it represent a natural object or creature?
- What kind of creature?
- Why was that creature important to the artist?
- Does it represent something supernatural?
- What sort of supernatural being?
- What did it mean to the artist?
- Is it a portrayal of something mythical?
- What sort of mythical being?
- Where did it fit into the beliefs of the artist and his or her people?
- Is there a story?
- What is the story?
- Who are the characters and places?
- Why was the story important to the artist?
- Is it a picture from the imagination?
- What ideas were going on in the imagination of the artist?
- How has he or she used materials to picture those ideas?

Aesthetic characteristics

- What are the rules of proportion used by the artist?
- How and why are particular shapes and forms used?
- Do the colours have special significance?

- Which realms of human experience are encapsulated in the representations?
- How is three-dimensional space represented or used?

Technical production

- What materials were used?
- What tools were used for fashioning them?
- What techniques for forming the materials are of special significance in the work of an artist or culture?

Knowing the artists

- Is the artist identifiable?
- What was the artist's name?
- When did he or she live?
- Where?
- How and when and why did he or she become an artist?
- Who taught him or her?
- Who paid him or her?
- What influenced the kind of art that he or she made?
  (See Sekules and Tickle 1993; Tickle and Sekules 1995.)

The number and range of questions which can brought to bear on the visual arts seems almost endless and it is not my intention here to propose a definitive list. The value lies in generating questions and deepening the categories of questions, as a means of extending enquiry as far as evidence and personal responses will allow one to go. Like the lists on representation, technique and biography, subsequent lists can be constructed, for example, on the purpose of art objects, on production methods, on production management (economic, commercial and social dimensions), and on patronage. Readers might like to extend such lists from the following starter questions, applied to any art objects of their choice.

Purposes

Is the object

- decorative?
- religious?
- an instrument of defence or aggression?
- self-expressive?
- autobiographical?
- the means to some other end?

Production methods

Did its making involve

- micro-electronic technology?
- expertise of more than one artist?
- traditional methods of fashioning materials?
- special knowledge of a material?

Production management

Was the object

- the work of the artist alone?
- made by a team of people?
- commissioned for a particular location?
- made on speculation of selling?
- expected as part of customary activity?
- overseen by ritual?

Patronage

Was the artist

- personally wealthy and independent?
- rewarded financially for his or her work?
- part of a social hierarchy?

Sometimes questions have to be put on hold until investigations of available evidence can be made. Sometimes the evidence is not available, and questions rest in the realm of the constant puzzle. The disposition to develop knowledge and understanding, rather than settling for cursory encounters with art objects, seems to offer depth of experience and a quality of intellectual, affective and even physical challenges which can be built upon over many encounters with just one object, a group of objects, and comparative studies of the work of particular artists and cultures. Depth of knowledge can be gained from the interflow of direct observation, the visual and affective examination of the object, and one's aesthetic responses. The search for material evidence might illuminate some of the questions asked, and provoke others to be asked. Knowledge can also come from encounters with other sources: catalogues, biographies, letters, anthropological studies, missionary accounts. It can also come from artistic practice, from the experience of working with material and equipment, directing one's attention to the processes which artists engage when they are making their work. This is especially possible in circumstances where practising artists offer workshops or residences.

REVIEWING ART EDUCATION

Since the beginning of the twentieth century arguments for making art an important part of the primary school curriculum have been commonplace in most industrialised and post-industrial nations. It was in any case a part of the elementary school curriculum in Western countries, steered by a mixture of interests in enhancing manual dexterity, extending the arts and crafts traditions, and child centred ideas about education and the place of creativity and visual imagery within it. It was, and is, also a part of the educational processes and curriculum content of other peoples throughout the world. Most societies show evidence of intention towards maintaining, renewing, and transmitting to new generations of artists, and to those who see and use their work, the individual's mastery of materials, opportunities for creative expression, and knowledge and appreciation of their accumulated cultural inheritances.

In Britain Herbert Read published a classic work, *Education Through Art* (Read 1943), in which he advanced the cause of visual art as a central component of the curriculum in our own culture. His ideas were backed by the then growing child-development psychology and emerging interests in the philosophy of education. A quarter-century further on, Dick Field published a (now little known) succinct and persuasive case for an art curriculum which included not only the benefits of making art, but also the development of understanding of art (Field 1970). The same cause has been pursued by many individuals, arts organisations, educational foundations, charitable trusts, policy makers, visionary teachers, and the like. There have been many encouragements to take visual art seriously, in the formal, school-based education of young children, both its making and its study for purposes of appreciation and understanding.

Yet in the final quarter of the twentieth century there was also, to put it mildly, widespread acknowledgement of the need for further action to reach that goal. Studies in Britain and America caused disquiet about the condition of art education in our schools (for example: Adler 1982; Alexander and Day 1991; Boyer 1983; Getty Center 1993a, b; Goodlad 1984; Gulbenkian Foundation 1982; Hargreaves 1982; Tickle 1987). Some showed that, in particular, the art curriculum in the realms of interpretation, appreciation and understanding (sometimes called perceptual, historical, and critical studies) has remained in a parlous state within many schools (Gardner 1990; Hargreaves 1983; Taylor 1986). A number of initiatives sought to establish the recognised but thus far unfulfilled potentials of a comprehensive art curriculum which goes beyond the visible surfaces of children making pictures and objects, and extends into the realms of understanding art as a universal (temporally and spatially) human phenomenon of considerable importance to us (Abbs 1987a, b; Arnheim 1989; Best 1985, 1992; Taylor 1986, 1992).

The tension between what might be regarded as an idealistic pre-occupation with art, and what actually is experienced by many children in formal education is summed up by Stake *et al.* (1991) in their description of American elementary schools:

> Art instruction was a regular guest in most schools. . . . With little arts preparation (training) and little resource teacher assistance, many classroom teachers chose projects easy to teach, easy to control, product oriented, tied to cultural events, and attractive to youngsters. The result was a jumble of short, little-articulated projects. If the teacher perceived growing creative skills, it seemed to be acknowledged in terms of the children's ages more than in terms of previous artwork. When asked what they would do with more time, more resources, or improved conditions, most of these (arts)-untrained teachers said they would do more of the same. . . . Most classroom teachers provided little guidance, verbally or by example, as to aesthetic quality. Many did not urge experimentation with materials or arrangements. Many did not suggest that tools could be used expressively. When choices existed (pink or blue, six or eight whiskers) they typically remained technical, not drawn to broadening vision or promoting understanding.
>
> (Stake *et al.* 1991: 340)

This is not the total picture of American elementary schools' art education nearing the turn of the millennium. Stake *et al.* also cite examples where art-specialist teachers and artists-in-residence provide encounters emphasising observation, planning, translation of ideas into visual form, and guided exploration of imaginations and of knowledge of art as a social and personal endeavour. But the first point of my selecting what might seem to be a hard-hitting and hyper-critical description of art education is that it provides a chance to look beyond our own classroom studios, to step outside them and to reflect back on whether activities within them would measure up any better to such scrutiny. The second point is that many primary school teachers, including those who are the authors of most of this book, acknowledge a certain if not complete accuracy in Stake *et al.*'s description. The third and most important point is that these same teachers would not just do more of the same. They have demonstrated that they are determined to do something different, to bring about changes in their practices, to create new educational ventures for themselves and their pupils. This has happened through recognition that they can offer more than they currently do, provided there are opportunities to develop their subject knowledge, their teaching strategies, and their children's access to the arts. It is in tribute to that determination and as an encouragement to others to join them that this book has been written. It is also in a different political context from the American one that the incentive to make those changes has arisen.

THE CHALLENGE OF LEGISLATION

The national legislation for the art curriculum in England and Wales has put in place requirements for primary school teachers to work to programmes which include what formerly was sometimes known as perceptual, historical and critical studies in art. While practical art has been a conventional activity in primary schools for over a century, and will continue under this legislation, the curriculum now requires that pupils should be taught about art and the work of artists, from diverse social and cultural contexts, through contact with original works of art.

Most primary school teachers gave up the practice of art at the age of thirteen, and will never have studied works of art, the working methods of artists, their social contexts, or their cultural origins, either for the purposes of their own art production or in its own right as an academic pursuit. The extent to which such study can be pursued during initial training programmes for teachers is severely constrained by time and the range of subjects to be mastered. A reasoned assessment based on evidence from research and on reports from many primary school teachers suggests that the task of innovation now being faced is such that they will all have to develop a working knowledge of art objects; of artists' technical ways of working; of the creative processes in which artists engage; and of the social, cultural and historical contexts of each of these factors. They will need to devise strategies for children to acquire such understanding, and in order to do so will need to understand how children learn such matters. Teaching strategies with any particular child or group will need to be accommodated within the overall curriculum design of a school. Implementation of co-ordinating mechanisms to ensure progression in learning will be needed. The innovation will also need to be researched, to accumulate sound knowledge of the educational potentials and effects of curriculum practice, and to disseminate that knowledge to colleagues.

The scale of the need is rather astounding. In two counties of East Anglia there are about 650 primary schools, catering for over 100,000 children age five to eleven. Over 4,500 teachers teach the art curriculum to all six year groups every year. In this small area these numbers of people will be engaged at some time within any one year in the study of original works of art in the school and the locality. Across England the scale is in the order of 175,000 teachers and four million pupils, in 18,000 primary schools. For all of them a particular challenge arises from the requirement that pupils should incorporate their knowledge of art and artists into the production of their own work. I will consider that next.

FURTHER READING

Abbs, P. (1987a) *A is for Aesthetic,* Lewes: Falmer Press.
—— (1987b) *Living Powers: The Arts in Education,* Lewes: Falmer Press.

—— (1989) *The Symbolic Order,* Lewes: Falmer Press.

Adler, M. (1982) *The Paedeia Proposal,* New York: Collier Macmillan.

Alexander, K. and Day, M. (eds) (1991) *Discipline-Based Art Education: A Curriculum Sampler,* Santa Monica: J. Paul Getty Trust, Getty Center for Education in the Arts.

Arnheim, R. (1989) *Thoughts on Art Education,* Santa Monica: J. Paul Getty Trust, Getty Center for Education in the Arts.

Best, D. (1985) *Feeling and Reason in the Arts,* London: George Allen and Unwin.

—— (1992) *The Rationality of Feeling: Understanding the Arts in Education,* London: Falmer Press.

Boyer, E. (1983) *High School,* New York: Harper and Row.

Elliott, J. (1991) *Action Research for Educational Change,* Milton Keynes: Open University Press.

Field, D. (1970) *Change in Art Education,* London: Routledge and Kegan Paul.

Gardner, H. (1990) *Art Education and Human Development,* Santa Monica: J. Paul Getty Trust, Getty Center for Education in the Arts.

Getty Center for Education in the Arts (1993a) *Perspectives on Education Reform: Arts Education as Catalyst,* Santa Monica: J. Paul Getty Trust.

—— (1993b) *Improving Visual Art Education,* Santa Monica: J. Paul Getty Trust.

Goodlad, J. I (1984) *A Place Called School,* New York: McGraw-Hill.

Gulbenkian Foundation (1982) *The Arts in Schools,* London: Calouste Gulbenkian Foundation.

Hargreaves, D. (1982) *The Challenge for the Comprehensive School: Culture, Curriculum and Community,* London: Routledge and Kegan Paul.

—— (1983) 'The teaching of art and the art of teaching', in M Hammersley and A Hargreaves (eds) *Curriculum Practice: Some Sociological Case Studies,* Lewes: Falmer Press.

Hopkins, D. (1985) *A Teachers' Guide to Classroom Research,* Milton Keynes: Open University Press.

Kaagan, S. (1990) *Aesthetic Persuasion: Pressing the Cause of Arts Education in American Schools,* Santa Monica: J. Paul Getty Trust, Getty Center for Education in the Arts.

Kemmis, S. and McTaggart, R. (1982) *The Action Research Planner,* Victoria: Deakin University Press.

McKernan, J. (1991) *Curriculum Action Research,* London: Kogan Page.

Read, H. (1943) *Education Through Art,* London: Faber.

Schon, D. (1971) *Beyond The Stable State,* San Francisco: Jossey Bass.

—— (1983) *The Reflective Practitioner,* New York: Basic Books.

—— (1987) *Educating the Reflective Practitioner,* London: Jossey Bass.

Sekules, V. and Tickle, L. (eds) (1993) *Starting Points: Approaches to Art Objects Selected from the Sainsbury Centre for Visual Arts,* University of East Anglia, Norwich: Centre for Applied Research in Visual Arts Education.

Sockett, H. (1994) *The Moral Base for Teacher Professionalism,* New York: Teachers College Press.

Stake, R., Bresler, L. and Maby, L. (1991) *Custom and Cherishing: The Arts in Elementary Schools,* University of Illinois: National Arts Education Research Center.

Stenhouse, L. (1975) *An Introduction to Curriculum Research and Development,* London: Heinemann.

Taylor, R. (1986) *Educating for Art: Critical Response and Development,* Harlow: Longman.

—— (1992) *Visual Arts in Education,* London: Falmer Press.

Tickle, L. (1983) 'One spell of ten minutes or five spells of two? . . . Teacher–pupil encounters in Art and Design Education', in M. Hammersley and A. Hargreaves (eds) *Curriculum Practice: Some Sociological Case Studies,* Lewes: Falmer Press.

—— (ed.) (1987) *The Arts in Education: Some Research Studies,* London: Croom Helm.

—— (1994) *The Induction of New Teachers: Developing Reflective Professional Practice,* London: Cassell.

—— (ed.) (1996) *Understanding Design and Technology in Primary Schools: Cases from Teachers' Research,* London: Routledge

Tickle, L. and Sekules, V. (eds) (1995) *Interpretations: Approaches to Art Objects Selected from The Sainsbury Centre for Visual Arts,* University of East Anglia, Norwich: Centre for Applied Research in Visual Arts Education.

Winter, R. (1989) *Learning from Experience: Principles and Practice in Action Research,* Lewes: Falmer Press.

Chapter 2

Art, art education, and the twenty-first century

Les Tickle

Walter Gropius, founding father of the Bauhaus, . . . urged his students to 'start from zero'.

(Pateman 1991: 115)

The practice of art retains a traditional place in the new art curriculum, but the ways in which practice is carried out is subject to what for most primary school teachers is a considerable new challenge: a dual emphasis on the study of art and the making of art, and the bringing together of the two. The requirement which teachers and pupils face, to make connections between the knowledge of art, artists, and their cultural contexts, and the pupils' production of their own artwork, is explicit and direct: 'pupils' understanding and enjoyment of art, craft and design should be developed through activities that bring together requirements from both Investigating and Making and Knowledge and Understanding, wherever possible' (DfE 1995: 2).

As it is presented, and taken at face value, this is an apparently simple idea. It might be thought to reflect the way in which artists themselves work, how they learn from or are influenced by the work of other artists. However, that is too simple an assumption, as the urging by Walter Gropius demonstrates. In the 'professional' world of artistic learning, given the diversity and range of the visual arts in multicultural and global communication networks, it is hard to pin down just what this might mean.

Some of the initial questions which arise are straightforward. For example, whether the study of art and the making of art are brought together by artists or whether artists distance themselves from the work of others, is an important question. The ways in which these relationships occur, and the consequences of such connections and/or disconnections, are not likely to be governed by any one set of rules; they are likely to be complex. If and how influences occur (or occurred) among artistic communities or particular cultural groups in different locations, in the diverse art world which is our global inheritance, are matters which stretch the minds of art historians, anthropologists, art critics and others. The nature of the relationships which accrue between different artists and works of art, in different societies, at different periods of history, are matters which rightfully would be part of any enquiry which leads to knowledge and understanding of art. Yet that must also be translated into an appreciation of how the relationships might develop into the next century. The very idea of working in ways which presume that artists connect their creative endeavours with those of others who have different biographies, working in other communities, in different localities, or from earlier times, and so forth, is a matter which cannot be treated simplistically.

Even looking back to the recent past, Pateman (1991), for example, provides a timely reminder that in Europe and America at least, during this century, sections of the artistic avant-garde have sought to disconnect from the past, break from conventions, disrupt tendencies towards consensus values, and generate continuous experimentation in search of originality. He says: 'The imperative to keep it new meant that one movement was destined to follow another, often with extraordinary rapidity' (Pateman 1991: 115).

He points out that 'modernism' as an umbrella term for perpetual experimentation left us with a rich legacy in the visual arts from within a short timescale and particular geographical region. In this century alone in our own continent this has included the Dada movement, the Fauves, cubists, futurists, constructivists, vorticists, surrealists, expressionists, abstract expressionists, pop artists, conceptualists, op artists, minimalists, landscape artists, installation artists, video artists, and so on. From a North American perspective Atkins (1990: 8) has listed fifty-eight movements in the visual arts between 1945 and 1990, many of them co-existing or overlapping in timescale. This richness of modern movements, according to Pateman, stemmed from an 'insistence on a contemporaneity without reference to the past [which] can be found in most of the manifestos and polemical declarations of the self-conscious modernists' (Pateman 1991: 115).

It has also meant without reference to, or rejection of, the work of others active during the same periods of time. That view of contemporary Western art consistently rejecting the past and even the present is itself too simple. There are examples of artists influencing artists. Reaction is itself a kind of influence. But it does reflect an important part of our own artistic heritage, which I will stay with for the moment. Eventually there was nothing left to rebel against, Pateman argues, and the constant attempts to disconnect from what had gone before washed themselves out (around 1980 in his view, but see below), to be replaced by 'post-modernism',

> which consciously opens itself to the past and to . . . our diverse human lives and plural cultures. [This movement is] concerned to make playful connections with the whole of the cultural continuum.
>
> (Pateman 1991: 118–19)

Pateman's summary of post-modernism comes with a strict warning against the possibilities of creating superficial likenesses of other art, or imitations of the styles of other artists, or items of 'fun' without deeper artistic significance. The essential spirituality (especially concern with aesthetic experience), and the substance of perceptions of the human condition, which in Pateman's view drive artistic consciousness and are at the core of its creative endeavours, form the basis of his (and others') appeal to recognise that art is more than mimicry. Teachers, and artists themselves, are left here to search for an understanding of what is significant art, and of what constitutes depth, meaning, value, and vision.

Modernism and post-modernism are the constructs of art critics, academics and observers of artistic endeavours who are trying to make sense of the contemporary Western phenomenon of art. As such they help to provide a sense of where art is at, an overview of developments. Atkins (1990) is helpful in this respect, pointing out that post-modernists challenged the

> notion of avant-garde originality by borrowing images from the media or the history of art and re-presenting them in new juxtapositions or arrangements that paradoxically function in the art world as celebrated examples of innovation or a new avant-garde.
>
> (Atkins 1990: 132)

One distinctive characteristic of the post-modern era is the breaking down of categories such as art, popular culture, domestic product, and media, and adjustments in outlook spurred by the electronic age. Manifestations of the developments in art production have included the use of mechanical devices, video formats, sound systems, and hybrids such as furniture sculpture and sculptured body apparel. These transitions have been reflected among some of those who think and write about art, to the extent that historians, journalists, and critics, for example, have transgressed the boundaries of the disciplines. In the world of art studies (anthropology, archaeology, sociology, etc.) there is a similar tendency to break down the boundaries of their disciplines which were substantially constructed during the modern era.

So we have a continuing dynamic in the production of art, as the activities of art are made up from the imaginations, ambitions and visions of individuals seeking to make sense of their world, and seeking to make their way in it, through the exploitation of art's materials. Fashioning them in their own metaphors of life experiences and perceptions as the twenty-first century appears will continue to be influenced by combinations of the elements of nature, human forces, inner feelings, bodily experiences, social life and electronic devices. It will also be influenced by knowledge and understanding of art, what it is, how it functions, and how it is made. And that knowledge and understanding will itself be socially constructed, by those who engage in the observation, enquiry and analysis of the phenomenon we call art. They will include not only artists, critics *et al.* but also primary school teachers and young children.

ARTISTS EXPLORING ART

Understanding this fundamental characteristic of art as a dynamic response to life's experiences, including responses to art itself, is part of a symbiotic relationship between knowing about and doing art. At least in recent Western societies the extent to which the rendering of artists' responses is done with reference to other ways of representing the world is subject to artists' individual imaginations, ambitions, and visions. Pablo Picasso's contributions to modern art for example – especially Cubism – reflect the spirit of an artist who was conscious of imagery, materials and techniques from many locations and cultures, and who exploited them to his own ends in ways which not only reflected the art of his time and place but also helped to create a new art which affected the nature of that time and place. It might also be thought that he exploited the social and economic opportunities of his time and place to the advantage of himself and the artistic community in general.

Bringing together the study of art and its production by artists themselves leaves little option but to open up questions about, rather than presume to know, how it happens, let alone whether it should happen. At the very time when Walter Gropius would have had his students at the Bauhaus starting from zero, for example, Henry Moore made his first visit to the British Museum (1921). At the Bauhaus (and elsewhere) the painters Paul Klee and Wassily Kandinsky paraded their explorations of the new, with their individualistic interpretations of images, abstract compositions, and uses of colour. Around the same time, as a scholar at the Royal College of Art, Moore explored the Museum displays weekly, especially in search of inspiration from what he referred to as 'archaic and tribal art' (Moore 1966: 7). Sixty years after his first visit he wrote that in his formative years nine-tenths of his understanding and learning about sculpture came from the British Museum.

What Henry Moore said he derived from the collection varied from piece to piece within both the Museum and his own work. He pointed out that each work of art, and each type of sculpture, emphasises some particular characteristic. The monumental nature of Egyptian sculpture – both in scale and in their vision – impressed him immediately. African and Pacific sculptures – which he also encountered in the personal collections of Jacob Epstein, Picasso, Brancusi and others – revealed to him alternative traditions of representing the human form with their own expressive intent.

The sculptures of the Cycladic room were appreciated for two particular qualities: their sense of form, their unity, and purity of style; and the fact that they are carved directly from marble, rather than cast in metal, or first modelled in plaster and then copied by a stonecarver. This gave Moore a sense of the possibilities of carving directly in stone, a possibility confirmed by figures from ancient Mexico.

From both of these sources he initially derived a sense of forming figures which remained faithful to the solid nature of the block of stone, but among the harp-players of the Cycladic figures he discovered how space as well as form could be incorporated into sculpture.

The fragility of stone might have restricted his exploration of the use of thin and free-standing forms, some of them large, which he saw in nature and wanted to reflect in his later sculptures. From a desire not to be constrained by any particular way of working, he extended his explorations into the use of metal. But his admiration for the simplicity of style of Cycladic figures remained with him, and his appreciation of the sculptors' achievements is on record:

> Although the images appear to be standing still, there is just a little suggestion of movement . . . the figures are very female in feeling; look at the lovely long legs . . . and the full thighs . . . each piece is so beautifully unified in technique and vision that the eye accepts it easily.
>
> (Moore 1966: 45)

In Britain such interest in, and influence of, the arts of other periods and cultures extended across different art forms, and generations. The influences were earnestly contained, though, by the artists' will to determine their own styles. Hans Coper and Lucie Rie were close friends and working colleagues, yet the nature and style of their ceramics is very individual.

Coper used sources of inspiration available to him during the post-second world war period in London: collections and gallery exhibits of archaic and tribal arts made a big impression; he admired other artists who had drawn upon these same inspirations, among them Pablo Picasso. Like them, creativity was also to be found in the exploration of materials and the search for aesthetic sensibility. He was well aware of, and especially admired, sculpture by Hans Arp, Marino Marini, and Constantin Brancusi – artists who were part of the modern movements of their time in Europe. His use and treatment of the materials, his methods of production, and the resulting effects of the forms, the textured surfaces, the colours, and even the ways in which the later characteristic forms were displayed, are individual and distinctive. They are Coper. His creativity was to draw from a wide range of sources:

> Hans' work at the germinal stage reflects the simplicity of primitive ceramics in which abstract decoration follows the form of the pot, as well as the work of Brancusi and the anonymous sculptors of the Cyclades.

These influences stayed with Hans throughout his creative career, and became even more strongly reflected in his own work at a later date.

(Birks 1983a: 27)

Birks advises us not to make too much of these connections (though he himself implicitly encourages it). He points out that like Alberto Giacometti and Constantin Brancusi, who also loved Cycladic figures, Hans was following his own inventive route, but making pots, not sculpture. He was seeking to solve his own formal, aesthetic and technical problems in translating the materials into the 'kind of balanced tension ... exploring the outer limits of pottery'.

Among painters, Francis Bacon's personal artistic search is claimed to have confronted the matter of derivation in a distinctively personal way. It is said that he saw the masterpieces of past European painters as a discouragement rather than an incitement – and that he gained as much from popular media photographs (Russell 1993: 39). One key to his paying attention to other works of art was his recognition of another artist's visual solution to a problem he was tackling. He adopted themes of his own, such as questions about the human condition, or violence, rendered through ambiguity and deformity of the figures he painted, and he looked to artists such as Goya out of an interest in their renderings of such matters. His searches included an interest in paint quality, and the use of motifs. However, they were directed by an intention to create in and for the context of the modern world, and in particular his personal world, rather than to ape the work of great but dead artists. His paintings were produced largely without planning, sketching and preliminary work. He preferred to work directly on the canvas. He also worked a great deal from photographs, exploiting technology to his own ends. 'The difficult thing is to keep open the line to the ancestral European imagination while at the same time producing something that comes across as entirely new' (Russell 1993: 46).

Bacon's work, like that of some of his contemporaries (Lucien Freud, Michael Andrews, Frank Auerbach, for example), did not follow the lines of 'modern' abstractionists, or pop art, or op art, etc. Those developments were led by another set. David Hockney, like his contemporaries Ronald Kitaj and Richard Hamilton, is one who forages among the work of other painters for its value as an existing repertoire of potential sources, and who used photographs extensively in his early work. He

recognises . . . that each artist who has conceived or perfected a particular technique can be said to have enriched the vocabulary and extended the range of expression of that [visual] language . . . by seizing in this way any technique that he deems suitable to his purposes, Hockney pays tribute to all his predecessors who have made a contribution to the medium.

(Livingstone 1987: 121)

In this sense Hockney and Hamilton are also known to pay tribute to new technology, from their exploitation of acrylic paint – a new medium in its time – to the use of photography, and explorations of electronic means of image production and communication, using computer software and the fax machine.

These few examples are chosen from among British/European artists whose intentions and purposes have been recorded. From these we are able to gain some insights into the influences and working processes of creative artists in our own recent past, and our present time and culture. It is a time and culture in which contact with a wide variety of art – from across continents and ages – has become available. Communication technology will make the vitality even more noticeable for the incoming millennium.

But let us not be only parochial in this matter. In contrast one might consider the evidence of those Cycladic figures which so apparently influenced Moore, Coper, and others. Those figures represent a tradition in marble sculpting which lasted several thousand years, and in which transitions from one style of figurine to another seemingly emerged very slowly, over centuries (Sekules 1995). The art of tattooing in a Polynesian culture was so controlled by ritual and reference to the gods that the accumulation of tattooing skills, and accurate transmission of images from one generation to the next, was assured by the quality control of watching elders (Tickle 1975). More locally the traditions of some textile arts, such as knitting, lacemaking, weaving and tapestry, draw upon the accumulated experience of generations of practitioners. The oriental tradition of batik-decorated textiles is similar in that respect, as are the traditions of glassmaking in Venice, potting in Nigeria, woodcarving in Vancouver Island, and so on.

In contrast, as the electronic super highway and multi-media resources reach more locations, contact with the arts may become even more diverse both in its means and in the objects in focus. An almost confusing array of possibilities among which to forage is presented: body decoration; carnival displays; stage sets; film and animation; product design; architecture; dress; installations; landscape art; performance art; graphic design; ceramics; painting; sculpture; printmaking; and so on. The communication systems provide an ever changing and expanding encyclopaedia from which to learn about how art forms are explored by artists.

In itself, that array suggests just how problematic is the matter of understanding art, let alone the matter of allowing understanding to influence artistic production. The would-be artist, or art historian, even at the professional stage, could not hope to master such a detailed, comprehensive and global compendium of the visual arts, except through the development of a meta-perspective which would permit continuous, life-long, exploration of art from a basis of understanding some of its fundamental (and perhaps universal) principles. From that standpoint the important thing is to investigate continually ways in which artists make use of art objects and other sources as a resource in the production of their own creative projects. Sources, derivations, stimuli, ideas, technical know-how, and so on are a perpetual concern of artists and artistic communities. They comprise a common referent in commentaries on the lives and works of artists, and descriptions of types of art.

The issues wrapped up in these matters range from how to stimulate and maintain the creative impulse by reference to others' work, to how best to use or create a visual language which can help to convey non-visible ideas (that is the essential task of the visual artist). There are some inevitable tensions (or perhaps complementary forces?), for example between the perpetuation of traditions of artistic production and the pursuit of innovative frontiers; between the expression of individual sense experiences and the transmission of universal meanings. What we are left with, then, is the question of exactly why and how artists refer to and use the work of other artists, from within or beyond their own cultures and traditions. The interface between former and future artists, and the former and future work of living artists (including novice artists such as pupils in schools) is an interesting phenomenon and a necessary contributor to understanding art.

CURRICULUM AIMS: KNOWLEDGE AND UNDERSTANDING

Within the national curriculum the development of knowledge and understanding of art, artists and artistic traditions from a variety of cultural contexts, through contact with original works of art, is the focus particularly of Attainment Target Two. The capabilities to be developed by children through the opportunities and teaching defined in the programmes of study are expressed as statements of learning outcome called End of Key Stage Descriptions. According to these descriptions, by the age of eleven pupils should have developed an ability to use a specialist art vocabulary when comparing images and artefacts. In particular they should be able to identify similarities and differences in the methods and approaches adopted by different artists. They are expected to be able to recognise how the purposes and intentions of artists affect what they produce(d), and the time and place in which works of art were made. The ability to evaluate their own and others' work in the light of what was intended by themselves or other artists should also be demonstrated.

It is expected that these capabilities will have begun in Key Stage One, where by the age of seven pupils should have learned how to describe and compare images and artefacts in simple terms, to recognise differences in methods and approaches used by artists, and to make links between this knowledge and their own work.

These capabilities are to be developed through the programmes of study, which are set out as a range of opportunities which pupils should be given, and things they should be taught, from the age of five. Their detail, characteristic of statutory orders, is very repetitive, much of it identical for different Key Stages, and it is not at all clear what distinctions, if any, are intended between the work of 5 and 11 year olds in many respects. (This is also true of Attainment Target One: Investigating and Making – see p. 25). The skills of critical evaluation are to be based on the development of knowledge of the work of artists, craftspeople and designers, including painting, printmaking, photography, sculpture, ceramics, textiles, graphic design, and architecture. The intention is to enhance appreciation of the diversity and richness of the pupils' cultural heritage, through contact with work from a range of cultures, times, and places.

Children in Key Stage One (5–7 year olds) are expected to be able to *identify* examples of art in their school and locality, and to *recognise* how colour, shape, line, tone, form, space, texture, and pattern are used in images and artefacts. They are to be taught to *recognise* differences and similarities in works of art from different times and places, and to be able to *describe* them. Teachers must teach pupils to *respond* to the ideas, methods, and approaches used in the work of different artists, and different styles and traditions. They must also be taught to *explain* what they think and feel about them (my emphases).

To achieve this, their lessons are to include introductions to the works of art in their locality, both from the past and contemporary work, and that from a variety of periods and cultures. These are to include a variety of genres and styles (*sic*). Pupils are to be taught to *select and sort* these images and artefacts, and to *recognise them as sources* of ideas for their own artwork. They are to learn how to *use* the source material as a basis for that work. They are to be taught about different ways in which ideas, feelings and meanings are communicated in visual form, through the use of the visual elements of line, colour, form, texture, shape, tone, and pattern.

Key Stage Two children (7–11 year olds) are expected to extend their knowledge of art available to them in the locality by being able to identify the materials and methods used by artists. How images and objects are created through the use of the visual and tactile elements (line, tone, colour, texture, shape, form, space, pattern) for different purposes is intended to add to their depth of understanding. Teaching about different ways in which ideas, feelings and meanings are communicated through the use of materials, methods, and visual elements is to continue. Their appreciation of cultural diversity is expected to be broadened through further attention to the work of artists, and children will be expected to recognise ways in which works of art, craft and design reflect the times and places in which they were made. That appreciation is to include the capacity to compare the ideas, methods and approaches to representation and expression used in different styles and traditions. Personal responses are to include the expression of opinion and ideas about their own work and that of others, using their knowledge through an associated, specialist, arts vocabulary.

CURRICULUM AIMS: INVESTIGATING AND MAKING

The relationship between the knowledge and understanding gained from the study of art and the art made by pupils themselves (Attainment Target One: Investigating and Making) is implied throughout the programmes of study, though there is a distinction in the end of key stage descriptions between the achievements expected in relation to the two attainment targets. Leaving room for interpretations was deliberate on the part of the Schools Curriculum and Assessment Authority, whose former chairman pointed out that the curriculum slimming was achieved in part by giving schools scope for judgement in implementing the new statutory orders. This may be in part an acknowledgement of the difficulty of defining the nature of knowledge and understanding and what its relationship might be to practical activities and the demonstration of attainments. What is implied and in places made explicit (see p. 24) is that the study of art and the work of artists is to provide a resource of information, ideas, perceptions, modes of working, language, dispositions, and strategies in a symbiotic relationship akin to that which is explored by, and manifest in variety among, practising artists.

In itself, the programme for practical art is very conventional. The opportunities to *record* observations; to *gather* resource materials and *use* them to stimulate ideas; to *explore* and use two and three dimensional media in different sizes of work; and to *review* and *modify* their work, provide the common threads of practical art throughout the key stages (my emphases). In much of the detail the programmes are the same for Key Stages One to Three. Creative, imaginative and practical skills needed to express ideas and feeling; to record observations; and to design and make artefacts are to be taught through experience of different approaches to art and different modes of classroom organisation – individual, group, and whole-class activities. *Experimentation* with materials, tools, and techniques in drawing, painting, printmaking and sculpture in Key Stage One is to develop towards *control* of these in Key Stage Two.

Experimentation with the visual elements in KS1 is to be encouraged in association with teaching about pattern and texture in natural and man made forms; through colour matching and mixing; in learning how images are made from line and tone; and how shape, form and space are used in images and artefacts. Variants on this for KS2 would have pupils learn about how colour is applied and experienced; about different qualities of line and tone; and about how shape, form and space are presented. Evaluative skills among younger children will be based on *reviewing* what they have done and *describing* what they might change in future work. Older children will be taught to *reflect on and adapt* their work in the light of what they intended, as well as thinking about future developments.

DEVISING A SYMBIOSIS

It is expected that throughout the primary school years children will learn to be able to apply their growing knowledge, understanding, and appreciation of works of art, and their capacity to discuss them, to their own production of art in more and more sophisticated ways. The ways in which connections between the two are to be made, and how the context of their own work is to be related to others' artwork at different stages in this development is an avenue which will need to be explored through the imaginative work of teachers, parents, and children. The devising of teaching and learning strategies which seek to bring together both realms will depend inevitably upon the ingenuity of individual teachers and children exploring the options available to them in their circumstances.

Creative and imaginative handling of the possibilities implied by these requirements will certainly be needed, especially to avoid the temptations of mimicry, imitation, pastiche. Submission to that temptation can occur when pupils look at the work of artists in order mainly to copy their subject matter, compositional forms, techniques in using materials, or, superficially, their use of visual elements such as colour, line, tone and texture. While appreciation of such factors are important dimensions within the study of art, it is necessary I believe to ensure that pupils' learning utilises their contact with art objects as inspiration, stimulus and resource. How that becomes relevant and meaningful to them in the context of their own lives and the production of their own work is a problematic which will need to be explored through an understanding of that relationship within the arts.

The teachers who have contributed to this book adopted the task of exploring with their pupils ways to use contact with art and artists. The extent to which this was or ought to be for the purposes of making their own work, or not, was judged by the individual teachers. There were several reasons for the decision not to prejudge and try to impose what that should mean. Among these was the fact that it was thought to be prudent to address the project in which the teachers worked to the development of approaches to understanding art first and foremost. It was thought impossible to predict by whom, and in what kinds of circumstances, different approaches to the study of art might be used. The development of subject knowledge was tackled in ways which left teachers to translate whatever is suitable and appropriate to their particular children, the opportunities they have, and the situations they are in. This is consistent with the principle of action research (see Chapter three) that educational practice and its development are context-bound, and context-specific. 'Circumstance' in this instance was deemed to include the teachers' own knowledge and understanding of art, of principles of art teaching, and the teaching practices which arise from these. It also includes the material circumstances – geographical location and availability of resources. And it includes understanding of the backgrounds, experiences, needs and potentials of the particular pupils in their charge. What was at stake, then, was literally an exploration of the challenge of innovation set by the headline charge of the art national curriculum: to bring together knowledge and understanding and investigating and making.

FURTHER READING

Atkins, R. (1990) *Artspeak: A Guide to Contemporary Ideas, Movements, and Buzzwords,* New York: Abbeville Press.

Birks, T. (1983a) *Hans Coper 1920–1981,* Norwich: Sainsbury Centre for Visual Arts.

—— (1983b) *Hans Coper,* Norwich: Sainsbury Centre for Visual Arts.

Department for Education (1995) *Art in the National Curriculum,* London: Her Majesty's Stationery Office.

Livingstone, M. (1987) *David Hockney,* London: Thames and Hudson.

Moore, H. (1966) *Henry Moore at The British Museum,* London: British Museum.

Pateman, T. (1991) *Key Concepts: A Guide to Aesthetics, Criticism and the Arts in Education,* London: Falmer Press.

Russell, J. (1993) *Francis Bacon,* London: Thames and Hudson.

Sekules, V. (1995) 'Carved figures from the Cyclades', in L. Tickle and V. Sekules (eds) *Interpretations: Approaches to Art Objects Selected from the Sainsbury Centre for Visual Arts,* University of East Anglia, Norwich: Centre for Applied Research in Visual Arts Education.

Tickle, L. (1975) *Taukuka: Tattooing of the People of Bellona Island,* Honiara: Solomon Islands Cultural Association.

Chapter 3

Children's responses to art

Les Tickle

> If one wants to enhance an individual's understanding [of art], the most likely route is to involve her deeply over a significant period of time with the symbolic realm in question, to encourage her to interact regularly with individuals who are somewhat (rather than greatly) more sophisticated than she is, and to give her ample opportunity to reflect on her own emerging understanding of the domain.
>
> (Gardner 1990: 17)

In a sense it is unsurprising that teachers and children in schools were not in step with the art vanguard in the making of art in Europe and North America during the twentieth century (see Chapter one). Teachers and students are in a no win situation. There is, for example, the conundrum of cohabitation between traditions and innovations in art, and that challenge of perpetual renewal over the acquisition of mastery and tradition. Pupils could hardly be engaged in shaking off (or throwing over) traditions, in favour of their own means of expression, when they are by definition, as pupils, engaged in a process of induction. Nor could their induction amount to schooling in the conventions of a particular artistic tradition if they were to gain a sense of cultural heritage in its broad scope. Into which tradition or traditions would they be inducted, and how? Would they, like rennaissance novice artists, be apprenticed to their teacher's style? Or would they be led around the pot-pourri of other masters, across the range of media which have been used by artists across the world, and throughout time? If they are not inducted into, or paraded around, the traditions they might be engaged in the self-expressive assumptions which some thought of as characterising certain types of both art and early childhood learning.

If school art practice provides little connection with the world of art in general, in the sense of reflecting that world, one must ask: how could it? If it neither addresses modern art in particular, with its experimentation, nor inducts into specific schools of art with their own traditions, conventions and norms, nor ranges across the global artistic inheritance, one should not necessarily be surprised. Somewhere among these possibilities curriculum designers and teachers have to make decisions built upon these inherent tensions. Curriculum conflicts also arise from the material conditions in which schools function. If micro-electronic equipment is not available to pupils; if ceramics facilities do not exist; if teachers are not updated through substantial retraining; and so on, then the pragmatics of curriculum provision invade. I do not offer these observations as excuses. They are, like critiques of school art which sought to change it, helpful in alerting us to some of the issues about art education in formal school settings (Bennett 1994; Bourdieu 1971; Boyer 1983; Gulbenkian Foundation 1982; Hargreaves 1983; Rittner 1983; Schools Council 1974; Taylor 1986; Tickle 1987; Wolff 1985). We might treat them as issues, as problematics which art educators and teachers have debated and will continue to wrestle with.

In the face of such questions, school art curricula have put an emphasis on making art in ways which have been driven by examination syllabuses and assumptions about art teaching in high schools which have been centred on the technical means of production. In primary schools, elementary school traditions of craft teaching, the use of drawing as illustration, and assumptions about young children learning to express themselves freely in visual materials, have combined with that drive for technical proficiency in handling tools and materials, to create a mixture of curriculum endeavours. In both primary and high schools unfamiliarity with works of art and artists has remained prevalent (see Taylor 1986; Gardner 1990 for summaries of evidence on this perspective).

There had been many calls for school art to adopt an emphasis on personal expression, and even idiosyncrasy, from the work of John Dewey (1934), Herbert Read (1943), the Schools Council (1974) and beyond. Appeals for school art to reflect the educational ideas and principles of child-centredness were very clear (see Taylor and Andrews 1993 for a review). This was partly linked to growing evidence (and appreciation) of children's learning, in school or out. Studies of the ways in which children create works of art, and why different children operate in different ways in their creating, are now well established, particularly within the psychological literature (see Gardner 1990 for summary). Branches of psychology concerned specifically with perception, personality orientations, visual imagery, and the visual representation of mental images and ideas are comprehensive.

They show that in these respects just as in intellectual, linguistic, physical and affective domains individual children, at least in Western industrialised societies, have their own means of acquiring learning (and demonstrating it) within complex general patterns of development among children at large. Approaches to education which seek to respect such individuality and emergent maturity are reasonable responses to learning theory. For teaching, a search for understanding of children in general, based on these observations and theories, presents a challenge in itself.

A search for strategies which can both accommodate to and extend the mental capabilities, motivations, physical dexterities, and life experiences of particular children in classroom settings, and specifically the capacity to manipulate ideas and materials towards the production of artwork, is one which exercises teachers constantly (see Gardner 1980, 1990; Perkins 1994 for summaries and further reading).

When the puzzle is moved on a piece or two, to how children respond to works of art, and what teaching strategies can be devised for developing responses, the picture of research and associated educational ideas begins to look as though the pieces have lost their colour somewhat. These are matters which have mainly become a focus of attention in curriculum and research literature as recently as the past decade. How we can understand the responses of children, and the effectiveness of teaching strategies in relation to children of different ages, is a research topic still in its gestation period. The extent to which race, gender, social class, or other cultural factors play a part in the construction of responses, and will need to play a part in devising teaching strategies, will be important pieces to contemplate in the overall picture of the puzzle. Since very little responsive, critical, or appreciation work was done in schools in the past there is not a body of practical knowledge among teachers to draw upon. As most of that which is done in galleries and museums is ephemeral, often related to transitory groups, single visits, or temporary exhibitions, opportunities to build a body of knowledge in those locations have largely evaded interested education officers and curators. With growing interest in this aspect of art education during the final two decades of the century, we have seen the emergence of 'educators [who] are searching for the optimal way in which to provide to ordinary students aspects of artistic knowledge that, until now, have only been available to those who continue formal study of the arts' (Gardner 1990: 37).

Significant contributions to this search have been documented by Dobbs (1992), Eisner (1988), Gardner (1990), Perkins (1994), Robinson (1987), Taylor (1986, 1992) and Taylor and Andrews (1993). In the USA since the mid-1980s the Getty Center for Education in the Arts has led a substantial and well resourced art curriculum movement based on the adopted principles of discipline-based art education. Other projects on both sides of the Atlantic preceded or paralleled this – the Stanford Kettering Project; Harvard's Project Zero; Critical Studies in Art Education; The Arts in Schools – and have contributed to its thinking. The principles of discipline-based art education are that the study of art should derive from the constituent disciplines of production, history, criticism and aesthetics:

> Artists, art historians, art critics and aestheticians contribute different perspectives about an artwork. These perspectives are instructive and useful because each one deepens our understanding and heightens our

appreciation of the various levels of meaning the work of art conveys ... in a discipline-based art education program, learning about art would occur not by isolating the content of each discipline, but by relating and integrating content of all the disciplines.

(Boyer 1985: 13)

In essence each discipline is concerned with the following:

- Aesthetics – conversations and reflections about visual appearances and the making of judgements about art; developing a language which allows oral discourse as well as direct visual and tactile experiences;
- Making art – concerned to know about how artists have used materials and solved problems of visual communication, to convey meaning or represent experiences; with its interests in objects as evidence of customs, beliefs, and social organisation;
- Art history – knowing about the relationships between works of art (individual works of one artist, styles, movements, and cultural traditions), the lives of artists, and the social/cultural contexts of art production; and the extent to which aspects of history can be revealed or imagined through the story of objects;
- Art criticism – through familiarity with particular qualities, properties, standards, and judgements across different works of art, or between different movements, trends and timespans.

In Britain Rod Taylor is a major contributor to literature on children's responses to art, focused initially on work at the Drumcroon Centre in Wigan and developed during a three-year curriculum programme known as the Critical Studies in Art Education (CSAE) Project (Taylor 1986). The approach is close to discipline-based art education: 'It is here that knowledge of traditions, awareness of history and culture, understanding of craft – the possession of an appropriate critical vocabulary – can develop and deepen aesthetic judgements and responses' (Taylor and Andrews 1993: 17).

Taylor's work was influenced in part by the concerns of, and proposals expressed and formulated by, David Hargreaves (1983). Hargreaves' case was, briefly, that poor teaching of art appreciation is likely to turn pupils off participation in the visual arts, through what he called the experience of aversive trauma. In short, a few bad experiences can create long-term aversion. On the other hand, he argued (using a model of religious experience as a basis), pupils can be converted, can experience a positive conversive trauma. This might be sudden and revelatory, or gradual and emergent. Taylor and his colleagues transposed these ideas into a curriculum experience model for aesthetic education which made demands on learners (and teachers) but was characterised by induction into long-term engagement with and enquiry into the visual arts. He summed up this vision as developing illuminating experience, through concentration of attention, generating a sense of revelation, memory retention, and the arousal of appetite for further aesthetic experiences. This is said to lead to commitment to explore works of art, and capabilities of discrimination, and the search for background information, all leading to heightened awareness of the arts.

The latter, Taylor argued, could act as a link between the study and the making of art (Taylor 1986: 27–8). The CSAE Project was based on a desire to redress the balance in the school curriculum from the predominantly practical towards the 'analytical, critical, historical and cultural domains' (Taylor 1992: 25). Indeed he set out the case perhaps more fully than anyone else for that link to be made, claiming that the Project demonstrated that relationships between study and making, far from causing children to imitate others' art, opened up 'a wide range of possibilities' (ibid: 27). Those possibilities, in Taylor's terms, stem from contact with 'the whole cultural cosmos of the arts as practised throughout time and across places' (Taylor and Andrews 1993: 24).

For primary school children specifically, Taylor and Andrews propose a curriculum model which, they assert, will help children to make connections between their own work and that of others. It is a model for the analysis of any work of art or craft in terms of its content (subject matter); form (use of colour, shape, etc.); process (materials, techniques and methods of making) and mood (feelings conveyed). They argue, too, that this content–form–process–mood model can provide a basis for extending and broadening knowledge and understanding of different categories of art and their social/historical/cultural contexts.

Perkins (1994) approaches the matter from a different perspective. He is concerned with the contribution art education and the study of art might make to the cultivation of thinking dispositions in general. He argues that three general categories (or sources) of intelligence and intellectual development can be found throughout contemporary psychology: those with a neurological basis; those with experiential/environmental bases; and those with a meta-cognitive, or self-reflective, or mental self-management basis. Since these are interactive he suggests that the experiential and reflexive in particular will be exercised and extended by the demands which guided study of the arts involves. This, he argues, occurs through the development and application of dispositions which make the act of looking prolonged; broad and adventurous; clear and deep; and organised. Art, in these terms, he says, is a training ground for dispositions which have wider application. The study of art in its own right is in turn an area of experience within the humanities which will be more generally enhanced by the application of these dispositions in the wider fields of learning.

However, how children might be encouraged to develop their knowledge and understanding of art, artists, and cultures from the age of five and to develop their practical art in parallel is, I believe, a matter which will reside in the realm of speculative research for a long time to come. General theses are straightforward enough, matters of common sense. Starting from the aim to develop understanding, for example, Boyer argues that that will be increased through working with materials and processes employed by artists to create the art in question (Boyer 1985: 13). A different starting point is offered by Abbs (1987), who suggests that creativity involves the complementary activities of inner stimuli and drives, and outer exploration of the artistic activities and products of others. Establishing a general thesis, though, does not resolve the curriculum and instructional dilemmas which arise from claims such as Taylor's:

> pupils can experience all the benefits and virtues implicit in making art: development of analytical and observational skills, sustained application, personal expression, etc. But simultaneously they can have opportunity to look outwards to the whole diverse world of the visual arts, and also see their endeavours as part of this larger whole with each aspect nurturing, affirming and enriching the other.
>
> (Taylor 1986: 280)

There is a grand case for exploring the relationships between ways in which children see and feel and think about the phenomena of their world; ways in which they represent their perceptions, feelings and ideas; how they interpret other people's renderings of their experiences; and how those renderings might play a part in the ways in which children create their own art. There are extensive fields of evidence on the first two of these but there is at best only a limited amount of research on the second two matters. Even if there were research evidence on these, bringing it together with the other two areas and converting it into practical classroom action would present a formidable task, even for the specialist art teacher.

The scope and scale of the problematic nature of curriculum endeavours faced by teachers in the implementation of the art curriculum can be sensed from this summary. What is apparent, and also problematic, is that the national curriculum requirements for art are based on a key (but in my view faulty) presumption that its designers (mostly people with substantial specialist expertise in the arts and art education) and teachers (including those in primary schools) know what is implied by its aims, how to achieve them, and how to implement its programmes.

I want to assert that that is not the case, particularly in the realm of children's responses to art, and the development of understanding. What is needed in this field is a predisposition towards enquiry – the adoption of a research stance to the curriculum proposals and their implementation in schools. In particular what is needed is a constant reminder of the warning made by Pateman in the context of making art (to avoid mimicry, pastiche, etc. by looking backwards or being cloned within a tradition). The same healthy scepticism can be applied to art teaching and curriculum models. A realisation of the enormity and complexity of the challenge which faces teachers, particularly primary school teachers who are not specialists in art, will be needed in order that there is scope for the exploration of teaching strategies in particular contexts, and for research of pupils' responses to those strategies by practitioners. Within that scope, scholarly models of curriculum and research literature about children's responses to art will make their own contributions.

CHILDREN UNDERSTANDING ART

Gardner (1990) provides a review of research literature from American developmental psychology concerned with children's responses to art, and an account of Harvard University's Project Zero (which focused also on children's perception and artistic production). He points out that (for most people) the capacity to see visible information develops very rapidly in infancy, but that knowing what and how to perceive within any field of study takes time, training, and experience. Empirical evidence in the visual arts, then, becomes immediately problematic in terms of general developmental principles, since so many contextual and instructional/tutorial factors play a part. He describes studies which show that young children naturally discriminate by size, subject matter, colour, and realistic representations. Sensitivity to artistic style (customary use of composition, etc.), use of metaphor, means of expression, and so on, have also been shown to develop with tutoring of the young. However, he cites Hayes' (1985) view that sophisticated discrimination, or connoisseurship, arises only after many years of careful study.

Perhaps more important is Gardner's summary of research into what children think about what they see, the sense they make of art and the ways in which they reflect upon it. Most significantly he points out that the extent to which tutoring can enrich their understanding remains to be studied. Its relationship to a need for research on the levels and kinds of prior understanding which are brought to encounters with art makes it clear that this is a domain inhabited by uncertainty. He none the less attempts to translate what is known about children's responses to the arts into a form of induction close to the general curricular and pedagogical principles suggested by Taylor (1986) and Hargreaves (1983).

Gardner proposes that the prior knowledge brought (by adults) to artistic encounters might consist of different general types:

- Intuitive knowledge – acquired through sensory–motor experience of the physical world, and interactions with other people;

- First-order symbolic knowledge – of words, pictures, figures, gestures, imbued with meanings;
- Notation systems – elaborate, culturally constructed codes such as in written language, music, mathematics, science, etc.;
- Formal bodies of knowledge – information, concepts, principles, canonical texts, frameworks of thinking, methodological codes, etc. of social groups or scholarly disciplines;
- Skilled knowledge – applied know-how of occupations and practical pursuits.

He suggests that the first four of these have a developmental/hierarchical/ sequential relationship to each other, but that the fifth overlaps them in terms of its acquisition from birth to adulthood. I will not dwell here on the details and the problematics of that dimension of developmental psychology, since Gardner himself expresses his

> belief that artistic forms of knowledge and expression are less sequential, more holistic and organic, than other forms of knowing (Dewey 1934; Read 1943), and that to attempt to fragment them and break them into separate concepts or subdisciplines is especially risky.
>
> (Gardner 1990: 42)

He shows concern for possible disjunctions in the way these types of knowledge might be transmitted/learned, and identifies a search among educators for ways to heighten their integration. Indeed he invokes 'an emerging consensus that the most promising methods involve situated learning' in which students encounter accomplished exponents within a field of study spontaneously calling upon the various forms of knowledge. In the Arts PROPEL Project which he describes, that search has been applied to discipline-based art education by deliberately merging the boundaries of the disciplines, and seeking connections with other bodies of knowledge which might be appropriate in the activities of reflection and response to works of art.

So what, from a curriculum and teaching point of view, can we glean from these ideas? I suggest that the best we can do is accept Gardner's summary of the need to accumulate knowledge of what works and what does not, in different settings, where different assumptions about learning and teaching might be at work, using different curricular materials and tutoring methods. This means, in his terms, recognising the nature of the problem, approaching it from complementary angles, and maintaining a flexible outlook on the kinds and levels of knowledge, skills and understanding that might accrue from different circumstances and teaching approaches. In effect, we should acknowledge that learning and teaching are context specific, and build up case-studies of practice.

Meanwhile one should not become trapped in a simple acceptance of, and acquiescence to, the current formal and legal definition of the art curriculum. Like any artefact, it is itself a part of the circumstances in which we work, a product of its particular time, place and creators. And its interpretation as a command to induct children into 'the richness of our diverse cultural heritage' holds its own inherent traps: not least, a danger of scanning, dabbling, and dipping. Unless, that is, there is:

- An approach towards a meta-perspective of the visual arts, seeking out its fundamental characteristics, which will constitute that authentic knowledge and understanding in our time which I mentioned earlier;
- Appreciation of the need to maintain a sense of enquiry about curriculum practices, and to research and record them;
- Awareness that the research has a number of possible strands – psychological, focused on how children see, feel, think, imagine, create, and learn; artistic, focused on how children interpret, record, represent and render images of their world; philosophical, focused on how children respond to other people's renderings; curricular, focused on decisions about access to knowledge; pedagogical, focused on strategies for maximising learning.

The teachers who have contributed to this book adopted the task of engaging, with their pupils, in ways which use contact with art and artists. The extent to which this was or ought to be for the purposes of making their own work, or not, was judged by them. This is consistent with the principle of action research (see Chapter one) that educational practice and its development are context-bound, and context-specific. Within that principle the value of general theories of education lies in their testing and application by teachers, as they take account of their own circumstances. 'Circumstance' includes their own knowledge and understanding of art, of educational values and principles of art teaching, and the pedagogical practices which arise from these. It also includes the material circumstances – geographical location and availability of resources. And it includes understanding of the backgrounds, experiences, needs and potentials of the particular pupils in their charge.

Plate 3.1 *My Mother Alone in her Dining Room*, Anthony Green, 1975-6 (Robert and Lisa Sainsbury Collection; photograph: James Austin)
© Anthony Green, R.A. c/o Piccadilly Gallery, W.1

Plate 3.2 The Bathroom at 29, Anthony Green, 1979 (Robert and Lisa Sainsbury Collection; photograph: James Austin)
© Anthony Green, R.A. c/o Piccadilly Gallery, W.1

Plate 3.3 Bucket Man, John Davies, 1974 (Robert and Lisa Sainsbury Collection; photograph: James Austin)

Plate 3.4 Head-dress Frontlet (wood, abalone shell, sinew) mid/late 19th century, Northwest coast of America, Kaigani or Haida peoples (Robert and Lisa Sainsbury Collection; photograph: James Austin)

Plate 3.5 Raven Rattle (wood, leather, pebbles) mid-19th century, North America, Haida or Tlingit peoples (Robert and Lisa Sainsbury Collection; photograph: James Austin)

Plate 3.6 *Petite danseuse de quatorze ans*, Edgar Degas, 1880 (Robert and Lisa Sainsbury Collection; photograph: James Austin)

Plate 3.7 Femme, Alberto Giacometti, 1958 (Robert and Lisa Sainsbury Collection; photograph: James Austin)

Plate 3.8 Mother and Child, Henry Moore, 1932, Green Hornton stone
(courtesy: the Henry Moore Foundation, photograph: James Austin)

Plate 3.9 Wolf mask (wood, feather) Inuit, West Alaska (Robert and Lisa Sainsbury Collection; photograph: James Austin)

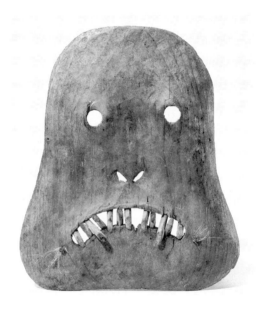

Plate 3.10 Walrus mask (wood) Inuit, West Alaska (Robert and Lisa Sainsbury Collection; photograph: James Austin)

FURTHER READING

Abbs, P. (ed.) (1987) *Living Powers: The Arts in Education*, Lewes: Falmer Press.

Adelman, C. (1987) 'The arts and young children', in L. Tickle (ed.) *The Arts in Education: Some Research Studies*, London: Croom Helm.

Arnheim, R. (1989) *Thoughts On Art Education*, Santa Monica: J. Paul Getty Trust, Getty Center for Education in the Arts.

Bennett, G. (1994) 'An Artist Teachers Portrait', unpublished PhD thesis, Norwich: School of Education, University of East Anglia.

Best, D. (1992) *The Rationality of Feeling: Understanding the Arts in Education*, London: Falmer Press.

Bourdieu, P. (1971) 'Intellectual field and creative project', in M. F. D. Young (ed.) *Knowledge and Control*, London: Collier Macmillan.

Boyer, E. (1983) *High School*, New York: Harper and Row.

—— (1985) 'Art as language: its place in the schools', in *Beyond Creating: The Place of Art in American Schools*, Santa Monica: J. Paul Getty Trust, Getty Center for Education in the Arts.

Csikszentmihalyi, M. and Robinson, R. E. (1990) *The Art of Seeing: An Interpretation of the Aesthetic Encounter*, Malibu, California: J. Paul Getty Museum and Getty Center for Education in the Arts.

Dewey, J. (1934) *Art as Experience*, New York: Capricorn Books.

Dobbs, S. M. (1992) *The D.B.A.E. Handbook: An Overview of Discipline-Based Art Education*, Santa Monica: J Paul Getty Trust, Getty Center for Education in the Arts.

Eisner, E. (1988) *The Role of Discipline-Based Art Education in America's Schools*, Santa Monica: J. Paul Getty Trust, Getty Center for Education in the Arts.

Gardner, H. (1980) *Artful Scribbles*, London: Jill Norman.

—— (1990) *Art Education and Human Development*, Santa Monica: J. Paul Getty Trust, Getty Center for Education in the Arts.

Goodlad, J. I. (1984) *A Place Called School*, New York: McGraw-Hill.

Gulbenkian Foundation (1982) *The Arts in Schools*, London: Calouste Gulbenkian Foundation.

Hargreaves, D. (1983) 'The teaching of art and the art of teaching', in M. Hammersley and A. Hargreaves (eds) *Curriculum Practice: Some Sociological Case Studies*, Lewes: Falmer Press.

Hayes, J. R. (1985) 'Three problems in teaching general skills', in J. Segal, S. Chapman and R. Glaser (eds) *Thinking and Learning Skills*, vol. 2, Hillside, New Jersey: Lawrence Erlbaum Associates.

Pateman, T. (1991) *Key Concepts: A Guide to Aesthetics, Criticism and the Arts in Education*, London: Falmer Press.

Perkins, D. N. (1994) *The Intelligent Eye: Learning to Think by Looking at Art*, Santa Monica: J. Paul Getty Trust, Getty Center for Education in the Arts.

Read, H. (1943) *Education Through Art*, London: Faber.

Rittner, L. (1983) Editorial, in *Arts Council Education Bulletin*, Autumn, London: Arts Council.

Robinson, K. (1987) 'The arts in the national curriculum', in *The Arts in Schools Project Newsletter* No. 7, December, London: Schools Council.

Schools Council (1974) *Children's Growth Through Creative Experience*, London: Van Nostrand Reinhold.

Sekules, V. and Tickle, L. (eds) (1993) *Starting Points: Approaches to Art Objects*

Selected from the Sainsbury Centre for Visual Arts, University of East Anglia, Norwich: Centre for Applied Research in Visual Arts Education.

Taylor, R. (1986) *Educating for Art: Critical Response and Development*, Harlow: Longman.

—— (1992) *Visual Arts in Education*, London: Falmer Press.

Taylor, R. and Andrews, G. (1993) The Arts in the Primary School, London: Falmer Press.

Tickle, L. (ed.) (1987) *The Arts in Education: Some Research Studies*, London: Croom Helm.

Tickle, L. and Sekules, V. (eds) (1995) *Interpretations: Approaches to Art Objects Selected From the Sainsbury Centre for Visual Arts*, University of East Anglia, Norwich: Centre for Applied Research in Visual Arts Education.

Wolff, J. (1985) 'Questioning the curriculum: arts education and ideology', in M. Ross (ed.) *The Aesthetic in Education*, London: Pergamon.

Chapter 4

Room for improvement

Jane Ackers

When I first saw the two paintings by Anthony Green, *My Mother Alone in Her Dining Room* and *The Bathroom at 29*, they immediately made an impression on me. They seemed alive and full of fun, with so much colourful detail. It struck me straight away that because the children I teach would be able to relate to each picture (as they contained so many common objects, clearly depicted and easily recognisable), I could link my teaching and research to a study of Anthony Green's work, and explore the children's capacity to observe and record pictorially and in accurate detail aspects of daily life and their surroundings.

I believed that Year 3 children 'see' objects but do not 'look' at them. My teaching aim was to encourage them to look more closely at objects and spaces, gaining more knowledge of everyday items and environments, discovering beauty in texture, patterns, shadows, and so on. By setting the group specific tasks I hoped to increase their enthusiasm for obser-vation and to develop drawing from what I regarded as their usual 'impressionistic' and schematic approach, to extend their modes of representing their 'everyday' world.

In order to research my initial beliefs, the children's modes of representation, their skills of observation and the influences my teaching strategies had on the acquisition of these skills, I planned:

- To set them specific tasks in order to channel their enthusiasm, limiting the media they used to what they were familiar with so far: water-colour, pencil and crayon;
- To discuss their work, in a group or on a one-to-one basis, depending on the individual children;
- To have the children study the two Anthony Green paintings, in addition to seeing as much of the collection as time would allow. (This was the first visit made to an art collection by most of the children.)

The following data were recorded:

- The tasks I set, week by week;
- Strategies, verbal and visual, which I used in teaching;

- The children's verbal responses;
- Examples of the children's work, before and after teaching strategies were employed.

For the purpose of storing data, I used written notes, audio tapes, photographs and examples of the children's work.

Gayton First School is a small country school about six miles from King's Lynn. It has sixty children on roll, many coming from fairly low income families. There are three full time teachers including the head-teacher, a part time teacher (myself), a welfare assistant and a part time secretary. For my project, I worked with my usual art group of twenty-four, Year 3 children, in a rather cramped mobile classroom. We made one visit to the Sainsbury Centre for Visual Arts, travelling by minibus with Mrs Muff (welfare assistant) driving one vehicle, and myself the second. The minibuses were borrowed from Springwood High School, the senior school in our area.

I SET THE BALL ROLLING

How should I spark the children's interest enough for them to make careful studies of individual objects? I decided to have them look at one object (i.e. the school hand bell) but to also bring in some objects to stimulate their curiosity. I collected some old fashion jewellery, a clarinet, a camera and a cine camera, showed these to the class, and we talked about shapes, patterns, the materials they were made of and the various colours. The children chose an object and made a pencil study of it.

I was really pleased with the results especially with Steven's clarinet. Steven has a very short concentration span and can be a disruptive child. For this lesson, though, he sat engrossed in his work and was rightly very proud of his results. All the group made a good attempt at an accurate image of their chosen object. This first lesson, however, had resulted in the objects being isolated and I wanted gradually to extend the studies to a whole room. To achieve this, my next lesson plan was to encourage the group to draw an object but this time to include a small area of back-ground. Again I found the results pleasing and Steven produced a piece of work which he was proud of and which showed he had the capability to concentrate and observe in detail.

I gathered background information about Anthony Green's work, and looked again at his painting *My Mother Alone in Her Dining Room*. Anthony Green had chosen to depict a room familiar to him, from memory. All the objects were clearly remembered, their positions, their relationships with each other and to the room itself. The contents of the room were just ordinary everyday things, but each had its own importance. Nothing was given what I call impressionistic treatment. All were recorded in minute detail right down to the two screw holes fixing the light switch to the wall. Even though the objects were familiar everyday things, Anthony Green had painted them as if they were just as important as the figure. The figure was the most prominent and significant part of the painting entitled *My Mother Alone in Her Dining Room*. She took up the central forefront position, looking outward, fixing the onlooker with a glassy stare. The painting was not called *The Contents of the Dining Room with My Mother Sitting at the Table*, yet the artist had treated all his mother's belongings with an apparent freshness and zest, which characterises the 'feel' of his work.

WRONG TACTICS!

On reflection, it seemed to me that the work I had set for the children was concerned more with recording individual objects in detail than it was with the whole composition of a picture, with representing space or environments. The tasks were based on observing and drawing an isolated item, then looking again at the object in its immediate background, and adding that background bit by bit until the children had built up a complete picture. I also came to think that it was a mistake to introduce them to unusual articles (which was aimed at sparking their enthusiasm for observing).

Realisation set in. The Anthony Green paintings I had admired were his representations of complete rooms full of everyday objects, and it is this familiarity that he treats with such individualism, seeing well known surroundings and belongings with a seemingly renewed vision. The composition is treated as a whole right from the start, as seen in his preparatory sketches (SCVA 1986), and not as a compilation of individual drawings. This realisation led to a quick change of teaching strategies and some thoughts on how familiar can also become unusual. If I wore the same clothes week after week, then wore something different, the children would be immediately aware of the change. I wanted them to notice the same clothes but look at them with a totally fresh outlook. If I gave them set objects to study, each object would be new to them and not part of a familiar everyday picture.

Because of my rethinking of object/space and familiar/unusual, I changed my approach and set the class a different task, as follows:

> Draw a picture of the classroom for a friend who wants to see what it is like but is unable to come and see it for him or herself. Think about all the things you can see in the room and how the tables and chairs are grouped. Where is the door? Where are the windows? Try to give your friend a really good idea of your classroom.

The children used pencil for this first lesson, a medium they were very familiar with, having done some sketching recently. Some remarked that it was just as well they were using pencil because of all the rubbing-out! The task contained few specific instructions. I wanted to see how the group coped with the task of drawing the whole room with minimum direction and little guidance. I also wished to test my belief that the children would not include much detail. I expected their pictures to be representations of small areas of the classroom with some sketchy impressions of a few items seen on desks or storage units. The resulting drawings provided data connected with three main questions:

- How much detail is recorded by the children?
- What is their mode of representation?
- Do they come across any problems and if so, what are they?

I was surprised at how much detail the children had put into their work. I had thought that they would sketch the rough shape of the room and then add details later (as was suggested in the next lesson by Matthew after seeing the Anthony Green pictures). None of the children attempted the whole room. Many had chosen to depict just the wall carrying the blackboard and charts. This was certainly carefully studied, with such details as writing on the board and pictures on the wall included. Most of the resulting drawings represented only one plane with no apparent attempt at perspective or the inclusion of volume. Listening to the general chat, there was no mention of scale either. At this stage I decided not to bring it to the attention of the group as I just wanted their raw efforts to test my own assumption that Year 3 children would only see objects and not look at them.

This first set of drawings completely upset that idea, as illustrated by the pictures by Tamsin, Sarah and Alison. Tamsin was one of the children who chose to draw the blackboard and recorded all the items stuck to the wallboard at that time. She also showed the board protractor which was hanging at a slight angle, and had taken the trouble to hint at the measurements around its edge. Sarah had drawn the wall which faced her table. She detailed all the items on the units and drew the land masses on the globe and the measurements around the axis. Each of the paintbrushes on the left was shown to be arranged according to height. I checked this, and she had made a very accurate observation. Alison had also chosen to make a study of the wall facing her table. She had made an attempt at three-dimensional representation, in that the chair was certainly drawn showing its depth and the fact that it sits on the carpet in front of the unit. The detail on the alphabet frieze surprised me. The spider even had the correct number of legs.

As the group worked I recorded three pieces of conversation to typify the problems which came to light for them as they sought to record the details of the room.

Figure 4.1 Sarah's drawing of the classroom

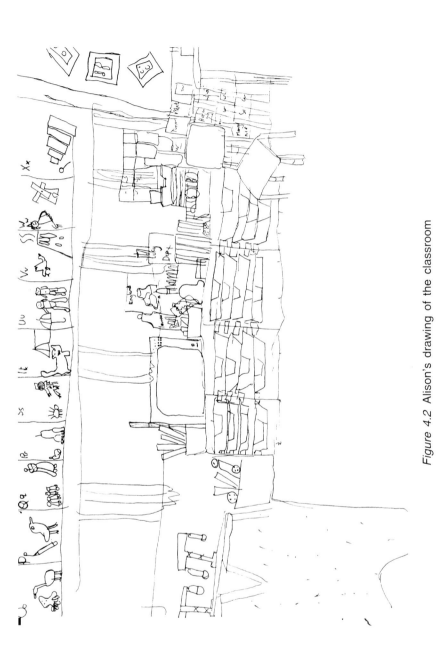

Figure 4.2 Alison's drawing of the classroom

MATTHEW   You can't fit the whole classroom into one little bit of paper; it's impossible!

Matthew solved this problem by depicting only one end of the room and did not attempt any other area of the mobile.

JOSEPH   There's so much in the room I don't know where to start.

The task seemed so daunting. He explained to me that he just did the television on the unit at the side of the room because it was close to his chair and was 'just a sort of rectangle shape and that's easy to draw'.

RACHEL   The mobile is like a big box but when I draw it, it just looks flattened out. I'm going to start again.

This remark indicated a different, reflective and evaluative view of the work she had done. I encouraged her to carry on with what she had done and then looked at her drawing again (Figure 4.3). She had not recorded in such detail as other children. The numbers and letters on the charts to the left of her picture were barely suggested by a squiggly line. She used a similar technique to depict the charts on the blackboard. However, the foreground of her drawing showed a different style. She attempted to show the 3D form of the chairs and tables by giving each piece of furniture four legs. Rachel's drawing showed a visual grasp of the concept of depth and a means of representing it. I wondered if this had been done consciously, thinking of what I had read: 'The seeing of depth must be discovered by the child. To take this discovery from him (*sic*) by "explaining" perspective would deprive him of an important experience' (Lowenfeld and Brittain 1966: 222).

However, a visual appreciation and conceptual knowledge of spatial relationships does not necessarily mean that a child can represent that knowledge graphically. I questioned Rachel as to the reason for her style of drawing:

J.A.   Rachel, can you explain why you've drawn the chairs like this?

RACHEL   Well, a chair has four legs and when it faces you, you can see two at the front and the two at the back but the back legs are away from you so that the seat sort of sticks out of the picture.

J.A.   And what about the writing on the chart? Why have you only drawn squiggly lines?

RACHEL   The charts are far away from me so they're not clear, but Charlotte's troll is near to me so I've drawn that in detail.

From what Rachel said I felt she had observed that part of the room with a good sense of spatial awareness, and understood the concept of perspective. We looked out of the classroom window and together we discussed how the trees in the distance appeared to be smaller than those

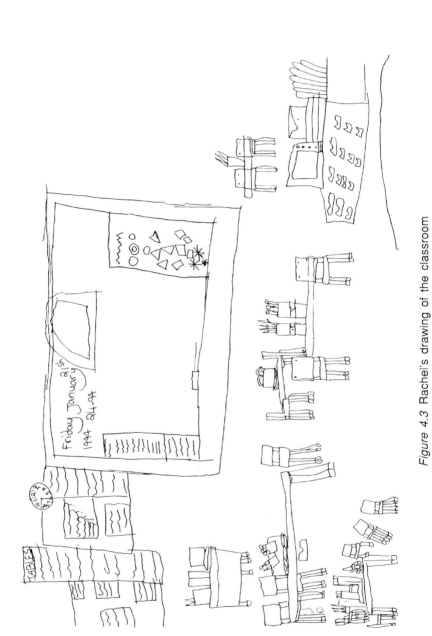

Figure 4.3 Rachel's drawing of the classroom

bordering the school playing field. Rachel noticed that the distant area was misty and, as she put it, blurred, whereas the closer trees and buildings were more brightly coloured and clear. By this time we had been joined by a number of other pupils who joined in on the discussion and agreed with Rachel's observations.

Thinking back to Anthony Green's work, I remembered that I had found his viewpoints intriguing. He seemed to be looking down on each scene but had then changed his viewpoint to embrace a representation of a complete room, looking up to the ceiling, down to the floor, sideways to the walls, yet also using perspective. How would the children deal with perspective, scale and multiple viewpoints in space? From the comments made by Matthew and Joseph, spacial concepts had yet to be linked to the range of possibilities of using devices to represent space and form on two dimensional surfaces. The idea of representing scale had not yet materialised either. I decided to explore these matters further after the children had seen the work of Anthony Green for themselves.

THE VISIT

I kept changing my mind about how this visit should be organised but, in the end, we were ruled more by time than by anything else. On arrival at the gallery the children were divided into groups of six, each group with an adult. They were allowed to wander around the exhibition to get the feel of the gallery. In turn, each group came with me to the two paintings by Anthony Green. I told them a little about each one and recorded their comments. As far as possible I wanted to record data which would tell me:

● How much did the children notice about the contents of each painting?
● How many of the everyday objects could they identify?
● Did any of the children comment on the artist's use of viewpoints?
● Were there any observations about the artist's use of perspective or scale?

There was a chorus of responses as soon as the children saw *My Mother Alone in Her Dining Room*.

LEAH   Look at the reflection on the table, and I can see the reflection of the lady in the mirror at the back.
SARAH   There's lots of reflections. Look at the one of the carpet in that thing on the left. [*Sarah was looking at the bureau on the left of the painting.*]
CLAIRE   He's shown us what's on the table and all the little patterns show up. He's added all the reflections and shadows and nothing looks flat.

J.A.   What do you mean, flat?

CLAIRE   Well, you could pick up all the things in the picture because they all look real.

The children were fascinated by the reflections and I was surprised that it was these that first took their attention. We played a game of hunt the reflection, and I noted how observant the group was. Leah noticed the mirror reflecting down on to the table. Claire's comment about everything looking real and not flat was an indication that she was aware of perspective and 3D representation.

MATTHEW   I can see my Nan's telephone. That's just like hers.

JANE   I've seen one of those china things in a shop in town.

Other children recognised the *After Eight* mints and the different types of fruit in the fruit bowl. Matthew looked deeper into the painting:

MATTHEW   The lady must know a cook. Look at the photo, he's wearing a cook's hat.

Sophie studied some detail in the foreground:

SOPHIE   The lady's quite old because her neck's crimpled and the artist has even shown that.

Now followed a discussion of all the items the children recognised. We played a game of I-spy and the group proved very observant. Sophie's letter was G for the grain in the wood.

RYAN   The door on the left is wider at the bottom than it is at the top. It looks downhill; the whole room looks a bit wonky and the door goes up there and the wall goes straight across but then the lines look as if they go backwards. That's all funny angles.

I asked Ryan if he thought there was any reason for this, but he could not think of any. He was able to recognise that the room was not depicted as he was used to seeing them. Apparently Ryan did not realise that the manner in which the artist had painted the room was a means to represent a feeling of depth and space, a pictorial device for including so much information. His description of the devices, though, opened up the possibility of discussing the matter further:

JODI   I think the telephone's going to slide off the table.

J.A.   Why?

JODI   The top of the table's tilted.

J.A.   Which way?

JODI   Out towards us.

J.A.   Why?

JODI   So we can see what's on it. All the flat bits are tilted except the big table and that's at the front, and anyway, the artist is looking down on that one.

Jodi was the only child to comment on one of the artist's viewpoints as being from above, although Ryan was able to describe parts of the painting which suggested different viewpoints: 'it looks downhill; the door goes up; that's all funny angles'. Other pupils noticed different pictorial devices:

JOSEPH   He's made the carpet look light up there and it's dark down here and the patterns are bigger at the front than they are at the back.
J.A.   Why?
JOSEPH   To make you feel you're looking into something. The big patterns are closer than the ones at the back. They're further into the room.

Joseph made a comment which showed not only close observation but also an understanding as to why the artist had painted the carpet thus. All the children liked the painting and were surprised to learn that it was painted from memory. One of the group noticed the fingers of the seated figure and pointed them out to the others. They did not like them and described them as too long and the hand too short. Leah said that most of the hand was obscured by the table and gave that as the reason why the fingers were foreshortened. They still did not like the hands. One described them as clumsy, and not like a posh lady's hand except for the nail varnish.
    We moved on to look at *The bathroom at 29.*

JODI   *Head and Shoulders*! We use that at home.
LEAH   And the hairbrush Jodi; that's like your Mum's.
MATTHEW   Look at all the coat-hangers. There's hundreds of them.

The everyday objects were soon recognised and the group found it strange to see items so familiar to them depicted in a painting for public view:

JODI   Our shampoo's famous. It's in a painting.

We talked about the reflections and the children noticed that although the lady's dress and the toilet brush were reflected on the side of the bath, the pedal bin's reflection was missing and this annoyed them:

JODI   He's really spoilt the detail on that bit because he's missed out the orange coloured reflection of the bin.

Matthew made an observation which indicated that he was aware of the artist's use of multiple viewpoints and Ryan noticed that the whole room was depicted in a similarly unusual manner as the first painting he had looked at:

MATTHEW   There's the toilet thing [*cistern*]. How can that be round there if the toilet's just here?

J.A.   Isn't that strange? Do you think the cistern is really in that position?

MATTHEW   No, otherwise you'd have to get off the loo and go across to pull the chain.

J.A.   Why has the artist painted it there then?

MATTHEW   Well, the artist is sort of standing where the tank would be and if he really painted what he saw, it would just be a black bit and that's all.

RYAN   There's lots of different angles again and this time even the picture's a funny shape.

I was asked why the lady and man were in the bathroom at the same time but Leah had made an observation which satisfied everyone's curiosity:

LEAH   The fingers on the wife are the same as on the mother ... and they've got the same colour nail varnish. The man's spectacles on the side wouldn't fit him because his head's too big. His head's so big it makes him look ill. Oh! he is ill, that's why the lady is having to give him a bath.

We had a vote on which painting was the more popular and *The bathroom at 29* won the day. The children found it hard to decide but said that the latter was bright and more cheerful whereas the other painting was darker and the lady looked very strict. All the children said how much they had enjoyed the visit. The only criticism was that there was not enough time for them to wander around on their own for very long or for them to do any sketching.

BACK AT SCHOOL

When I first set the task of drawing the classroom, I gave little guidance on how to tackle the idea of perspective as this was not my initial interest. Following the conversation with Rachel, and having noticed other attempts from members of the class which suggested a visual appreciation of depth and spacial awareness, I introduced their next task as follows:

J.A.   Last time we met, I set you the task of drawing the classroom. Since then you've seen two rooms painted by a famous artist and one of you remarked that in one of the paintings you felt as if you were looking right into the room. This week, I want you to have another try at painting the whole room and to think about that phrase 'looking into'. What shape is the classroom?

GROUP   Cuboid.

J.A.   Right! Now see if you can make your drawing show that it's that shape. Just before you start, let's have a look at some of the work done last week and try to discover if anyone has found some tricks to help to sort out the problem.

At this point we studied two drawings: one by Alison who had represented the room as if viewed from the ceiling; and one by Jonathon, who looked down on the room from behind my desk. These were discussed and compared with the paintings seen at the gallery. As the children worked, I recorded some of their conversation which illustrated how they reflected on Anthony Green's work as they tackled their own:

JODI   In the bathroom one, he moved some of the things to fit them in; can we do that, please?

MATTHEW   If you stuck your head through the wall so you can see the classroom, can we move things on the board like Anthony Green did with the toilet, so they can still be in the picture?

J.A.   Listen to Tiffany's idea. She suggests a sketch of the room first then add the details after that. Do you think the artist did this?

MATTHEW   Yes! He must've done it that way because he couldn't rub out paint if he made a mistake.

J.A.   Did Anthony Green finish the whole picture in just one day?

MATTHEW   No, I shouldn't think so; there's just too much in it to finish that quickly.

J.A   Then what do you think he did first?

MATTHEW   A sketch!

One or two of the children had imagined the room from above and when asked about this, all replied that by doing so they could fit the things into the paper more easily, but no one could explain why. Charlotte then had a statement for me:

CHARLOTTE   Mrs Ackers, I can't get the door in on my paper. It will be all squashed up.

J.A.   Suppose you wanted to get all the things on that wall on the top width of your paper. What would you have to do?

CHARLOTTE   Well, I'd have to do the blackboard smaller.

With Charlotte's permission I stopped the rest of the class and briefly described the problem which she had found. The discussion between Charlotte and me continued with the whole group listening in.

CHARLOTTE   So that's OK then. I'll do the board smaller then everything will fit in.

J.A.   Will the clock look right if you do the blackboard smaller?

CHARLOTTE   No, because the clock will look too big.

J.A.   Right. I'm going to introduce you to a new word connected with sorting out this problem: scale. Now let me explain. Let's all look at the clock. How many times do you think I could fit the clock along the bottom of the blackboard? [*The children estimated twelve times.*] So, in your picture, how many times should your clock fit along the bottom of the board?

CHARLOTTE   Oh! that will have to be twelve too or it won't look right, will it?

J.A.   Now, Charlotte, can you suggest what you might do to make the drawing look right?

CHARLOTTE   Well, if I just make the board smaller, the clock won't fit in so I'll have to make the clock small too. I'll have to make the clock the size that will fit into the bottom of the board twelve times just like the real one would.

J.A.   Yes, then they would both be the same scale. If you made the board small and left the clock alone would that be in the same scale?

CHARLOTTE   No, because the clock would only fit in about two or three times. Oh! I know how to explain it! If you have to make things smaller everything has to be made smaller just the same; it's all got to be smaller against each other!

Here, with Charlotte's co-operation, the whole group had become aware of the concept of scale by using her sense of size and comparison. Although I did not introduce the word 'proportion' at this time, the children were also dealing with that concept. These would be important considerations too with regard to the ideas of viewpoints and perspective. They were ideas which I was having to think about myself in relation to the children's awareness of devices for representing objects and space.

In his book *Strategies of Representation in Young Children* Norman H. Freeman (1980) asks: 'What would a child have to know in order to draw, even crudely, in perspective?' He feels that four things are essential:

- A grasp of the idea that the observer has to play an active role in construction so that the final representation is a recombination of aspects of the real objects which explains their structure and relationships;
- Some degree of abstract understanding that the best way of explaining a scene is to rescale and possibly violate isolated aspects of its appearance;
- A certain grasp of measurement and geometry as these are much concerned with scaling and co-ordinating scales;
- A concept of space – this deals mainly with a child's ability to analyse the structure of a scene whereas a concept of geometry deals with his or her ability to reconstruct that scene to form a picture.

It is little wonder that the children were taxed in their exploration of their own solutions to the tasks I set, and in their interpretation of Anthony Green's use of his solutions. But their tasks had been based on direct observation. Often they try to work from memory; this offered further possibilities and problems to be explored.

FOOD FOR THOUGHT

Anthony Green painted his rooms from memory, his vision of each room and all its detail stored away then reproduced from his own recollections. We talked about Anthony Green's rooms and decided that the artist remembered them with affection and that the moment captured in the bathroom painting was a scene recreated with tenderness.

I asked the children to think about a room at their house in readiness for a new task the following week. I changed the subject matter because I thought the children would benefit from drawing a room of their own choice. I asked them to walk around their homes and to decide which room they would like to draw. They were to have a good look at it in order to memorise it in as much detail as possible. I began by reminding them of the paintings we had seen at the gallery. I asked them to close their eyes and to 'walk' around the inside of their own house. As I did not know what their house looked like, they would have to picture it in their own mind as I walked through each room with my voice, guiding the class, asking them to try to visualise the members of their family who might be in the rooms. I suggested that, as they could draw only one room, they choose the one they liked best.

FINAL TASK

The task for the following week was to depict their chosen room from memory, and again to attempt to draw the whole room and not just part of it. We looked at the drawings which Alison and Jonathon had done the previous week and recapped on the discussion we had had on viewpoints and scale. At this stage I still had not mentioned 'perspective' as I was continuing to test the children's visual concepts and levels of understanding.

J.A.   How has Alison made us feel that the blackboard and the charts on the wall are going down into the room?

TAMSIN   She's made the board wider at the top and narrower at the bottom. Even the curtains are done like that.

I then introduced the word 'perspective', using these two pieces of work to help to clarify its meaning. I felt that during discussions the group had grasped a visual concept of depth and were also discovering ways to represent it.

J.A.   I'm going to introduce a new word to you now. If I got out my sketch pad to draw a picture of us all sitting here, I'd have to show that the real scene has a near area, an area a bit further away from me and an area that is in the distance. I'd have to show that the tables, chairs, units and all the other things in the classroom aren't just flat as if they'd been run over by a steam roller. I'd have to give whoever looked at my picture the idea that some things are in front of others; some are behind, beside, near to me, far away. I'd have to show all their different positions. The way I'd have to do this is called drawing in perspective.

RACHEL   That's what I meant when I said things had to stick out of the paper. I've said that to Sophie.

J.A.   Right. Well, you know a word to describe that idea now. I wonder if you'll remember it? Try to think of that word, and how I explained it, while you're doing your work this week.

A request from Jodi soon spread among others: could they use crayon to colour their pictures? I agreed to the request, and set them a supplementary task: to pretend to dust the room which they had drawn, noticing anything they had forgotten to include in their picture, and trying to visualise everything in the room clearly, and then to crayon it if they wished.

My overall impression from this lesson was that the children were relieved to leave the confines of the classroom, but found drawing from memory quite difficult. We had a number of false-starts and requests to start again. For the purpose of research I chose to examine the work of children whose pictures I had previously used as examples. I needed to compare the earlier and later drawings to discover whether any new ideas had been conceived and whether the task had widened their knowledge or left them floundering. My notes included the following items.

Alison

A changed viewpoint: Alison viewed the classroom from above but is now looking into her sitting room at home from a standing position. There are indications that Alison has spatial awareness and a grasp of perspective and has also discovered a means by which her awareness of space can be represented. For example, the carpet pattern attracts the eyes to the back of the room as does the line of the settee on the left. All the chairs are drawn to show a solid shape and the schema for drawing the chair in the foreground is repeated in the settee. This schema changes for the chair at the end of the carpet as that is viewed from the front and not the side. I asked Alison about the top surface of the slope-top bureau and she replied that if you could see the sloped front you would not be able to see the top part . . . an observation which shows a good understanding of space, viewpoint, and a close scrutiny of the scene.

Rachel

Rachel included plenty of detail in her drawing. Rather than drawing her bathroom as a whole unit I feel she has visually 'walked around the walls', drawing small scenes. The bath (viewed from above) and the basin beside it are both drawn to the same scale even though Rachel has drawn them from two different angles. The window shows that Rachel has the ability to see depth and is discovering how to represent this in her drawing. She has drawn the view through the window. In terms of depth, the window has been depicted with the sill tiles as the foreground, the window frame as the middle distance and the view as distant. The toilet has proved more difficult for her to represent. She seems to have realised that the whole rim would be visible from this viewpoint and she has drawn it in, but the whole thing is tilted forwards. Rachel can see and comprehend the 3D form of the toilet but has not yet discovered how a rounded shape can be shown to have this property in her drawing. Rachel explained to me that her viewpoint for looking in the mirror was behind and slightly above the figure, but, although she could easily draw the back view, when she looked at the result, the figure appeared to be nose downwards on the floor.

RACHEL   That mirror's meant to be on the wall with Mummy standing in front of it. I've tried to draw it but it won't go right.
J.A.   Why not?
RACHEL   The mirror looks as if it's flat on the floor with Mummy lying on top of it! I don't know how to show that the mirror is sort of upright on the wall.

Rachel showed a concept of depth but had yet to discover a way to represent what she knew and saw. When I first explained the meaning of perspective, Rachel said that it was like making things stick out of the paper. Now she was faced with a different problem, where she knew what the figure, mirror, and reflection were meant to look like but was unable to represent them in a way suitable to her.

Tamsin

TAMSIN   I feel just like Anthony Green. Do you think I'll be famous, Mrs Ackers?
J.A.   You'll just have to wait and see, but tell me why you feel like Anthony Green.
TAMSIN   Well, this is my Mum looking in the mirror and it's like Anthony Green's Mum but the other way round. We could see his Mum's face

in the picture but the back of her head was reflected in the mirror and I've done it so my Mum's face is reflected in the mirror but we can see her backview facing out at us.

Both the figure and its reflection are relative in size and shape. The way she has left a gap between the mirror and the standing figure illustrates that Tamsin has found a way to represent her mother standing away from the wall in order to suggest depth. In Tamsin's first picture her drawing was detailed but the only representation of depth was the double outline of the blackboard and protractor. Tamsin also drew from a base line but in her later work she found a way to represent the idea of a complete room by drawing the items around its perimeter.

Ashley

Ashley's imagination took him above his room and he found a way to represent it looking down, by angling the lines of the walls on to the area of the floor. He had not realised that the pictures on the walls could be represented in the same way, or had not chosen to do so, so they do not appear to hang down the walls.

Natasha

Natasha found that, by sloping the corner of the walls into the area she has drawn to represent the floor, she is able to give an impression of looking down into her bedroom. She has realised that anything on the wall needs the same treatment ... some of the hearts on the wallpaper are elongated as are the door and window. Natasha became disorientated in her thinking and drew the window on the floor. However, she has discovered a method of representation for perspective and has repeated the schema in the curtains and the sides of the bed.

LEAVING THE ROOM

I realised that my original thoughts about children's capacity to observe and record in detail were wrong, and that Year 3 children both see detail and are able to record it in their drawings. To discover what the children had understood about perspective and scale, I asked them to give me some of their own definitions.

TAMSIN   If you did a picture, the things at the front have to be quite big and the things at the back have to be quite small. The bits in the middle are middle-sized ... well, that's how you draw them.

ALISON   When you do a room or something, it shouldn't look just flat on the paper, you have to draw the sides as well to make it look solid.

RACHEL   Whatever you see, there are bits that are close to you and bits that are far away. When you draw it, your drawing has to show that things are all in those different places, otherwise the picture would just look flat and it should look like the things are coming out of it.

JODI   When you draw something, like a table, you have to make it smaller to fit the paper. If you make the table twice as small, all the other things in the picture have to be twice as small too.

I had judged that in order to acquire the skills of representation children must first acquire the skills to observe and to understand those observations. Even when the children could verbally explain the juxtaposition of objects, in some cases they had not yet discovered a means to represent them as they wished. I was confident that, by the end of my teaching strategies, the children were observing with a heightened awareness and, judging from their comments, had improved their techniques of representation.

RACHEL   I've always wanted to be a dentist but I think I could probably be an artist when I grow up. I can draw things better now!

WITH DOOR AJAR

The children had not yet fully explored the use of colour when implementing their ideas. I wanted to extend their present knowledge by using teaching strategies designed to encourage them to experiment with paint in order for them to discover how it can be used effectively in their representations. Time for further consideration of the Anthony Green paintings . . .

FURTHER READING

Bell, J. (1987) *Doing Your Research Project*, Milton Keynes: Open University Press.

Freeman, N. H. (1980) *Strategies of Representation in Young Children*, London: Academic Press.

Gardener, H. (1980) *Artful Scribbles*, London: Jill Norman.

Hopkins, D. (1985) *A Teacher's Guide to Classroom Research*, Milton Keynes: Open University Press.

Lowenfeld, V. and Brittain, J. (1966) *Creative and Mental Growth*, New York: Macmillan.

Sainsbury Centre for Visual Arts (1986) *Anthony Green's Mirror*, Norwich: SCVA.

Taylor, R. (1986) *Educating for Art: Critical Response and Development*, Harlow: Longman.

Chapter 5

Representation, emotion, and special educational needs

Sue Allen

The aim of this research was to investigate how Year 7 children, all of whom have statements of special educational needs, respond to emotion as represented in visual art. I describe how children observe, express and articulate their interpretations of emotion in art. The lessons in which the data were gathered were structured to provide opportunities for the children to respond to different art objects. Verbal responses were also encouraged through describing, questioning and discussing. The group in the study is a Learning Support Centre class of seven boys and five girls. Three main issues are considered: the utilisation of art objects in teaching art; artistic maturation; and the development of expression and communication by visual and verbal means.

It is my belief that children need to be visually literate to function effectively in a world where so much information is presented in text and pictorially. This need for children to become confident and competent in understanding and interpreting the images and symbols of visual communication, and in using them, is well recognised: 'pupils should become visually perceptive, develop powers of observation, and be capable of selecting, interpreting and recording what they see, think, feel, and know, using art media' (DES 1991: para. 4.5).

Countless studies exist of the progression of children's artistic maturation, for example Barnes (1987), Gentle (1975), Larkin (1981), Clement and Page (1992c, d, e). A common view within them shows that at a very early stage all children who can hold a pencil (or similar) make marks with it. The quality and meaning invested in those marks is something which is not always obvious, and the development of image-making may depend upon constructive teaching and progress in understanding how to use certain tools and techniques. Children's ability to recall their experience has considerable bearing upon the way in which they make their images. When they begin to draw, images are often made from recall. Attention is absorbed in the image as it emerges and children are not always evidently concerned with the differences between the images they make and appearances in the real world. This partly accounts for the flexibility and spontaneity attributed to children's art in early childhood.

As children progress through primary school they become more self-conscious about how images they make correspond to their perception of the real world and are received by others. Towards the approach of adolescence children become more acutely concerned with 'realism'. They start to question the value and point of their artwork, and become increasingly critical of it. Their artistic maturation and modes of visual representation do not always satisfy their 'perceptual maturation'.

The children I teach all have special educational needs. Many experience communication and expressive language difficulties because of delayed language development or specific speech disorders. They have reached that level of artistic maturation, somewhere between childhood and adolescence, where they lack confidence in their ability to make visual representations successfully (in their terms) through drawing alone. At the same time, for some children, the constant effort of communicating through speech results in frustration and a sense of inadequacy. There is the possibility that this could lead to a reduction of effort in speaking, especially where the risk of embarrassment exists. However, children who think that their drawings do not 'look right', that 'the paint won't mix', or that they 'can't draw', reveal another tension between what they experience, what they visualise, and what emerges through the use of art media.

Early adolescence for such children is extremely important in the growth of the individual's sensitivity to both the use of oral language and the use of visual images, and the way the latter can arise and be given form. Clement and Page liken the acquisition of drawing skill, for example, to that of oral language: 'Drawing depends on an individual's confidence to "say" in a drawing what they want to convey to others' (1992b: 127).

One of the starting points for the visual art project reported here was my belief that children who feel vulnerable, insecure and inadequate are even less likely to express ideas visually or discuss their world, yet their exposure to 'real' art in circumstances other than school might overcome those inhibitions. I wanted to test out the possibilities of new opportunities for both the children and me.

The broad teaching aims of the project were:

- To encourage realisations that art is more than the representation of visual realism in drawing and painting;
- To increase the children's confidence both in artistic expression and in verbal communication in relation to art;
- To utilise original art objects within my teaching strategies, aimed at developing observation skills, expressive skills, articulation and confidence.

In other words, I hoped that the expressive experience of the children would be extended by developing their ability to communicate both visually and verbally without the emphasis on 'realism'. The focus was primarily on the expression of feeling as portrayed by art objects and interpreted by the children. I also hoped that the children would begin to understand, enjoy and discriminate between images and art objects of different kinds in familiar surroundings, such as their homes and school, and in less familiar environments such as an art gallery. The development of the pupils' visual perception was an important consideration within the teaching aims, since I believed that the promotion of learning through direct observation about the appearance and structure of objects, and about their own responses to them, provided the key to understanding the link between art and emotion. That approach is encouraged in the National Curriculum: 'In order to develop visual literacy pupils should be taught about different ways in which ideas, feelings and meanings are communicated in visual form' (DfE 1995: page 4, para. 3).

The National Curriculum orders also require that children should be taught the skills they will need if they are to become visually perceptive and artistically competent in relation to the expression of feelings. So far as possible that is to be achieved by relating the study of other artists' work to their own direct experience and responses to the world. I chose to use the theme of faces and feelings as a focus to test out my aims.

The research which I carried out as part of this 'testing' is in the interpretative tradition which uses naturalistic enquiry to generate theory, from data collected through careful observation and recording of participants' views. The work of Lawrence Stenhouse (1975) on curriculum action research influenced my choice. Action research 'offers to inform the judgement of actors ... by opening the research accounts to recognition and to comparison and hence to criticism in the light of experience' (Stenhouse 1975: 78).

I was aware of Schostak's (1985) distinction between the observer and the narrator in the process of research (when recording and analysing the data) and regarded myself more as the latter: 'an observer records observations as they occur; the narrator reflects upon these observations and orders them to preserve the lived quality of the drama' (Schostak 1985: 8).

The research aims were:

- To seek evidence of how children observe, express and articulate emotion;
- To observe and investigate how children respond to emotion as represented by visual art;
- To observe and investigate how children show emotion in their visual representation of faces.

The school is an 8–12 middle (deemed primary) situated on the outskirts of Great Yarmouth. It was opened in 1938 and the buildings reflect the architecture of that era. It has 270 pupils on roll, with twelve full time and three part time members of staff. There is a triple-unit Learning Support Centre (LSC) for thirty-eight children. Each LSC class has one full time teacher and a full time classroom assistant. Most of the children live outside the school's immediate area and are transported by taxi.

The project was conducted mainly within school, utilising my mobile classroom and the specialist art room in the main building. Two visits to the Sainsbury Centre for Visual Arts were made during the early part of the Spring term. Exploratory work on the theme preceded the first visit, with follow-up activities based on the children's observations and interests, sketches and responses. This chapter focuses mostly on the visits.

My outline time scale and teaching plan was as follows:

Week 1 Discuss and explore the feel of our faces. Look at facial muscles and their function using biological diagrams. Represent the feel of the faces using simple lines.

Weeks 2–3 Continue by experimenting with representing facial feel using string.

Week 4 Self-portraits using hand mirrors to observe detail.

Week 5 Visit gallery.

Weeks 6–9 Mask making.

Week 10 Revisit gallery.

The Year 7 LSC class has seven boys and five girls. For the research I originally intended to focus on six of the children as I thought it would be difficult to monitor accurately the reactions and responses of the whole class. I selected the children by taking every other name on the class register: Russell, David, Alan, Joanne, Tara, Emma. At the time I thought this was the best way to obtain a representative sample of my class. However, as the initial teaching project progressed I soon realised that valuable data were being lost by excluding the other class members. The children I had selected were constantly working with the other pupils on collaborative tasks and it became impossible to credit the selected group with responses since they were often arrived at jointly either through an exchange of ideas or group discussion. Therefore Lisa, Jasmine, Mandy, Clifford, Jason and Kerry were also included. None of the children had ever visited the Sainsbury Centre before. I felt that none would be inhibited by being tape recorded and photographed, and they agreed to be.

Teaching decisions, actions and interactions in the normal course of the teaching project were recorded using various methods. I made detailed observation notes after all my art lessons and kept a research diary, recording anything which I judged relevant to the research aims. Children often spoke to me about their work or their feelings outside of art lessons. Photographs were taken of the children engaged in the various tasks set, both at school and at the gallery. Photographs were also taken of their finished pieces of work. A video recording was made of the visits to the gallery. Both served as an *aide-mémoire* for me and the children, and as a basis for further discussion. The children also used tape recorders when discussing their work and transcriptions of relevant conversations were made. Samples of their visual representations and written responses were also kept and analysed. In particular I sought to construct records of the children's expressive language, physical reactions, and visual representations of emotion.

The research was carried out according to the following principles:

Co-operation   I explained to the children why we were learning about faces and feelings. I explained that the visual artwork was new to me and that the research formed an important part of my own learning about teaching art. I emphasised my desire that the project would be a co-operative venture, in which we would all share our ideas.

Sensitivity   I was aware that I had to be responsive to the children's different experiences and personalities. In talking with them and in my interactions I had to discover: 'how to learn from them without being too inquisitive, how to be interesting without talking too much, how to take great interest in their troubles without patronising them, how to inspire confidence without perplexing them' (Zweigg, in Logan and Schostak 1984: 19).

Negotiation   Use of the data was through negotiation with those involved in the research. All of the children were keen to be involved and were willing for their work to be used. They attached importance to being asked to contribute to the project through their verbal responses, written work and art activities.

INITIAL CLASSWORK

I introduced the theme of Faces and Feelings a month before the visit to the gallery. In my teaching I aimed to extend the range of materials and methods used in representation to give the children a variety of experiences and tasks at which they could succeed. Through discussion we decided to approach the subject of drawing faces from an unusual angle. Instead of drawing faces that showed differences between each other, the children used their fingers to find similarities, to feel gently the shape of their own faces and those of others in the class. To help them to concentrate on the shape and 'feel' of the facial features, each child was given a life size paper shape and asked to represent the 'feel' of the face by using simple lines in soft pencil. The children developed their work further by using string on dark cardboard.

Their representations of faces were full of expression and the combination of string and PVA glue produced an interesting visual and textural effect. Some of the children were able to say how their characters 'felt' or how they themselves felt about the expression on the faces they had produced. Emma's person 'wanted to frighten you like a ghost or something'. Jason's 'looks like he's smiling because he's just got a surprise like a present'. Kerry thought her face was 'serious', while Clifford's 'was like an alien'. Other children indicated only that their face showed happiness and sadness. It was more difficult for them to say how they felt when looking at the display – happy, sad, and scared were the only responses.

However, more evidence arose a few weeks later when the children were asked to draw a self-portrait. All of the children expressed concern at attempting to draw their own faces and in Joanne's case there was reluctance to try, as the diary records.

Joanne

Joanne sat and stared at her blank piece of paper for what seemed a long time – several minutes. She looked around to see what the other children were doing, then drew a circle for a face, heavily, in pencil, screwed the paper up, and asked for some more. The same thing happened again. Eventually Joanne picked up her pencil and asked me what she had to do. I re-explained the task emphasising the use of the hand mirror. 'I can't draw,' she said. 'I can't do it.' I encouraged her to try by looking at a small part of her face at a time. With persuasion Joanne looked in the mirror and saw that her face was not a circle. We discussed the shapes of the features. Joanne thought her eyes were 'long egg' or 'lemon' shaped. She carefully drew an eye and gradually added to her face, calling me over for reassurance at each stage.

I encouraged her to check her mirror frequently and to draw what she saw. In this way she was able to answer many of the questions she asked herself. For example, 'Where do I put my nose?' 'Where shall I put my freckles?' Ironically Joanne insisted on staying in at break time to finish her self-portrait (Figure 5.1). Afterwards she smiled as she showed it to me. She said, 'I think it looks like me – a bit. You can see all the hairs and my eyebrows.'

I felt it was important to provide a framework for drawing so that the children could achieve success as they tried to represent each facial feature. As their portraits progressed they became generally more confident, observant and critical of their own work. Clifford commented, 'My eyes have grey in them as well as blue.' Mandy's eyes were 'lemon shaped, not round'. She also noticed that 'If you measure, my eyes are half-way down. I put them at the top. That's wrong.' Joanne said, 'I couldn't do it at first . . . it's easier if you do a bit at a time.' Jasmine concluded, 'It's good, Miss, I know it's me – and that really looks like Russell' (Figure 5.2).

It was evident that these faces were drawn by children who had studied the shape and form of the face and the features. These faces resembled their owners. They were drawn by children who were beginning to understand the positioning of ears, eyes and noses, not through looking at pictures but by using the evidence discovered through direct observation and through their own sense of touch.

THE GALLERY VISIT

Before the visit to the gallery I spent a lesson discussing with the children what they thought they might see there. We talked about what an art gallery was as none of the children had ever visited one. They suggested there might be 'drawings, models, paintings and ornaments', some of which might be 'very old, unusual, precious and expensive'. We discussed the research I was aiming to do while we were there.

Clifford brought in a folder containing photographs and slides of the Sainsbury Centre the following day. They were mainly of the building and promoted much discussion about its huge size, the patterns formed by the windows, use of building materials, and the Henry Moore sculptures outside. Joanne thought that 'there must be some really big things in there because it's a huge building'. I explained that we would see some very small objects too.

Sensible behaviour is also a personal target area for some of the children so it was necessary to outline appropriate behaviour for the visit and this was recorded by the children on a worksheet. I also asked them to write down what they were looking forward to. Responses included 'looking at all the different things', 'going all around the big building', 'seeing the masks', and 'eating my packed lunch'. We had discussed feelings and explored some of our own responses to situations in recent Personal and Social Education lessons, and the children made a list of words and ideas which they could refer to on the visit.

Figure 5.1 Joanne's self-portrait

Figure 5.2 Russell's self-portrait

Initially the children worked in two groups looking at objects that I had pre-selected because of their striking facial features and expressions, and the possible feelings associated with them and evoked by them. The objects also presented a wide range of materials with which the artists had worked, and were from different cultures and times in history: John Davies' *Bucket Man*; Anthony Green's *The bathroom at 29*; head-dress frontlet (North West Coast of America); and reliquary head (Central Africa, Fang peoples; Plate 5.1).

Later the children worked individually, observing and sketching things which they selected and which interested them. All of them had sketch book, worksheets and pencils and were encouraged to use them to record the visit. The worksheets were intended to provide a framework for their thinking and for further discussion when we returned to school.

Bucket Man immediately captured the children's imagination. Clifford's first response was 'wow' as we approached the exhibit. Some of the children immediately started sketching while others attempted their worksheet. Russell said that *Bucket Man* was 'life-size and realistic – like a prisoner of some kind because of his scruffy old clothes'. Tara wanted to know what was in the buckets and Kerry suggested that she looked without touching them. Tara was disappointed to find them empty as 'they should have stones or water in them because they're heavy'. Jason intervened, saying, 'he was a workman or a builder then'.

I asked the children about how *Bucket Man* might feel and how he made them feel. Most thought he was sad although other suggestions were made, including 'mad – just look at his eyes!' (Russell); 'tense' (Alan); 'fed-up' (Jasmine) and 'concentrating – serious' (Clifford). Reasons for such feelings were also discussed and responses included 'because he's got to do a lot of work' (Tara); 'he doesn't like carrying the heavy buckets' (David); 'he's just switched off' (Russell). It was interesting that several children imagined the buckets to be full and heavy despite their being visibly empty.

Everyone agreed that he made them feel 'nervy and uncomfortable' especially if they looked into his eyes. 'It's like he's really looking right inside you,' said Russell. 'He's staring you out,' said Clifford. Tara disagreed, saying: 'He's not looking at anyone – just down at the ground.'

I also drew attention to the materials used and the children listed all the different ones they could see – clay, rubber, board, real clothes, plastic, metal, string and plaster. Joanne noticed the ball on *Bucket Man*'s head and the shield around the back of it. Russell suggested the former was part of his hair 'like Japanese or Chinese people have'. Clifford commented that they looked odd and asked me if they were really meant to be there. 'Did someone fix them on later – someone else I mean – not the man who did it?' he asked.

Plate 5.1 Reliquary head (wood), Central Africa, Fang peoples (Robert and Lisa Sainsbury Collection; photograph: James Austin)

Bucket Man promoted great interest and made a lasting impression on the children, although no one liked his appearance and he made them feel uncomfortable. I was interested in how fascinated, observant and responsive they were and how confidently they expressed their ideas and feelings. David's description afterwards is typical:

> We saw lots of things. I liked the *Bucket Man*. He looked very sad and serious. His eyes were looking straight ahead into space. Someone made the *Bucket Man* because they wanted everyone to see what they could make and how good it was. They were proud of it. *Bucket Man* looks real. He makes me feel a bit nervy too.

Our conversation about *The Bathroom at 29* (Anthony Green) centred on the identity and feelings of the people featured. The children started to talk as soon as they located the painting. It was obvious to them that the man and woman were in love and cared for each other. Joanne found it strange that 'two people were in the bathroom at once'. Emma giggled, saying she thought it was 'a bit rude because the lady is watching the man having a bath'. Alan commented that she was wearing a 'sexy nightie'. I was surprised and pleased that these observations did not result in any silly conversation or infectious laughter.

Lisa thought the painting was 'pretty real' and Alan felt 'you could reach out and touch it'. The everyday objects such as soap and shampoo were easily identified and this encouraged the children to look more closely for detail. Russell noticed the odd shape of the painting and everyone agreed that the bathroom was very small and old-fashioned. Clifford and David said the coat-hangers made it look untidy.

All the children were able to identify with the subject (setting) of this painting and observed the detail carefully. They also noticed perspective. Tara saw that the light was on and David noticed the reflection in the mirror and the shadows on the tiles. He thought this was 'really clever' and like 'an optical illusion'.

When asked about the feelings the painting evoked Lisa said: 'squashed in because it's too small'. Kerry thought it made her feel 'sleepy and warm – like you are when you have a bath', and Alan liked it because 'there is a bit of romance'.

I was surprised at the depth and complexity of their thinking and their sustained interest in the painting. Russell's description afterwards illustrates this:

> I looked at the painting of the bathroom. It is a funny shape painting. But it looks like a real bathroom with all the soap and shampoo and other things in it. The man looks sleepy because that's what happens if you have a long hot bath. The lady is his wife or girlfriend because she is touching him. She cares about him. They will soon be kissing

each other. They are in love. I like the picture because it is realistic. I don't like all the coat-hangers.

The crouching animal head-dress frontlet appealed to the children because of its colourful shell inlay and because of its animal associations. It was in complete contrast to the other objects studied. They were quick to notice that the 'mask' was made of wood but did not identify the shell, saying it was 'plastic, glass or metal'. Clifford deduced that because it was hollow it would be light to wear. Emma, Lisa and Kerry discussed the kind of animal it was – dog, wolf or bear. They looked carefully at the paws, ears and claws and dismissed dog because 'it looked more wild than that'. No one could suggest who might wear it apart from Tara who thought it was for a fancy dress party. It was also very difficult for anyone to say how the wearer might feel. David said 'hidden' and Russell said 'silly'. The children had not studied any other civilisations, cultures, or mythology, and could not relate to the frontlet in terms of its history or purpose. It seemed beyond their comprehension that the characteristics of the animal might be superimposed on to the wearer, and I did not pursue that line of instruction.

The children recognised that the Fang reliquary head sculpture was made of wood and was shiny. Emma suggested 'someone must have polished it', and Jasmine thought 'that would keep it looking nice'. The girls thought it might be an ornament in someone's house although 'it's a bit big to put on the shelf'. Clifford said that the head was definitely foreign. David added that it was a black person's face because of the shape of the lips and nose. There was little agreement on whether the face was male or female, although more children thought the latter because of its size, hair style and small features. Emotion was hard for the children to identify and 'sad' was the only word used. Nobody had any strong feelings towards the sculpture, saying that it was 'OK' and 'quite good' or 'nice'. However, Clifford appreciated that 'whoever did it must have been clever – it must have taken them ages'.

EXPLORATIONS

I encouraged them to draw some of the masks in the Collection, and videoed their choices so that we could discuss these back at school. The children were tired by now and lacked concentration in this final 40-minute period of the visit. However, they were disappointed when it was time to leave, saying that they needed more time to look at things. Everyone wanted a return visit.

The worksheets proved a valuable framework for directing the children's thinking. It helped that we had been through them in class before the visit so the children already knew what to look for and were familiar with the questions. Joanne especially was keen to complete hers. In retro-spect, I thought, I tried to cover too much ground and it was only just possible to fit everything into the whole-morning session. I felt that the activities were rushed. Previously I had anticipated that some of the children would lose concentration and interest fairly quickly, and had intended not to linger too long on each exhibit. This did not happen, and the children became engrossed in *Bucket Man* and *The Bathroom at 29*. Not wishing to deter them, and recognising the quality of learning that the children were engaged in, I allowed them more time studying these exhibits than I had planned for. Consequently time spent on the frontlet with crouching animal and the reliquary head was much shorter than intended.

Unfortunately the quality of the video recording made was rather poor. I had not used the camera before although I had practised in the class-room. This was very disappointing since it was to be my main source of recorded evidence. It was difficult to pay attention to what the children were doing and saying and to video them. Joanne also found the video a distraction and most of the time was more concerned about my recording than the tasks she had been set. It would have been more successful if another person had taken charge of the camera, releasing me to concentrate on my work with the children.

The dictaphone provided more useful evidence and was less distracting for the children. In places the conversations were muddled and unclear as the children all talked at once. However, it was possible to transcribe accurately extracts of conversation that provided a record of the children's thinking.

The children were made aware that faces could be represented in many different ways. At the end of the visit they could remember several of the different faces and art forms they had seen. They were highly observant and made detailed studies of *Bucket Man* and *The Bathroom at 29*. I was surprised at how carefully they tried to notice detail. They also noticed the materials and some of the techniques used by the artists. Tara and David noticed the perspective in *The Bathroom at 29*. We had talked about optical illusions recently in a science lesson and both children noticed how the painting played tricks with their eyes. I considered this a hard concept for children of their age to understand in relation to art and had not intended to draw attention to it.

The level of talk was another surprise. Mandy, Kerry and Jasmine are usually the least to contribute in group discussions, but on the visit seemed to forget their inhibitions and joined in fully. All the children were articulate and able to express their ideas and feelings with the minimum of prompting. They learned collaboratively about the art objects by sharing and sorting ideas, justifying points of view, questioning and refining observations.

Perhaps the biggest surprise for me was that the children wanted so much to return to the gallery to continue sketching. In the past they have been reluctant to draw from direct observation and had lacked confidence in their ability to do this. I thought originally that one visit would be sufficient for the purposes of the research project and the needs of the children. However, having seen the enjoyment and quality of learning gained I was as eager as the children to visit again before the end of term.

When term resumed we spent time reviewing the visit, including looking at the video, and discussing what the children had enjoyed and found interesting. They remembered *Bucket Man* and other John Davies sculptures. They also recalled the Anthony Green paintings and wanted to look at *My Mother Alone in Her Dining Room* again. The masks were objects of fascination and I suggested they could make some of their own, based on what we had seen. We embarked on mask-making using papier mâché, and it took several weeks for the children to discuss their ideas and to make and decorate their masks. They co-operated well together making suggestions and discussing ideas. When it came to decorating their masks some were keen to preserve their 'own' ideas. Clifford and Alan had quite a discussion about this, and their final masks were quite different from each other's compared to the initial stages, where one seemed to have followed the other (Plates 5.2, 5.3).

A SECOND GALLERY VISIT

I felt more relaxed this time because I was less concerned about how my class would behave. I also knew that they were well motivated, having set the agenda for the day themselves. As we walked from the car park towards the building they looked more like older students than school children, clutching their clipboards. The frenzied excitement of the first visit had been replaced by a sense of purpose which was evident from the way the children walked, said 'good morning' to the security staff, and generally went about their work. They quickly settled down to sketching the things they had been discussing as we approached the building.

I had taken a few lessons from a colleague on using the video camera and I felt more confident about focusing on the children sketching. (The quality of the recording turned out far better than my previous attempt.) I had more opportunity to concentrate on collecting evidence on video because the format of the day was less structured, and there was less need for the children to involve me in what they were doing.

I had anticipated that the children's reactions on our first visit to the gallery would be less productive than they turned out to be. They had behaved more maturely and had concentrated better than I had expected. The light, warm atmosphere in the gallery, perhaps, had a calming influence. The impact of the art objects commanded attention. In view of this,

Plate 5.2 Alan and Clifford
mask making
(photograph: Sue Allen)

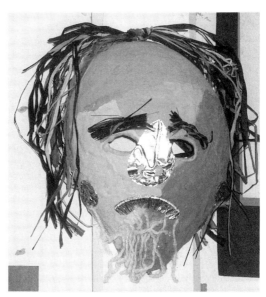

Plate 5.3 Clifford's mask (photograph: Sue Allen)

our second visit was less formal and structured by the pupils themselves. They were allowed to pursue their own interests. Everyone wanted to see *Bucket Man* again and several children decided to draw him this time. They were also keen to talk about their drawings, although I did not interrupt whilst they were concentrating. I only discussed things when children brought work to show me or asked me questions. Less discussion occurred than on our previous visit as the children were absorbed in their sketching. I was not concerned about this, since we had talked at length about the exhibits in our first visit. In addition, the video recording would provide a stimulus for further discussion later on. We went together to look at Anthony Green's painting, *My Mother Alone in Her Dining Room*.

The children observed carefully and were quick to notice the reflection in the table and the mirror, the patterns on the carpet, pottery and furniture and the mixture of old and new things, for example the old clock and the new telephone. I was again surprised at how observant they seemed to have become in just a few weeks, and they answered my questions with confidence. Alan was particularly interested in this painting and talked about it later whilst the others were sketching. He thought the carpet looked real but was a bit too bright. He also decided that the lady was lonely, her husband had 'died, or left her' and that 'not many people visited her'.

I explained to the class that the lady was Anthony Green's mother. Much discussion followed. No one thought she looked like their mother – 'she's too old, posh and serious,' said Emma, whilst Russell thought 'she'd be strict with her kids, a bit like a teacher – I'd be scared of her a bit.'

At lunch time I asked the children to show each other their sketches. All the objects selected were easily recognised by other children and I was encouraged by the positive comments made. No one criticised another's work. Responses ranged from 'Miss, look at Tara's *Bucket Man* – it's really good,' or 'That's brilliant, David,' to 'Show me where that was after lunch – I want to draw it too.' For the children this was as much a lesson in social living as it was in representing faces. Very few of the children had recorded drawings or paintings in their sketches and I thought that this showed that they were becoming more aware of what counts as art, by selecting sculptures and art objects from different cultures and times.

We talked about the two Anthony Green paintings and the children were interested to find out that both rooms were in the same house. Tara deduced that the lady in the bathroom was probably the artist's wife or girl friend, but did not suggest that the man in the bath was the artist himself. When I pointed that out the children found it confusing. Mandy wanted to know how someone could paint themselves in the bath. Russell humorously said: 'No wonder his mother looks cross if that's what's going on upstairs.' I suggested that it was unlikely that the pictures were painted at the same point in time, or to represent the same moment!

The children found the John Davies sculptures fascinating, particularly those displayed *en masse*. Clifford thought the display was like a prison camp, the pointing figure being in charge. Russell commented on their 'prisoner clothing'. Their imaginations then ran riot and they concocted stories of escapes, shootings and punishments.

FOLLOW-UP AND REFLECTION

Back in the art room the children added the finishing touches to their masks – patterns, hair, ears and jewellery, based on what they had seen. They talked about their masks in relation to those in the gallery. Tara recognised a similarity in eye shapes, and David commented that their masks were people, whereas many of the ones we had seen were animals. All the children preferred their own masks because they were 'different and colourful'. Clifford thought his was particularly impressive with its long hair and bespeckled appearance. When the children wore their masks most said they felt 'silly' or 'funny'. Only Clifford and David said their masks might scare someone. No one thought the masks in the gallery were frightening because they were 'too plain and dull'.

It was evident to me from the paintings by Anthony Green and the John Davies sculptures that emotions are essential to artistic activity. No work is solely a manipulation of paint, plastics, or other materials, and 'content free'. Each tells us something about the subject and sometimes, as with Anthony Green, I thought I could infer something about the relationship of the artist to the subject, depicted in the materials and elements the artist chose or had available. Sometimes the 'emotional content' was less easy to link to the artist, as in Davies' work. In the case of the more stylised work of the frontlet and reliquary head there was not much 'contact' with emotional content in the objects themselves. Indeed, it strikes me that the *context* in which these originate is where the 'feelings' would reside.

My main teaching and research aims addressed the issue of communicating feelings by attempting to record and investigate the children's responses and reactions to emotion as represented by visual art. I found that they generally expressed only a superficial view of feelings when initially engaged in their own artwork and when studying the objects in the gallery. They could say that a face represented 'happy' or 'sad'. Beyond this they had difficulty in expressing and articulating emotion. This was particularly evident when the head or face was seen in isolation and devoid of context, which is the case with the objects displayed in the gallery.

This is illustrated by comparing the children's responses to the reliquary head and to *Bucket Man*. They could only say that the former was 'sad'.

With *Bucket Man* many suggestions were made along the 'happy'-to-'sad' continuum and beyond: 'tense', 'serious', 'concentrating', 'fed up' and 'switched off'. The children put these feelings into a context themselves by imagining possible reasons for his stance and appearance:

happy	sad	upset	astonished
weary	dizzy	worried	grumpy
cold	hot	sweaty	down
angry	jittery	amazed	guilty
excited	surprised	shocked	sins
relaxed	nervous	tired	sleepy
hungry	frightened	sorry	

However, these were in response to work which could be called 'super-realism'. At the time I was disappointed that they had not articulated such ideas in response to other works of art, and in their own artwork, since much time had been spent before the visit exploring different feelings through a variety of classroom activities. I had made an effort to link the work on faces and feelings to other areas of the curriculum such as English and Personal and Social Education. Their verbalising of emotion was becoming quite extensive, sparked by the question of 'possible' feelings. However, while the expressive mouths of the string faces were indications of partial success in making this link in their own work, there was little transfer of ideas when we observed heads and faces, as distinct from whole figures. Retrospectively I wonder whether, as I had imagined, feelings *are* conveyed, through facial depiction, and whether artists can truly represent feelings. For example, a smile can be interpreted in many ways – as a sign of joy, recognition or tolerance. It does not necessarily convey one partic-ular feeling. Tone of voice, body language, an action or a prolonged mood make a more accurate interpretation of feeling possible in a way that inanimate materials and techniques, such as are used in painting or sculpture, cannot achieve. Perhaps the children could not frame the expression shown on the faces of the art objects within their own expe-rience and could only comment on a superficial level for those reasons.

I also came to question the suitability of the single heads and faces in the gallery for this project. Many have unanimated expressions. It was almost impossible for me and the children to attribute feelings to many of the subjects we studied. The only single head which provoked any reaction was that of a baby. This bronze sculpture is open mouthed, which the children thought indicated that 'he was crying or screaming because he wanted his mummy'. Again, the point of reference to personal experience and the attachment to 'realism' seemed to play a part.

The children in my class are approaching the start of adolescence. Their own emotions are often unstable and they may experience great mood swings, as demonstrated by Joanne's being pleased with her work on one occasion, then destroying it saying that it was 'no good'. With the onset of puberty children sometimes find it difficult to understand and articulate how they feel and the reasons for their rapidly changing emotions. It was, perhaps, unrealistic of me to expect them to express emotions clearly in relation to visual art, when they are still struggling to come to terms with their own, often contradictory, feelings and tensions.

I became very aware, however, of how the capabilities of children with special educational needs are frequently underestimated. My colleagues in the mainstream greeted my suggestion of visiting the gallery with this class with humour and scorn, saying nothing educational could be gained by these children on such a visit and that it was 'a waste of time'. In the light of this study I can firmly refute such allegations. The benefits in the development of observation skills, expressive skills, articulation and confidence are well evidenced and illustrated in the records which I made.

I also underestimated the children's ability to listen, observe and behave 'appropriately' on the visits, and was surprised at the quality of artwork produced both before and afterwards. Perhaps this was partially because I involved the children at every stage of the project, and in decision making with regard to the work undertaken. This evidently had a significant bearing on the way they focused upon the art objects. I found that: 'when children share through talk the purposes for their learning, their interest and involvement in the learning activities increase' (Badderley 1992: 14).

Evidence from this project seems to commend the idea that children should be involved in the planning and review of their work, as well as in the practical activities themselves.

FURTHER READING

Badderley, G. (ed.) (1992) *Learning Together through Talk*, London: Hodder and Stoughton.
Bancroft-Hunt, N. (ed.) (1979) *People of the Totem*, London: Orbis.
Barnes, R. (1987) *Teaching Art to Young Children 4–9*, London: Allen and Unwin.
Capon, R. (1976) *Making Three Dimensional Pictures*, London: Batsford.
Clement, R. and Page, S. (1992a) *Investigating and Making in Art*, Harlow: Oliver and Boyd.
—— (1992b) *Knowledge and Understanding in Art*, Harlow: Oliver and Boyd.
—— (1992c) *Principles and Practice in Art*, Harlow: Oliver and Boyd.
—— (1992d) *Primary Art*, Harlow: Oliver and Boyd.
—— (1992e) *Resources pack and teacher's book*, Harlow: Oliver and Boyd.
Department for Education (1995) *Art in the National Curriculum*, London: Her Majesty's Stationery Office.
Department of Education and Science (1991) *Art for Ages 5–14*, London: Her Majesty's Stationery Office.
—— (1992) *Art in the National Curriculum*, London: Her Majesty's Stationery Office.
Gentle, K. (1975) *Children and Art Teaching*, London: Croom Helm.
Glaser, B. G. and Strauss A. L. (1967) *The Discovery of Grounded Theory*, Chicago: Aldine.

Hopkins, D. (1985) *A Teacher's Guide to Classroom Research*, Milton Keynes: Open University Press.

Larkin, D. (1981) *Art Learning and Teaching*, Dublin: Wolfhound Press.

Logan, T. and Schostak, J. (eds) (1984) *Pupil Experience*, London: Croom Helm.

Mendelowitz, D. (1963) *Children are Artists*, Stanford CA: Stanford University Press.

Sekules, V. and Tickle, L. (eds) (1993) Starting Points: Approaches to Art Objects Selected from the Sainsbury Centre for Visual Arts, University of East Anglia, Norwich: Centre for Applied Research in Visual Arts Education.

Schools Council (1974) *Children's Growth Through Creative Experience*, London: Van Nostrand Reinhold.

Schostak, J. (1985) 'Creating the narrative case record', *Curriculum Perspectives* 5 (1).

Stenhouse, L. (1975) *An Introduction to Curriculum Research and Development*, London: Heinemann Educational.

Chapter 6

More than Moore

Rex Barker

> Children can learn a lot about the process of producing art through the example of artists like Henry Moore: in his copious drawings and embracing interest in the sculpture of other cultures and periods of time and in the importance he placed on drawing in his work as a 'help towards making sculpture ... as a means of generating ideas ... and developing them'.
>
> (Wilkinson 1977: 21)

With a concern to avoid the possibility of children's artwork resulting in imitative copies, and with the intention of introducing the work of a major twentieth-century sculptor to young children, I decided to focus my teaching on some of the sources influencing the artist's work as well as the work itself. In focusing upon some of the sources of influence in investigating and understanding the artist's work, I do not wish to suggest that Moore's work (or any other artist's work) can be fully appreciated from this approach alone. The approach does, however, have the advantage of emphasising the relationship between knowledge and understanding of influential artists, and activities using materials aimed at developing observation, visual perception and imagination. The intentions of this project were:

- To test whether the approach adopted can enable children to explore their individual responses to the themes and objects which inspired an artist, without feeling the need to produce work which simply imitates the appearance of that work;
- To consider some of the artistic sources of influence in an attempt to link the appreciation of an artist's work with a wider tradition of sculpture;
- To approach practical work in ways which open up a creative space in which the children may explore their own ideas and responses using similar sources (existing art, natural objects, the human figure, etc.).

For the purposes of this study Henry Moore was chosen for a number of reasons:

- A major artist whose work increasingly departed from the representational towards abstraction provided a challenge to children normally exposed to representations of the human figure which are largely naturalistic;
- Connections could be made between the work of a modern sculptor and some of the works in the Sainsbury Collection produced from a range of very different and sometimes remote, social, historical and cultural contexts;
- Many of Moore's themes are universal and could be adopted and explored by the children as appropriate in their own artwork;
- Moore's work and some of the natural sources of his work have a local connection;
- Moore's work has fascinated me personally.

Twelve Year 4 children (aged 8 and 9) of mixed ability were chosen as a focus for the research, although all the class followed the same programme of work, in a modern middle school of average size on the edge of Norwich. The children come from different social and cultural backgrounds. Most had never visited a gallery or art exhibition previously.
The teaching aims were:

- To develop children's appreciation of the way in which the exploration of sources of influence on artists' work as well as the work itself can stimulate both enquiry and artwork;
- To improve the knowledge of art and artists available in the community;
- To develop teaching strategies to improve the skilled production of visual art by children in ways which took account of that knowledge;
- To open up a creative space in which children's responses to natural materials, textures and forms, art materials and other artwork allowed children the freedom to explore their own expressions of ideas and feelings.

The research aim was:

- To investigate the extent to which teacher and pupils were successful in achieving the teaching aim through a consideration of the children's work, their talk and my reflections upon the teaching.

The following sources were used as teaching aids and learning resources:

- Works by Henry Moore (see Appendix, p. 110), video recordings of Moore's work;
- Art of other cultures which was recognised as influential on Moore's work;
- Found objects, such as stones, bones, pebbles, driftwood, and shells, which had been identified by the artist as a source of stimulus for his work;

● Writings and transcripts (secondary sources) and in particular statements made by the artist relevant to the works studied.

In the course of the research the data which were collected and analysed
included:

● Visual evidence in the form of sketches, drawings and sculptural objects
produced by the pupils;
● Transcripts of taped pupil–teacher talk during introductions to lessons;
● Videotaped recordings of children engaged in practical activities;
● Field notes made in the form of a diary.

Natural objects were clearly an important stimulus and a readily available
source of sculptural ideas for Henry Moore. With a vast range of natural
forms at his disposal, Moore was able to study structures, form, rhythm,
subtleties of shape and texture, and to develop his methods of 'transformational drawing' whereby natural forms could be 'metamorphosised' into
human forms: 'I have always paid great attention to natural forms, such
as bones, shells and pebbles, etc.' (Henry Moore, quoted in James and
Moore 1966: 64).

Moore's sketches and drawings before the second world war often
began with studies of closely observed small, natural forms which became
figures or parts of figures. The idea that found objects can bridge the
distinction (often used in art education) between observational studies
and 'imaginative work' led me to encourage the children to collect a
variety of small objects as a resource during the project (Plate 6.1). The
objects would, I hoped, serve three purposes: as examples of the kind of
source material used by Moore; as source material for observational
drawing; and as a stimulus for the children's individual imaginative
response in the course of their own artwork.

The collection provided the children with visual resources which they
could seek to represent accurately, more so I believed than, for example,
large trees. The lessons began with a brief talk about Moore's use of natural
forms, his fascination with stones, pebbles, bones, trees and pieces of wood,
and the way in which he had used such objects within his work as a stimulus
and source material. The children were also shown copies of drawings from
Moore's notebook of 1930/32 and I explained what Moore meant when he
referred to some of his drawings from natural objects as 'transformational
drawings': 'One doesn't know really how any ideas come, but you can
induce them by starting in the far little studio with looking at a box of
pebbles' (Henry Moore, quoted in Arts Council 1978).

With the intention of having the children emulate these processes,
they were issued with drawing paper, 2B pencils and conté crayons. They
were asked to select objects, to study them from different viewpoints, and to make well-observed line drawings. As many of the objects

Plate 6.1 Classroom collection of natural, found objects
(photograph: Rex Barker)

were quite small, the children were encouraged to enlarge them in their drawings. They were asked to concentrate on looking carefully at the shape and form of the objects they had chosen. While the children worked from direct observation there were opportunities to talk to them about their ideas, feelings and imaginative responses to the objects they worked with.

I stood back from the class and did not intervene with instruction, to allow their individual responses to the objects and the creation of their own images. An atmosphere of intense and contemplative study was interrupted only when they returned their chosen objects and quietly exchanged them for further objects to draw. The children thought the atmosphere was productive and helpful to their contemplation. I used the opportunity to contrast this sort of working-condition (in which many artists work) and that often experienced by pupils in the more commonly busy atmosphere of classrooms.

Most children chose to draw shells. The collection contained a large number of cockle shells and some whelks which had been eroded by the sea. My own feeling was that the cockle shells had little inherent suggestive power to make the imaginative leap Moore had made with his 'transformational drawings' when compared to pieces of wood and irregular-shaped pieces of flint. Perhaps most of the children had chosen to draw shells because they were attracted by their easily discernible patterns. More children chose cockle shells than sea-eroded whelks. Fir cones and feathers seemed to be chosen for their easy recognition of pattern and shape. Pattern was certainly a criterion for some choices:

R.B.   Which of those objects do you find the most interesting ... and why?

ROSA   I think it's the snake skin ... because it's got a lot of pattern.

All the drawings except one showed evidence of a strong use of line and about one-third of the children had attempted to represent textural qualities. A few had attempted to suggest three dimensional form through tones of shading. Four had attempted to enlarge the objects or extract details. Most drew the objects actual size. About one-third produced drawings from different points of view, although this included depictions of objects such as shells which had been simply rotated rather than viewed from an entirely different plane.

The children had been very immersed in studying the objects they had chosen to draw and produced a range of careful drawings. A few had attempted to produce the imaginative work which had been expected and exemplified by Moore in his 'transformational drawings'. Most, though, had concentrated their efforts on making objective depictions of a range of objects and many had become interested in the patterns which the objects displayed. The children's approach did not easily lend itself to transformational techniques. Several children, it seemed, did not make this imaginative leap because they had become absorbed in the creation of representations, focusing their attention on the qualities of the objects themselves.

Without intending to do so, I found myself intervening and helping some of the children who were wrestling with a need to produce a 'correct' depiction. Rosie, for example, felt she could not represent the pattern of ribbed and fan-like lines which gave her shell its form and structure. I pointed to the configuration of lines on the shell and helped her to represent them in her drawing as they appeared. A few children indicated an 'imaginative' response verbally and may have been uncertain or reluctant about converting their observational drawings into figurative ideas for sculpture. They were able to point to images which the objects invoked, but found it difficult to draw out those imaginative images. It appeared that, despite a seemingly large collection of found objects, the children may have lacked what Moore referred to as 'form-interest' to shape their curiosity. An example of this occurred when discussing some 'whistling thorns'. Rosa's comments clearly suggest that the unusual thorns which her father had brought back from Nigeria had stimulated her imagination. However, her drawings never really progressed beyond an attempt to record their appearance.

R.B.   What does it make you think of when you look at that, Rosa?

ROSA   It sort of looks like a body with two horns and that's the body
... and this bit's the head.

R.B.   Right. Which way round would you put that if you were to draw
it as a body ... as a figure? You'd do it that way round, would you?
Facing which way?

ROSA   Ummm ... I think like that [*demonstrates by turning the object
round*].

To extend the exercise using the school plantation as a stimulus, the
children began collecting pieces of wood and making drawings from
old trees, roots, decaying branches, and so on (Plate 6.2). Some began
to put pieces of wood together, building sculptures by using the found
materials directly. Adrian, for example, having found a large piece
of twisted and weathered oak suggesting a bird's wing, began eagerly
to collect other pieces with which to construct a complete bird. Carina
sat down and began carefully to observe and make a drawing of a sting-
ing nettle. When I asked her why she had chosen the nettle she said
the serrated leaf shapes reminded her of a dragon and pointed out the
body parts. She went on to make further drawings and eventually a
painting in which the dragon emerged more strongly. Discussing some
of these sketches with the children, it became clear that their responses
required time to develop. The approach had placed a high expectation
on individual creativity and I realised it was wrong of me to expect all
of the children involved to produce inspired results at the same time
and over a short time-scale. With the aim of encouraging their use
of imagination (without the constraining pressure of creating faithful
depictions) and of introducing a medium which might produce more
spontaneous and expressive results, I initiated different activities with
a view to producing sculpture on a figurative theme using clay. This
would be based primarily on a visit to the Sainsbury Centre for Visual
Arts.

THE VISIT

A class of twenty-seven children of between 8 and 9 years of age visited
the gallery on a cold but bright day in January. The children were divided
into two groups, alternately taking turns to view the work exhibited in
the main gallery and the large sculptural works by Henry Moore situated
outside the building. The aims of the visit were:

● To introduce children to a range of sculpture representing the human
figure;

● To look specifically at works from other cultures considered influential
on Moore's work;

Plate 6.2 Children drawing natural forms found in the school plantation
(photograph: Rex Barker)

- To enable the children to look at and discuss some of the works by Henry Moore and make sketches;
- To allow time for children to view other works in which they were also interested.

Most of the children had never entered an art gallery before and were excited by the building and the diversity of work on view. Several discussions took place inside the gallery in relation to sculptural representations of the human figure, particularly the collection of Cycladic figures, a Standing Figure from Mexico and Moore's *Mother and Child*. These discussions continued during the following week with the aid of a video recording of the works seen on the visit. The children were then shown works by Henry Moore (see Appendix, p. 110) including drawings and maquettes. Before leaving the gallery the children spent some time on their own or with friends looking at other sculptural works in the gallery and making sketches.

Outside, children were able to spend more time viewing three large bronze sculptures by Moore: *Draped Reclining Woman* (1957–8; Plate 6.3); *Reclining Figure* (1956); and *Two-Piece Reclining Figure No. 3* (1961; Plate 6.4). They studied and discussed the sculptures and made sketches from different points of view in pencil and conté crayons. These three works, together with *Mother and Child* and the other art-objects mentioned above, formed the focus of my teaching and were referred to in different contexts throughout the lessons which followed.

The first follow-up talk was designed to consolidate some of the teaching points of the gallery visit and to explore what children had understood, perceived or felt from looking at the sculpture. A further aim was to extend their thinking about the ways in which sculptural objects from other cultures, as well as natural objects and landscape, informed Moore's artistic practice.

The initial talk referred to Moore's interest in sculpture from many different countries, cultures and periods of time which he was able to study in books and in museums such as the British Museum. Similarities between the art considered as influential on Moore's sculpture and work contained in the Sainsbury Collection were pointed out, such as the fact that nearly all the artefacts seen represented the human figure. Several of the sculptures could be linked to themes which had preoccupied Moore throughout his working life, such as seated, reclining and standing figures, mother and child. Others were made from materials which had been carved or cast and could be related to Moore's methods of working in stone or bronze.

Our discussion initially focused on the Cycladic figures (Plate 6.5). The transcripts give some indication of the children's understanding and how much they remembered from the visit. The talk contains evidence

Plate 6.3 *Draped Reclining Woman*, 1957–8, Henry Moore (Robert and Lisa Sainsbury Collection; photograph: James Austin)

Plate 6.4 *Two-piece Reclining Figure, No. 3*, 1961, Henry Moore (Tate Gallery, Millbank, London. Bronze, presented by the artist, 1978.))

Plate 6.5 Female figure
with arms folded (marble)
Cyclades Islands, 2,700–2,400
BC (Robert and Lisa Sainsbury
Collection; photograph: James
Austin)

Plate 6.6 Standing figure (basalt) Mexico, Vera Cruz, 1,200–400 BC (Robert and Lisa Sainsbury Collection; photograph: James Austin)

of the ways in which children were able to make sense of the work they saw by comparing sculptural objects from widely different cultures and times.

R.B.   We looked at some pieces of work which are very similar to the sort of work which Henry Moore looked at when he was studying sculpture in the British Museum and when he was looking at sculpture in books. We looked at Cycladic figures. Put your hands up if you remember the Cycladic figures. What did they look like? Do you remember?

RACHEL   Crossed arms, folded. ... You couldn't see their faces very clearly.

R.B.   You couldn't see their faces very clearly, they all had folded arms. Can anyone remember anything else about the Cycladic figures?

RACHEL   Some of them didn't have any heads.

LUCY   They were very small.

BARNEY   Some of their heads were the shapes of dinosaurs. Some of their heads were in the shapes you get on ... like pterodactyls.

R.B.   You thought they looked like dinosaurs.

PUPIL   Yeh! the back bit.

NATHAN   Their heads were leaning back.

DANIELLE   They were standing on tip-toes. They looked like they were dancing.

RACHEL   They were all nearly the same.

ADAM   They didn't really look like they were supposed to stand up ... because their backs were flat.

NATHAN   We thought they could have been painted.

ROSIE   We thought their eyes and mouths had been painted on and might have been scratched off.

BARNEY   Their backs had most of the detail. They had a big line for the spine.

[...]

R.B.   ... sets of figures that Henry Moore also was impressed by was sculpture from Africa, and sculpture from Mexico, very early Aztec sculpture. Can you remember a piece of Mexican sculpture we saw?

LUCY   It was the Standing Figure (Plate 6.6).

R.B.   Oh, you've made a drawing [*holds it up to class*]. It was called Standing Figure and it was made in Mexico ... when?

PUPIL   1200 to 400 BC.

R.B.   Right. As a comparison, how would you say that the Mexican Standing Figure which Lucy has drawn ... is different to the Cycladic figures?

EMILY   He hasn't got his arms folded and he's got his eyes and nose.

R.B.   It has features on the face. What else?

ROSIE   It looks like it's crouching down.

R.B.   You feel it is crouching rather than standing? What do you think it represents anyway?

GEMMA   It's got little holes in it.

R.B.   Right . . . it's got little holes in it . . . why?

DANIEL   It's got something to do with the rock it was made of.

R.B.   Can anyone remember what rock it was made of?

BARNEY   It had like . . . red . . . chalky stuff inside it.

DANIELLE   That was volcano rock.

R.B.   Volcanic rock . . . was it called basalt?

PUPILS   Yeh.

R.B.   How was the face different in a very obvious way apart from features which are actually carved into the face?

TONY   It looks like he's angry.

R.B.   Right. It's got expression. Do you think the Cycladic figures expressed anything?

RACHEL   The Cycladic figures haven't got much of a face, the standing figure has got features.

R.B.   And what sort of features are they?

PUPIL   He's angry.

R.B.   He's angry . . . right . . . you sense anger there. Do you sense anger or any other emotion in the Cycladic figures' faces?

ROSIE   I think he represents the devil.

R.B.   Well, we're moving into an area that's quite interesting. What did you notice about the Henry Moore sculptures? When you looked at the faces what did you notice about the faces?

ROSIE   The heads are smaller than the body. He does the bodies really big and then he does the heads very small.

R.B.   The heads are small . . . right. Let's just think about the three big pieces of sculpture outside. Rosie said that the heads are very small. What else?

ROSA   [referring to 'Draped Reclining Woman'] The lady was like . . . she was like . . . lying sort of with her elbow holding her up like that [demonstrates with arm] and it kind of looked like she was relaxed and it didn't show you so much the way she was feeling.

R.B.   You didn't think so? [To class] So what expresses the feeling and emotion in the Henry Moore sculptures? We said that the Mexican figure expressed feeling very much through the face. Is that the case with Henry Moore's figures?

BARNEY   No.

R.B.   So how do they express feelings?

BARNEY   Through the body.

R.B.   What do you mean 'through the body'? How? What does he do to the bodies?

PUPIL   Puts them in different positions, like that lady ... he put her in a position so she was all relaxed.

R.B.   Right ... through the position of the body.

ROSIE   [*referring to 'Reclining Figures'*] He made them look like they were really relaxed and, with the other lady, it looked like they [*referring to 'Two-Piece Figure'*] was fitted together.

R.B.   [*referring to 'Mother and Child'*] How does that figure express feelings or emotions?

ROSA   She looked like she was trying to protect the baby.

R.B.   How then did the sculpture make you feel that she is trying to protect the baby?

LUCY   She was looking away ... and it looked like she was protecting her really because she was looking away.

EMILY   She was looking very protective and when she was looking away she looked like somebody was coming.

R.B.   Right. Was there anything about the figure that is different to how the proportions of a real person would be and maybe that has something to do with how it expresses feeling?

ADRIAN   She has a big shoulder.

R.B.   Right. The shoulder was really exaggerated, wasn't it? So this huge shoulder, as it were, protects herself and the child from what?

BARNEY   [*interrupts*] An intruder.

R.B.   Can we see an intruder?

ROSA   No. ... It looks like she was looking at an invader who's burst in. ... It doesn't really need an intruder because it shows it through the two anyway.

R.B.   [*clarifying*] Through the figure?

PUPIL   Yes, so it didn't really need it.

ROSIE   I didn't think the figure looked like she was looking at things. I thought she looked like she was thinking into the future ... about what future her baby would have.

The children were able to describe individual pieces of work. For example, the Cycladic figures were described as 'small', 'about 20 cm high'. It was pointed out that the figures are very similar and feature 'crossed arms'. Heads are sometimes missing and 'you couldn't see their faces very clearly'. Their heads are depicted 'leaning back' and 'they were standing on tip-toes'. It was thought that 'their faces could have been painted' and that the figures 'looked like they were dancing'.

The Mexican Standing Figure was compared with the very different Cycladic figures to draw out the qualities of expression in different materials. Through comparison with the Cycladic figures the children were able to appreciate some of the formal qualities and characteristic features, such as differences in the material from which the object was made, the way in which it represented its subject and what it appeared to express. One child suggested what the figure might represent.

Comparing Moore's works with these ancient art objects, it was possible to lead the discussion towards a description of the qualities perceived in some of Moore's sculptures. This approach enabled the children to consider the formal features and qualities of different pieces by direct comparison which required close observation. Looking back at the lesson and my role, I felt that my contributions moved the discussion along selective paths of enquiry. Occasionally the children's talk deviated from these paths, as when Gemma talked about the stone of which the Mexican figure is made, perhaps not fully understanding my question and the word 'represent'. There is also evidence that the children were able to understand and adopt as their own some of the words used in the teacher's discourse, for example 'I think he represents the devil'.

The class discussion began to approach the formal qualities of Moore's sculpture which is in varying degrees abstract or moving away from naturalism. There is evidence in the talk of an appreciation of what Herbert Read referred to as the departures from naturalism and exaggerations in 'depictions which convey the feelings of strength and dependability' (Read 1965: 78). However, the children appeared more interested in the feelings of the figure than the 'sense of monumentality' and 'contained power' which impressed Read, concepts which are not, perhaps, so easy for children to articulate.

Focusing on one piece of work (in this case the *Mother and Child*) and questioning the children's comments enabled the children to reflect on their observations. They were able to arrive at insights about the significant formal qualities by examining the apparent distortions and exaggerations of Moore's figures. The idea arose that the figure expresses feelings 'through the body' positions, and that the distortions of the shoulder expresses a feeling of 'protection' and 'threat'. Some were able to point to realms of human experience outside that which is immediately depicted, by suggesting what that threat might be.

TOWARDS PRODUCING SCULPTURE

The aim of a sculptor like Henry Moore is to represent his conceptions in the forms natural to the material he is working in. . . . His whole art consists in effecting a credible compromise between these forms and the concepts of his imagination.

(Herbert Read, cited in
Sylvester 1957: Introduction)

The next lesson began with a talk about Henry Moore's life, to vary the children's interest. It focused on his childhood, his education, family and home background, and was illustrated with statements made by Moore himself and photographs selected from reference books. Reference was made again to the sources of influence on Moore's work as a sculptor: natural forms, such as trees, rocks and cliffs, and sculptural objects from other cultures. The children were also shown photographs of Moore at work in his maquette studio, surrounded by small sculptural objects made from a variety of materials. These helped to focus on the distinction between modelling and carving in Moore's work. The importance of life drawing and his thorough knowledge and grounding in the study of the forms of the human figure was also illustrated.

In order to offer a manageable introduction to making sculpture and to attempt to develop the imaginative and expressive potential of the children, one group was given blocks of grog-clay to work with. The clay was very firm, too stiff to manipulate easily by hand. Accordingly, a number of methods were quickly demonstrated to suggest that the hard clay might be approached with a view to carving rather than modelling (although the distinction in practice was not always obvious). Another group was given soft clay to work with. The remainder of the class were set to making figure drawings using volunteers from the class as models. Instructions to the life-drawing group were simple: to observe the figure carefully and draw from observation; and to make line drawings of the whole figure with an emphasis on looking at proportions and shape and not at details.

The children working with the clay were given the theme 'family group' to work to, with instructions that the family group might include two or more figures in any arrangement of their choice. At first the children attempted to manipulate their slabs of clay and found the material difficult to mould into the forms they wanted. Two of the children pressed their soft clay fairly flat, drawing figures on the surface with the intention of cutting out the scratched outlines of the figures with a table knife.

It appeared that little had been learnt from looking at the sculptural objects in the collection; works which owed so much to the material from which they had been wrought. (Afterwards, I realised that these children's approach might have been influenced by their use of clay in a different context. As part of a technology project they had made cut-outs for a mobile by rolling out clay to a specific thickness and using templates to draw around.) I had hoped that the children might be able to use the clay in a free and spontaneous manner but I soon realised that I had taken for granted their ability to express their ideas using the clay in a three dimensional and plastic way. The children's methods of working seemed to owe more to past experiences and schema than anything they had seen in the gallery or discussed after the visit.

After I suggested a different approach, the children spent the rest of the lesson producing 3D figures. All of the figures were initially conceived as standing, symmetrical and erect. All had discernible torsos and heads but no limbs and little in the way of facial features. This fact was pointed out and Peter, having created a figure from welding two separate blocks of clay together, added a preformed arm using the same technique. Barney also added legs and arms to his figure and attempted to make it stand up. He was very disappointed by his apparent failure. Carina and Phillip left limbs and facial features until the schematic bodies of their family group had been established (Plate 6.7).

For both groups technical instruction was given as problems occurred. Some children were shown how to make effective joins between two pieces of clay, the use of carving and modelling tools was demonstrated, and modelling and textural effects were suggested. We talked about the Cycladic figures again and debated whether they were designed to stand up. Barney reminded me about the wire which had been attached to the backs of the figures to display them erect. We agreed that this was one solution but not a preferred one and that an aesthetic and technical solution might be sought by looking at other examples of standing figures and family groups.

After several failures and continued struggles, some of the children began to feel happier about the compromises they were making with the material. After a period of thirty minutes Phillip exclaimed, referring to the vaguely formed but free-standing shapes he had carved from hard clay: 'I've made a man and a woman. . . . Now I'm going to make three children.'

Barney's first attempt to remedy the problem of making a free-standing figure was to reduce the size of the body with a hooped cutting tool and then to broaden and thicken the legs. As the children began to abandon their earlier method of tackling their subject, a different aesthetic slowly emerged. The material constraints were beginning to be considered and worked through as the children sought to produce figures within the theme which I had set them. As Keith Gentle points out: 'simply stated, the problem is one of giving form, through a medium, to their ideas and responses' (Gentle 1985: 76).

For Gentle, this content/form tension, which includes 'quality of observation, sensitivity to materials and power of imagination', is 'the source of real understanding in art'. This tension, between the children's ideas and responses and their attempt to realise them in the material at their disposal, was fast becoming a dominant issue in the project and one which related directly to the works studied at the gallery. Another important issue was the extent to which exposure to other artwork influenced the children in the process of their individual artistic production.

In the following lesson I gave the children no instruction or guidance

Plate 6.7 Carina's first family group (photograph: Dennis Whitehead, Eastern Counties Press)

in how they were to approach their work. I decided to intervene as little as possible and see what emerged from the children's individual attempts to tackle the task. The children worked in groups with different lumps of clay, most using an easy-to-model grey clay. A few chose to work from blocks of hard grog-clay, using knives and cutting-tools. Some began by making separate pieces for the parts of the body (constructional approach), carefully rounded balls and cuboid shapes, which they then attempted to join together. One or two remembered the techniques of joining masses of clay together which I had demonstrated on previous occasions. Rachel imparted this skill to Lewis, who was struggling to keep his figure in one piece. One or two children adopted a different approach, using one whole piece of clay. Callan, for example, quickly created forms which he modified and reshaped by squeezing, prodding and extruding the clay with his hands.

Each of Rachel's free-standing figures appeared on first sight to have been little influenced by the work she had seen (Plate 6.8). However, on closer examination the minimal features (eyes and mouth reduced to holes) were comparable in some respects to the heads of some of Moore's sculptures, for example the *Draped Reclining Woman* of 1957–8 which

Plate 6.8 Rachel's free-standing figures (photograph: Rex Barker)

Rachel had spent considerable time drawing at the gallery. Furthermore, the simplicity, although not the shape of the head, might have been suggested by the Cycladic figures we had discussed on previous occasions. The plinth-like, rectangular base resolved the problem of making her figure stand and could have been derived from the *Mother and Child* of 1932. Finally, the arms, crossed in a loose but still quite formal manner, were probably an attempt to overcome a problem experienced with the material by other children (the fact that arms and legs, if made too thin, tend to drop off as the clay dries). Rachel's solution might have been suggested by this very feature of the Cycladic figures which she had pointed out in the previous lesson. During the discussion which followed this practical lesson the children considered the issue of influence.

R.B.   What other art did we look at which we felt might have had some influence on Henry Moore? What other art was he interested in?

CALLAN   Cycladic figures.

R.B.   Yes, Cycladic figures. Was there anything else we said had inspired him?

EMILY   Those heads ... the idol.

BARNEY   The way the figure was formed?

R.B.   Sources are things which artists draw upon in doing their work. You saw the pictures I showed you of Henry Moore holding stones and looking at them. What was he looking for in those stones, do you think?

TONY   Transformation?

R.B.   Transformation. What do you mean by that?

TONY   He could change it into, like ... a person or an animal.

R.B.   Absolutely. Very good answer. Right, now what do you think he would be looking for when he was looking at other art? He would be admiring it, but do you think in doing so it might find its way into his own work as well?

EMILY   He might try to transform other people's work into things?

R.B.   That's a nice way of looking at it. He might have tried to transform other people's work. Any people in mind?

BARNEY   Other artists. They might draw things and you can like ... ummm ... look at them and ... ummm ... draw them again and ... ummm ... then like make a plan of it ... and ...

R.B.   Well, he did actually do that, yes. We do have evidence from his sketchbooks and his drawing books, his notebooks, that he did actually make drawings of other art ... but a very wide range of other art. Looking at those drawings, perhaps the most common work he studied was African art.

Referring to the folded arms on Rachel's figures, one child said they reminded her of the Cycladic figures. I pointed out that the feature might have been equally arrived at as a way of tackling the problem of creating limbs from soft clay.

R.B.   Was it anything to do with the problem of handling the clay ... limbs falling off? Attaching them close to the body like that ... it makes it much stronger. Nothing to do with that?

RACHEL   [*shrugs*] That's the way I hold my hands.

Rachel's aim had been to create a set of figures, representing various members of a family. In carrying out that aim, she became immersed in the seemingly simple technical problem of making a recognisable figure, in proportion, and capable of self-support. In that process she might well have absorbed influences which would help her achieve that aim. Apart from her comments and the work itself there is no real evidence of mimicry, copying or influence. The issue of influence in the children's art was proving difficult to ascertain. Mimicry and copying other artists was not an issue (there was more evidence of the children copying each other). There seemed to be some evidence of that 'influence', but this was not consciously recognised by the children as they produced their work.

   None of them at this stage (with the possible exception of Carina) had attempted from the outset to create figures as a one-piece grouping, or in any posture other than 'standing' (almost all of the works by Moore depicted figures seated or reclining). This left me with the view that they were using a simple schematic mode of representation coming from 'within' themselves, rather than from looking at others' schematic modes. But it was hard to tell. Rachel's figures, carefully and competently produced, appeared to contain a formula of her own devising (comparison with developmental studies would perhaps suggest the degree to which they depart from the typical figure-forms produced in this medium at this stage of 'artistic development'). She appeared quite happy to go on making similar figures with the same features.

   Later, during a follow-up session, one of the children (Carina) abandoned the 'one figure at a time' approach to create a family group in which three figures are physically bound together in one mass (Plate 6.9). This may have been derived from a comment I made referring to the fusion of the mother and child in Moore's sculpture. Carina said she was happy with the rounded semi-abstract forms and satisfied with her figures despite the lack of detail and only slight indication of limbs. The problem of depicting a group of standing figures in the soft clay had been resolved in a form which imbued her group with a different feeling and significance from the free-standing figures, which the children would discuss later. Despite the apparent 'unfinished' look of Carina's piece, I felt that as a response to the problem, based on Carina's developing personal experience, the piece should be considered complete.

Plate 6.9 Carina's second family group (photograph: Rex Barker)

> Apparent distortions of shape, idiosyncrasies of colour, oversimpli-
> fication of form, exaggerations of scale or relationship are not just
> 'mistakes' or 'incompetence'. There is always the possibility that such
> elements in a child's work show the beginnings of a capacity to
> form personal statements arising from a genuine response and visual
> perceptiveness.
>
> (Gentle 1985: 79–80)

Carina's work opened up an opportunity to consider other approaches
to the subject and this departure was discussed with members of the group.
A lot of the talk was focused on perceived qualities of the different family
groups through comparing one piece with another rather than with the
work of Henry Moore and other work seen at the gallery. At this stage
in the development of the children's work there seemed to be more value
to be gained from a comparison of the ways in which the children had
approached the subject than from further investigation of the extent to
which their gallery experiences might or might not have influenced
their work. With the production of sculptural work of their own, the
teaching project had turned full-circle; discussions focused on other
artists' work had moved on to discussion of the pupils' work. The quality
of the later discussion is exemplified in the following extracts, in which
differences in the formal approaches to sculpture were pointed out. The
conversation referred to the handling of significant details and features of
their figures:

LEWIS   The figures get bigger.

Qualities such as texture were referred to:

DANIELLE   It's ... like the ... rock. Rock from a volcano.

The children talked about the feelings and emotions conveyed:

ROSIE   Phillip's look happy and Carina's look sad.

Similarities with some of the qualities of other sculpture were highlighted:

CARINA   It looks like the Mexican figure.

The children's intentions were brought out:

CARINA   I wanted them to look normal.
RACHEL   I thought it was a good way to do it.

The groupings and relatonships were commented on:

AMI   Carina has joined hers together.
GINA   Phillip's figure has got eyes, ears and nose. Carina's hasn't.
MARY   They're a close family.
R.B.   What makes you think they're a close family?
TONY   Because they're all huddled together.
R.B.   They're physically close together ... they're attached together ... the figures are attached together physically.

[...]

R.B.   Carina said she didn't want to do any faces because she was interested in the shape and she wanted them to look normal. I'm not sure what you mean by 'look normal'.
CARINA   ... an ordinary family. Because it reminds me of once when I sat with my nan and grandad in a line watching telly.
R.B.   Was that a good memory or a bad one?
PUPIL   A good memory.

It was very important during this discussion that the children's understanding of their own work was articulated and shared, and that their interpretations of the task and their evaluations of responses to it were seen as a valid part of the process. In this way the children were encouraged to increase their confidence, perceptions and ability to look at and talk about art. This involved being prepared to look carefully at the work without being judgemental and listening to what the children had to say: to allow space for individual responses, memory and associations.

As the children's experience with clay increased, their sculpture developed in increasingly different directions. Some produced seated and reclining figures using constructional techniques which I had demonstrated at the beginning of a lesson, others chose to create heads, and some produced figures from thin wire nailed to blocks of soft wood. Their art had developed in directions according to the interests, feelings and sensitivities of each child. At the same time their competence in handling the media at their disposal increased. Evidence of their concern with materials was sometimes linked to recognition, after the event, of the possible influences of other sculpture. Mary, referring to her wire figure, said: 'It reminds me of the dancer [Degas' *Petite danseuse de quatorze ans*] I drew.'

SUMMARY

The data showed something of the ways in which the children made sense of art, through discussions which focused upon the sources of an artist's work, on some of the works themselves, and on their own search for solutions to the tasks set for the production of their own work. In many ways, not least through comparison with other sculptures depicting the human figure which may have been influential to the artist, it was possible for children to discuss and focus upon the nuances of form and expression, significant details of surface qualities, materials, and the feelings to which various formal attributes gave rise. To some extent they were able to infer influences on an artist's work by looking at works considered influential by critics and commentators. More importantly, perhaps, they were able to carry this appreciation of sources of influence into discussions about their own work and its relationship to the art they had studied.

Through their own work, the children were able to appreciate the potential of natural forms as a source of ideas as well as the inherent qualities of the objects in their own right. Through the children's verbal comments, and gradually through their drawings and paintings, it was clear that many were able to value natural objects beyond their immediate qualities and to begin to develop their individual imaginative responses to them. Difficulties were encountered by the children in transforming and embodying those responses in their practical artwork at first. Their experience was that of many artists. Not all children expected, or could be expected, to be successful in any one lesson, especially in achieving 'transformation' of observations into imaginative form.

There would have been greater opportunities for children to explore the potential of using natural sources through visits to the coast and woodlands, where they could collect and explore the use of found objects as materials with which to build sculptures directly. The collection of large pieces of wood and branches made by children in the final days of the study suggests that many of the shortcomings experienced in the attempt to work along the lines of Moore's transformational techniques might have been overcome by using the materials directly. At the time I judged that the children's lack of experience and ability in handling tools and in

Plate 6.10 Emily and friends enjoying her sculptured head (photograph: Dennis Whitehead, Eastern Counties Press)

Plate 6.11 Phillip working on a wire support for a figure (photograph: Dennis Whitehead, Eastern Counties Press)

sculpting from resistant materials favoured the use of clay and more easily formed materials at this particular age. That judgement was reviewed in the light of the evidence I gathered. However, there was not time to explore this avenue fully during the project.

As the children engaged in their own artwork throughout the project, it became increasingly necessary to teach some of the basic skills in handling materials and equipment. This was addressed largely as the individual or group need began to emerge. Children's techniques in handling materials such as clay appeared very underdeveloped and this was apparent in the appearance of their early work as well as the methods they used, most of which followed the simple schema of the human figure.

The notion of 'influence' continued to be an important one and related directly to the use of other artwork which had been identified as a source by Moore. The children were able to recognise some of the formal similarities which exist between some of Moore's work and other artworks in the Sainsbury Collection. Many of these connections between one artist's work and another's were discussed in a similar way by the children as they engaged in their own artwork, and as they were able to compare similarities and differences between their work and the art they had studied in the gallery. The problem of imitation never really emerged, and ceased to be an issue throughout the children's practical work, at least in so far as the children did not attempt to mimic or copy the works they had studied. There was more evidence of the children imitating each other both in their choice of objects to work from and in their methods of working.

FURTHER READING

Arts Council (1978) *Henry Moore at the Serpentine*, London: Arts Council of Great Britain.

Bell, J. (1987) *Doing Your Research Project*, Milton Keynes: Open University Press.

Bogdan, R. C. and Biklen, S. K. (1982) *Qualitative Research for Education: An Introduction to Theory and Methods*, London: Allyn and Bacon.

Bowness, A. (ed.) (1957–88) *Henry Moore: Sculpture and Drawings Vol. 2 1949–1954*, London: Percy Lund, Humphries.

—— (1965) *Henry Moore: Sculpture Vol. 3 1955–1964*, London: Percy Lund, Humphries.

—— (1957–88) *Henry Moore: Sculpture Vol. 4 1965–1973*, London: Percy Lund, Humphries.

—— (1957–88) *Henry Moore: Sculpture Vol. 5 1974–1980*, London: Percy Lund, Humphries.

—— (1957–88) *Henry Moore: Sculpture Vol. 6 1981–1986*, London: Percy Lund, Humphries.

Eisner, E. W. (1972) *Educating Artistic Vision*, London: Macmillan.

Elliott, J. (1991) *Action Research for Educational Change*, Milton Keynes: Open University Press.

Gentle, K. (1985) *Children and Art Teaching*, London: Croom Helm.

Golomb, C. (1974) *Young Children's Sculpture and Drawing: A Study in Representational Development*, Cambridge, Mass: Harvard University Press.

James, P. and Moore, H. (1966) *Henry Moore on Sculpture*, London: Macdonald.

Leeds City Art Galleries (1981) *Henry Moore: Early Carvings 1920-1940*, London: British Museum Publications.

Levine, G. and Mitchinson, D. (1978) *With Henry Moore*, London: Sidgwick and Jackson.

Marlborough Fine Art (1970) *Moore, Picasso, Sutherland*, London: Marlborough Fine Art.

Metcalfe, G. (1975) *How to Use Modelling Materials*, London: Studio Vista.

Mitchinson, D. (ed.) (1981) *Henry Moore: Sculpture*, London: Macmillan.

Moore, H. (1966) *Henry Moore at the British Museum*, London: Tate Gallery.

Read, H. (1965) *Henry Moore: A Study of His Life and Work*, London: Thames and Hudson.

Roberts, D. (1978) *Teaching Art*, London: Batsford.

Robertson, S. M. (1963) *Rosegarden and Labyrinth: A Study in Art Education*, London: Routledge and Kegan Paul.

Sylvester, D. (ed.) (1957) *Henry Moore: Sculpture and Drawings Vol. 1 1921–1948*, London: Percy Lund, Humphries.

Taylor, R. (1986) *Educating for Art: Critical Response and Development*, Harlow: Longman.

—— (1992) *Visual Arts in Education*, London: Falmer Press.

Thistlewood, D. (ed.) (1989) *Critical Studies in Art and Design Education*, Harlow: Longman.

Wilkinson, A. G. (1977) *The Drawings of Henry Moore*, London: Tate Gallery.

APPENDIX

Works by Henry Moore in the Sainsbury Collection

Half Figure No. 2 (1929)
concrete

Girl (1929)
conté crayon and wash

Reclining Figure (1930)
ironstone

Mother and Child (1932)
Green Hornton Stone

Study of Seated Nude (1935)
pen and wash

Square Form (1936)
Green Hornton Stone

Sculptural Object in Landscape (1939)
watercolour and pen

Reclining Figure for Metal Sculpture (1940)
watercolour and pen

Group of Shelterers (1940)
watercolour and pen

Drawings for Sculpture (Standing Figures) (1940)
  watercolour and pen

Sleeping Shelterers (Two Women and a Child) (1941)
  watercolour and pen

Two Shelterers Eating (1941)
  chalk, watercolour and pen

Miner Drilling (1942)
  chalk, watercolour and pen

Studies for Shelter Drawing (1943)
  watercolour and pen

Madonna and Child (1943–4)
  bronze

Odysseus in Despair and Exhaustion (1944)
  chalk, pen and wash

Family Group (1945)
  chalk and watercolour

Two Women in an Interior (1948)
  chalk, pen and watercolour

Reclining Figure (1956)
  bronze

Draped Reclining Woman (1957–8)
  bronze

Two-Piece Reclining Figure No. 3 (1961)
  bronze

Chapter 7

Facing feelings

Linda Cadmore

> A face is probably the first thing we recognise with our eyes and we soon understand the meaning of certain facial expressions.
>
> (McHugh 1992: 4)

The decision to focus on the communication of feelings through facial expression as experienced and expressed by 4 and 5 year olds was originally made because I felt that the children I teach could probably relate best to a familiar idea, providing a way in to the study of art. Children coming into my reception class are usually able to draw some sort of recognisable face. These early drawings range from the combination of face and body to more mature representations with clearly defined features and sometimes the suggestion of a particular emotion. I wanted to know more about factors which influence the children's ability to convey emotion through their own representations of facial expression, and whether this could help, and be helped by, the study of other artists' work.

The children had some experience of looking at and discussing reproductions (mainly prints) of works of art, but I wanted to extend this, focusing particularly on work which might convey emotion through facial expression. I would present some work by non-Western artists for the children's consideration, including some examples of 3D work. They had little experience of both. The Sainsbury Collection includes numerous facial representations from a variety of cultures, in both 2D and 3D form. Taking the children to look at some of these was a new opportunity and a chance to extend their ideas. The visit to the Sainsbury Centre for Visual Arts would be the climax of our work rather than the stimulus for it. Building on the children's existing knowledge and perception of faces, these new ideas and experiences were monitored to gauge their expressive and perceptive abilities as they responded to them, with regard to two aspects of their topic-related activities.

The reception class of twenty-eight is a mixture of full and part time 4 and 5 year olds. I worked mainly with the sixteen full time children, concentrating particularly on a group of eight for the research. A welfare assistant and an NNEB student were involved in classroom activities. The school has 250 children on roll, including a nursery. It was built in the early 1950s on a large council housing estate and some of the children are from socially deprived backgrounds.

The teaching aims were:

- To develop the children's ability to look carefully;
- To develop the children's confidence in using and understanding descriptive language relating to works of art;
- To provide opportunities for the children to work with a wide range of materials, including some which are new to them;
- To enable children to make connections between their own work and that of other artists;
- To extend the children's ability to communicate feelings in their own representations of the face and to perceive expressions of emotion in the work of other artists.

The research aims were:

- To gain some insight into the children's ability to convey emotion in their own representations of the face:
- To identify factors which affect the children's ability to express emotion in their own work;
- To explore the children's responses to visual representations of emotion by identifying the types of response;
- To understand some of the factors influencing these responses.

CLASSROOM ACTIVITIES

Any successful teaching takes place in the context of a planned and structured programme of learning. You need to know how one experience builds on another and how to ensure that what the children learn gives them the opportunity to explore and express their ideas.

(Clement and Page 1992b: 8)

Before embarking on the topic I felt it was essential to help the children to extend three vital skills: to observe, to listen carefully, and to use simple descriptive language. These skills are necessary to some degree in all areas of an Early Years curriculum. I realised that they were absolutely crucial to the work on the communication of feelings through facial expression. Looking and listening skills are encouraged and developed daily in almost all classroom activities and particularly during story time, both with and without a visual focus, in order to develop children's visual and auditory responses. However, I wanted to introduce more specific looking activities in preparation for later work.

Our school topic for the autumn term was Lights so our Looking Table soon had a display of torches, lamps, bulbs, batteries and candles, to be handled and examined at the children's leisure as well as in small group or whole class sessions with me. We spent several short sessions looking at a large print of Van Gogh's *Starry Starry Night*, finding more detail each time and giving the children the opportunities to listen to each other as well as voice their own opinions.

Alongside work on recognising and naming colours we looked at Van Gogh's *Sunflowers* and Nicholas Hilliard's portrait of Queen Elizabeth I, full of intricate detail in numerous shades of brown. The children were encouraged to make spontaneous comments but also to listen to others and to me while I asked and answered questions about the prints.

During the first week of the spring term I used Gladys Blizzard's *Come Look With Me: Enjoying Art With Children* for short sessions of 5–10 minutes with one or two children. This book is a collection of coloured photographs of paintings about children, with suggested questions about each picture to assess the observational (and also language) skills of the children looking at them. In her introduction Blizzard says, 'The book may . . . help children to learn how to look at paintings so they will be able to see original works of art with greater understanding' (Blizzard 1990: 7).

Throughout the 'careful looking' activities, responses such as 'It's nice' or 'It's good' were common. Some of the children probably knew no other words to convey their approval of what was in front of them and although they needed to feel that their comments were valued they also needed to be introduced to new vocabulary. The situation is well summarised by Angela Anning:

> The challenge is to get beyond the superficial responses – 'I like it because it's nice' – to stretch the children's ability to talk about their feelings, or to help them to make connections with their own experiences when talking about the work. They will need your help to build up a vocabulary of evaluation which includes technical, mood and descriptive words.
>
> (Anning 1993: 21)

I tried to introduce new descriptive words as often as seemed appropriate, especially in stories and poems. I welcomed the children's own invented vocabulary (which often seemed more effective than conventional words) and encouraged their tentative use of difficult words.

I planned the teaching to include whole class, large and small group, paired and individual activities, but with the emphasis on group work. The children were used to working individually and co-operatively and to being observed. Some had previous experience of their comments being tape recorded or written down, but the use of a video camera in the classroom was new to us all.

Most of them could name eyes, ears, nose and mouth. A few could name chin and cheeks, but none could name eyebrows, eyelids, eyelashes or forehead. To teach these unknown names to the children, I read the poem 'My Face', by Deborah Humphries:

My Face

The shape of my nose feels like
    the side of a mountain.
My lips feel soft and tender like meat.
As I feel my ears they remind me
    of a helter skelter and mazes.
My cheeks feel podgy and squashy like
    a soft quilt.
My eyebrows feel like a soft and
    furry caterpillar.
And my eyes feel like children
    fidgeting under a blanket.
    (in McKellar and McKellar 1980: 13)

The children looked at their own faces in mirrors and felt their features, then painted a picture of their own faces, putting in all the features they had seen in the mirror. The paintings clearly showed reasonably accurate records of their features, in realistic positions! Emma B. made an oral checklist of features as she painted; 'I done the eyebrows, now I got to do the nose. Shall I do the ears?'

None of the children included references to emotion in their painting. Later they drew a face using thick felt pens, with no instructions about expressions or feelings. Descriptions of this work included several references to a specific emotion conveyed in their drawing, for example 'My mummy laughing at my daddy upstairs' and 'My mum walking to the shops with pretend teeth in to scare people'.

Next was an activity which involved feeling changes in their own features and seeing changes in each others' faces as they made a face to show a particular mood. The children sat in a circle so that all their faces could easily be observed and together showed me in turn a happy, sad, angry and surprised face. They found it harder to make an angry or surprised face than a happy or sad one – some children had to look at others for clues as to how to change their features to show anger or surprise.

I then asked the children to identify which part of the face told us that the person was happy, sad, etc. Smiling mouths were easy for the children to recognise but I had to work very hard at questioning, prompting and encouraging the children to look carefully. However, the language used by the children was fairly limited and often repetitive. Few children were able to make accurate comments after careful observation of, for example, Karl's angry face:

KANE   He's got his teeth out.
RYAN   He's growling with his eyes.
MISHA   He's screwing them [*his eyes*] up.

or Amy's sad face:

KANE   Her eyes look sad.
RYAN   Her mouth is getting upset.
MISHA   Her mouth is a bumpy shape.

The children each made a face showing an emotion of their own choice. These were almost all happy faces, with two or three children making angry faces. I asked the children to paint faces showing a particular feeling. No one said what sort of face they planned to paint before they began. The children talked as they painted or when they had finished. Several children changed the mood of their face as they went along:

LEE-ANN   I'm doing happy. No, it's gone sad now. The mouth is sad. Look.

Comments ranged from a very few words, such as:

JASON   A sad face.
EMMA S.   It's got a smiling mouth.

to longer descriptions offering an explanation of the mood conveyed:

KARL   I'm doing a happy face. He's happy 'cos his mum's happy.
ZOE   She's smiling 'cos she's on a photograph.

Kane gave a running commentary as he painted:

'I'm doing an angry one.
He wants to get rid of his hair and his mum won't let him.
I done a straight line for a mouth.
He's gone and cut it off when his mum's not looking.
It's gone all different [*Yellow and red paint run together*].
There he goes [*paints another, smaller face*] to get his hair cut.
Look. He's cutted it.
Now he i'n't angry no more.'

In order to help the children to identify and describe moods other than happy and sad, the same children sorted a collection of photographs, pictures, prints and cuttings into categories according to the mood they conveyed: happy, sad, angry, surprised and worried face (plus an empty hoop for any other categories the children might suggest). Each child chose a picture, showed everyone, described the mood of the face and then put it into the appropriate hoop. The sad and happy faces were easily recognised and sorted. Faces with a worried or surprised expression were harder for the children to describe. Misha said that one picture showed 'a thinking face' and put it into the spare hoop.

Prints of *A Clown* by Georges Rouault and *Self-Portrait* by Max Beckmann were looked at for two or three minutes, then comments about them were invited. Lee-Ann and Benjamin both thought the clown was sad: 'It's a sad one. Her mouth is sad. The eyes have started to water,' commented Lee-Ann. Misha thought the clown's mouth was giggling and his eye was winking. Ryan described him as mad. Misha and Ryan concentrated well and both suggested a story to explain the way the clown looked, based on the well which Ryan could see in the picture and the forest Misha saw. Lee-Ann and Benjamin were less responsive and needed a lot of questioning and prompting from me to focus their attention.

Karl and Kane appeared not to be very interested in *Self-Portrait* at first. Karl made only a short comment when asked, but when Kane thought he saw paint and blood on the man in the picture he became more animated and studied it with greater interest. Emma and Charlene also needed specific questions from me to focus their attention on different aspects of the picture. Emma seemed distracted and eager to return to another activity, while Charlene was preoccupied with peeling glue off her fingers. They both eventually talked about what they could see in the picture in response to my questions.

I showed the group a set of five black and white prints made between 1914 and 1920 by Karl Nielsen, Karl Schmidt-Rottluff and their contemporaries. Some responses described the emotion the children perceived in the faces, others were statements regarding the general appearance of the figures:

KANE   They're all soldiers. They're strong. And fierce.

LEE-ANN   The faces are like rectangles. My mum's got them lines on her face. And spots.

RYAN   One is longer and longer.

BENJAMIN   That one [*with a beard*] is like Father Christmas.

I asked the children to remember the angry, cross, strong faces we had looked at and to draw faces showing similar moods. One group drew faces with thick, black felt pens on white paper, another made prints. The original prints remained on the wall. None of the children went to look at them before drawing/printing their own faces. The drawings were made quite quickly with bold strokes of the pen. The children liked all the black lines on the white paper and were pleased with their own results. 'Look he *is* angry,' said Charlene. I felt that the children had really captured the aggressive mood of most of the prints. They could see a link between their work and the original prints but no one had attempted simply to copy the originals.

Printing was a completely new experience for the children, who seemed astonished when we spread thick black paint over the table! To avoid excessively black hands (and aprons!) the children drew faces in the paint with a variety of tools – corks, lolly sticks, bricks, paint brush handles, etc. They were thrilled to peel off the paper and find 'their face' on it, and also to discover that they could take a second print from the table-top. A few children were so involved in the mechanics of the print-making that they were unable to concentrate on producing an angry face and just drew a neutral or happy face.

We looked at photographs and pictures of decorated faces, including natives of Papua New Guinea and Australian Aborigines, as well as Western examples of painted faces, with theatrical make-up. The children said that people paint their faces 'to look more prettier' and could relate this to their mothers' use of make-up on their faces. I pointed out that most of the people in the pictures were men and asked how they looked with painted faces. 'Pretty' and 'scary' were the children's comments. 'Dads don't wear make-up,' said Lee-Ann. Kane thought men painted their faces to look more scary.

The children decorated their own faces with face paints, sitting in front of our big mirror, and said how they felt and looked. The pictures we had looked at earlier were left on the table and I noticed that Nicholas seemed fascinated by one particular photograph of a native of New Guinea whose face was decorated with a bold yellow and red pattern. Nicholas made a very good attempt at producing a simplified version of this pattern using the same colours. He said he felt different with his face painted. Other children's comments were: 'funny', 'scary', 'fierce', 'happy', 'mad', 'pretty', 'like a clown', 'like an Indian', and 'like a princess'.

I felt that the children were beginning to make longer, more descriptive comments about their work and were becoming more confident and adventurous in their use of language: 'curly eyes', 'angry cheek', 'rectangley eyes', 'thin, grumpy mouth', 'ugly face', 'stripey mouth', and 'small eyes'. They were also associating emotions with particular facial features. Two more prints of faces were discussed: Van Gogh's *Self-Portrait* and Mary Cassatt's *Child with a Red Hat*. Comments were recorded, varying considerably in length and in the amount of detail observed.

For the *Self-Portrait*:

BENJAMIN   It's sad. The eyes are sad.
KANE   His face look bumpy. He look sad. He's got a beard and a lip
    mouth. He's thinking about old people.

and for *Child with a Red Hat*:

KARL   It's a sad face. Her eyes look sad and her mouth too.
CHARLENE   A baby. She's sad. Her mouth and nose look sad. She's looking at her dad. When he laugh she feel sad.

The children identified strongly with *Child with a Red Hat*

KELLY   Look, the eyes are like me.
LEE-ANN   It's my mummy and she's happy in her mouth.

I left both prints on the table and several children returned to look at and discuss them, often with a friend.

A collection of paper and papier mâché masks made in China, India and Tibet were shown to the children and I asked them what they thought the masks would be used for. They decided they would be worn 'to frighten people', 'for fun', 'to go to a party', 'to hide in', or 'to make you look special'. Two mask-making activities followed, one using paper plates as a base plus assorted decorative materials, such as paint, tissue, foil, straws, bottle tops and fabric; the other an opportunity to paint a mask in the style of the big red, black and gold Chinese mask.

The children took a long time exploring and selecting materials to use. Some of the masks clearly conveyed a mood of happiness or sadness but others were purely decorative and showed no particular emotion. The use of all the available materials became almost an end in itself for some children, tending to obliterate the task of conveying a mood through the mask. The paintings of the Chinese mask showed variable evidence of both careful observation and hand control. Most children had managed to capture something of the stern and menacing mood of the mask.

Tony Ogogo, a Nigerian painter and potter from the Benin region visited the school (to work with Year 3 children). I took the opportunity to borrow a small collection of West African masks, one made by Tony Ogogo, for my class to see and handle. I asked the children to identify the materials they were made of. They easily identified wood and clay or pottery. They liked touching the masks and talked about the emotions portrayed in them and their own feelings, generated by the masks:

He looks tired and asleep.
He looks laughing and happy.
He looks like a robber.
He's cross, especially his nose.
The eyes look sad.
It makes me feel frightened.
I feel sad and a bit sick.
It's a bit like a Chinese face with eyes.
The eyes are like little bananas.

Some of the Year 3 children brought the masks they had made with Tony Ogogo to show us. My class noticed that they were all made in a similar style ('They all look a bit the same,' said Misha), with long noses and thick lips. They made clay masks in this Benin style, following the instructions the Year 3 children had been given. These were prescriptive. The masks were made by working on a base of clay smoothed over a thick twist of newspaper. Additional pieces of clay were used for the features, for example using a 'sausage' shape for the nose, making hollows for the eyes and filling these with small balls of clay. This method of working was a new experience for the children whose previous clay work had been 'free' with no specific directions or restrictions.

The following day the children drew pictures of their own masks and dictated their comments about them to me. By now the children were spontaneously associating emotion with particular features:

STACEY   The eyes look surprised.

CHARLENE   He's mad with a square mouth.

LEE-ANN   Her eyes are a little bit angry.

BENJAMIN   A happy face and big happy eyes.

We looked at an African wooden mask and discussed how it made us feel and how it looked. Kelly covered her eyes and said she did not like looking at it. Kane gritted his teeth and said he liked it. Most children thought it was scary and Ryan said it made him feel 'killing'.

The children had another chance to look at the mask, individually. Almost all the children were able to explain why the mask made them feel as it did. Some were also able to elaborate on the very short comments they had made during the earlier observation session:

EMMA B.   He frightens me because of his teeth – they're too big.

KELLY   His eyes make me feel unhappy.

STACEY   The eyes shape make me feel funny.

RYAN   It makes me feel I want to punch it because of the shape of his mouth and nose and eyes.

BENJAMIN   He has angry teeth, it makes me feel angry, and I feel frightened when I look at him.

ZOE   His teeth make me feel dirty. I feel horrible.

AMY   My tummy feels all funny. His teeth make me frightened.

LEE-ANN   When I go to bed I feel scared because I think it is going to bite me.

Only Kane showed a definite liking for the mask: 'He makes me feel all right. He's not scary. I'm not scared of him. I like him.'

Masks made later by folding and cutting black paper conveyed a wide range of expression. Scissor skills were generally not accurate enough to enable the children deliberately to cut features conveying a specific emotion. The results were therefore more accidental, any mood conveyed depending largely on the haphazard way the children cut their paper.

Paul Klee's *Senecio* face was introduced, to consider his use of shapes. They immediately noticed and referred to the shapes they could see: 'It's a circley, triangley face. ... Look at all the shapes. ... It's round and nice.' None of the children mentioned any emotion except that they liked the picture and especially the colours. When I asked if they thought it was like a real face, they said, 'yes'. As a follow-up activity the children were asked to make faces similar to *Senecio* using shapes cut from assorted papers. After cutting out a paper head they were free to stick on the shapes as they chose. The children became very absorbed in this and especially in using coloured tissue paper shapes which over-lapped to produce new colours. Most children put the features in conventional positions but some did not. None of the children commented on features which had been placed unconventionally and there were no references to feelings.

Four children looked at a reproduction of Picasso's *Weeping Woman*, individually. Ryan and Charlene were quick to identify triangles, squares and rectangles, while Kane defined the eyebrow as a stripe. When I asked Misha which shape she could see, she said it was 'rectangley and circley'. None of the children commented on the 'unconventional' representation of this face. They interpreted its mood differently:

KANE   It's a mask, like tears. A mask like a princess.

CHARLENE   Sad tears. Everyone smacked her in the face.

MISHA   It makes me feel good 'cos the hair's got all colours in. I like the long eyelashes. It might be a her. I can see some tears.

THE VISIT

None of the children had visited a gallery or museum before. As we were able to make only one visit to the Sainsbury Centre I decided to use it as the climax to our topic work. I hoped that the children's observation and expressive skills would have developed sufficiently during the previous half-term of work in school to equip them for a fairly intensive session of looking at and describing what they saw at the gallery. They were in groups of three, each led by an adult. The adults each had a note-pad to record comments made by children in their own group.

At school we had discussed what a gallery might be like. I explained that we would see pictures and sculptures of people and animals and some masks made of different materials. The children's responses to the gallery in general and to individual exhibits were extremely varied. The video provides a record of the children's physical and verbal reactions and was especially useful to me. Several children found it hard to concentrate on the objects and explanations of them. They can be seen fiddling and looking elsewhere. Some were clearly distracted by, and interested in, other exhibits or just by the novelty of being in a completely new environment. Others listened and looked but made little verbal response. The children were generally less talkative than I would have expected, although some answered and asked questions spontaneously and showed great interest in the exhibits. We looked at the following works.

Femme (Alberto Giacometti)

The children seemed shy or reluctant to respond to questions about this. They did not appear very interested in the figure at all. Comments included: 'It's old', 'It's made of metal', It's thin, like Tamara', and 'It looks like a skeleton'.

Petite danseuse de quatorze ans (Edgar Degas)

This provoked a quick response of 'It's metal' from several children. They went closer to the figure and made further comments, including 'It's a ballet skirt' and 'The eyes are peeping open'. There was no response to questions about the mood of the girl – the children were more interested in copying the pose of the dancing figure.

Bucket Man (John Davies)

This was one of the children's favourite exhibits. Their replies to the question 'What do you notice about him?' came thick and fast:

> He's being rude [*bare chest!*].
> He's painting.
> He's got string in his mouth.
> It's a beard.
> I can see his belly-button.
> String's holding his trousers up.

No one mentioned the ball on his head until asked to look carefully at the head. Misha said, 'It's got a little round ball on his head, like a hat.' In response to questions about his face, the children said he looked worried and sad.

Wolf and walrus masks

The children were convinced that the wolf mask was a reindeer. No one knew the word walrus – they thought this was either a big spider or a monster. The children had to be prompted before they could see and say that these were actually masks. It seemed that as they were in animal form and made from materials which we had not found in the masks at school the children had not recognised them as masks. They identified wood and feathers and noticed the decorative dots on the wolf.

Head-dress frontlet with crouching animal

The children described this as 'a man with a monkey on top', or 'a man with a baby on his head'. They said it was wooden and eventually realised that this too was a mask.

Seated male

The children related immediately to this 'baby' as they called it (Plate 7.1) and commented that he looked upset. Kelly said, 'His mummy's died.' Emma B. thought he was crying, 'cos he's up there'. Misha identified the material he was made from as 'china'. (At school, Emma B. drew pictures of 'the poor baby' for several weeks after the visit, always drawing the toes first and a rectangular frame around the figure.)

The children were given pencils and clip-boards and asked to draw a picture of one of the exhibits we had looked at in the gallery. Their response to this was very enthusiastic – almost all of them went straight off to their favourite exhibit and sat or lay on the floor looking and drawing in a very relaxed way. It seemed that the children's ability to concentrate and look carefully was enhanced by drawing. In order to produce the sketches they had to focus their attention specifically on a particular object or on several parts of it. The most popular objects drawn were *Bucket Man*, the wolf and walrus masks, and the seated male (known as 'the poor baby'). The drawings ranged from very crude representations to easily recognisable figures showing considerable detail. The observation and expressive work in which the children had been engaged at school had been a useful and productive experience, preparing them for the visit.

REFLECTIONS

By the end of the project I felt that I had begun to achieve my teaching aims but I was conscious that each aim needed to be continued beyond the duration of the project. Most children were certainly able to sustain longer periods of careful looking and were growing increasingly confident in talking about what they saw, often using vocabulary which was new or unself-consciously using words of their own invention (aims 1 and 2). The children had worked with a variety of materials including paint, assorted papers, pencils, pens, scissors, glue, straws, clay and junk materials. They

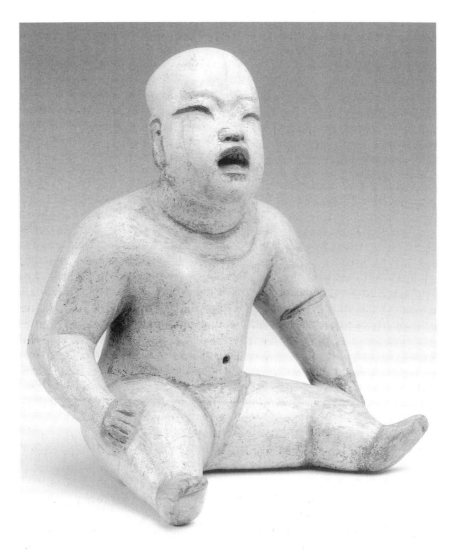

Plate 7.1 Seated male (clay) Mexico, Puebla (Robert and Lisa Sainsbury Collection; photograph: James Austin)

had made table-top prints for the first time. I had planned to include some papier mâché work and will certainly do this at a later date (aim 3). The children had looked at a variety of 2D and 3D work of artists from different cultures, in school and at the gallery. I felt that the children were developing the ability to reproduce specific styles or moods in their own work. An important implication of this work was my awareness of the need to build up a collection of school resources to enable the children to continue to make these connections (aim 4). I was encouraged by the children's growing ability to express feelings in their own facial representations and their increasing awareness of the emotions conveyed in the work of others (aim 5).

EXPRESSING EMOTION

Having observed the children at work during most of the activities recorded in the previous section and studied the evidence, I am aware of four main factors which seemed to influence the children's ability to express emotion through their own representations of the face. The first (self-evident) one is their own experience. The second was their ability to use language. In *Two to Five*, Parry and Archer (1975) say: 'Children judge every sensory impression in a peculiarly personal way, based on previous experience. No two children will have the same experience, so they are unlikely to see the same things at the same time' (1975: 3). It was apparent that in addition to 'seeing' differently, the children represented what they saw in distinct ways. There are faces which children painted early in the investigation in response to the instructions to paint any sort of face. (This was mainly an exercise in the positioning of features.) Each child's use of space, colour, technique and the combination of available materials produced a range of results, each quite distinctive and each with merits peculiar to that child. Each child's unique and individual response meant each piece was valid evidence of a child's attempt to express an emotion.

In many paintings and drawings the children's own experiences were clearly distinguishable. Some were able and willing to talk about the person (often mum or dad) involved, or the incident which they had been part of and which was being 're-run' through their work. The talk sometimes revealed more than I could interpret from the painting: 'Quite often the implicit content is greater than is evident on the surface – there is more in child art, in fact, than meets the eye' (Parry and Archer 1975: 72).

On the other hand there were a number of children with either speech or language difficulties in the class. Of the sixteen children involved in the research project two were having speech therapy. Five children are deemed to have 'limited' language capability and need special help for all aspects of their language development. All these children show some difficulty in understanding or interpreting the instructions given to them before embarking on a particular activity. Only one of them spontaneously talked about her work. When asked to describe their work this group tended to reply in very short phrases and seemed either reluctant or unable to say very much at all. There was also a tendency for these children to repeat descriptive words or phrases already used by others, often inappropriately, for example to use 'sad' to describe a beaming, happy face they had drawn, when the child next to them had just described his own drawing as sad. The language ability of this group of children did not affect their physical ability to draw or paint, but to some degree it affected what they drew and, presumably, in some cases, their understanding of the relevance and theme of our topic work.

Lack of confidence showed when these children either did or said nothing while other children began their task, or when they simply copied what others were doing. They often showed dependence on others to lead. Those who were articulate and had a wider vocabulary were confident in their approach to the activities, able to talk about their own work fluently and often in considerable detail, and took the lead.

Table 7.1, comprising verbal descriptions of their own prints given by 14 of the children (2 absentees) on two consecutive days, demonstrates that some children used almost exactly the same words on both occasions, whereas others gave very different descriptions. It appears that the language they used about their own work depended on when they talked about it, and may have been influenced by opportunities to reinterpret their images.

The combination of a child's own experiences together with the ability to describe and elaborate on them produced some imaginative work. It was sometimes difficult to distinguish between fact and fiction in a child's description of his/her work: 'A child's factually based story or picture easily tips over into fantasy' (Parry and Archer 1975: 64). For very young children there often appears to be no dividing line between what is real and what is pretend, and they seem able to move happily between the two, sometimes presenting fiction as fact. This third factor seemed an important one in their expression of emotion.

I realised that four or five children consistently worked and talked 'imaginatively', and that four of them were from families which have had a variety of problems. Perhaps, for this group of children, their expressive work was some sort of emotional release providing a way of coming to terms with painful memories or current experiences, or temporarily moving into another frame of reference.

The children's ability to draw, paint and make models was dependent to a considerable extent on their physical control in using their hands to hold and control brushes and pens and to manipulate scissors, clay, papers and other materials. For children who still seemed to be at the

Table 7.1 Children's comments on their own black and white prints, given on two consecutive days

Pupil	Day 1	Day 2
Zoe	It's got a happy mouth.	It's a happy face, eating his dinner.
Lee-Ann	It's a angry face, his cheek is angry and his eye. That one's a bit angry and that's a nice one, that eye.	An angry face. His eyes look angry and his nose and a rectangle mouth.
Ryan	A Chinese face – it was a bit mad and angry. His mouth is mad. He kicks.	A Chinese face. His eyes are looking for food, licking his lips. His nose is a clown shape and it fights.
Stacey	It's an angry face. His eyes are angry.	An angry face with eyes that are small. His mouth is a funny shape.
Charlene	A sad face. The mouth is sad and the eyes are – look. Because somebody told him off. Now he's crying – look. He hasn't got any hair 'cos he's sad. He's got lines on him so he's sad.	[Absent]
Misha	An angry face – a circley, rectangley mouth and her eyes are a bit rectangley. That's my mum that is. She's going to a disco and Tamara is getting on her nerves.	A yawning face, one ear fell off, his eyes are funny. The lines on his face are all wrong.
Jason	It's sad.	A rough face with sad eyes.
Toni	Grumpy. The mouth is thin. The eyes are thin too. He's painted them lines on him.	An ugly face with lines all over him and a big nose, stripey mouth and dotted eyes.
Benjamin	It's a sad face – look, the mouth is sad. The eyes are circles. The mouth is down.	A happy face and mouth and eyes.
Karl	It's a sad face. His eyes and his mouth are sad. His nose looks a bit sad and all the lines.	A sad face with sad eyes and mouth.
Emma S.	An Indian face. He's happy in his mouth.	An Indian face with curly eyes and a laughing mouth.
Amy	I made a sad face but it's got a smiley mouth.	[Absent]
Emma B.	[Absent]	A scary face, really angry and going into the house and scare everybody away.
Kelly	A sad face. It's me. Leanne is dead. I'm crying 'cos she's dead.	She is dying and crying and it's very sad face.

stage of 'beginning to appreciate the possibilities of controlling and directing marks' (Clement and Page 1992a: 16), the request for a drawing of 'a surprised face' must have been a tall order! Their drawings and paintings were likely to be little more than exploratory marks and their aim before starting to paint or draw was usually very different from their description of the final result. They tended to interpret the marks they had made, often changing this as they painted and sometimes giving completely different interpretations of their work when it was finished: 'The four to six year old ... may start to draw one thing and find that it suggests something else and immediately adapt his drawing' (Parry and Archer 1975: 72).

Particularly when manipulating clay or sticking boxes together in a fairly haphazard and random way, the children could 'accidentally' produce a facial representation and then interpret an emotion suggested by the result afterwards. Kelly's drawing of a face, in which she drew around small wooden shapes for the features, had a similar accidental quality. This face had an angry feeling but the emotion portrayed was probably coincidental with the manipulative demands, as Kelly had moved most of the shapes while drawing round them.

Children with good hand control were able to work competently with the whole range of materials and techniques available. They tended to produce work which conveyed an emotion they planned to show right from the outset of the task. This was most noticeable in drawings and paintings which required more deliberate control in execution. The drawings made after looking at twentieth-century prints which children had identified as 'fierce' and 'angry' conveyed similar intended emotions.

A few of the children with good hand control had already developed a recognisable style in their representation of faces so that their work, regardless of the medium used, is easily identifiable.

The use of some materials and techniques appeared to inhibit some children's ability to focus on their aim, and this became a fifth factor in my evidence. They tended to explore the materials themselves and to wander off task, pursuing the intrinsic satisfactions of the materials rather than concentrating on the making of their face to represent emotion. Collage and junk materials especially had this effect. Although the results of working freely with a wide range of materials in this way were colourful, the feelings conveyed in the faces produced were often unclear to both the artist and the observer.

INTERPRETING OTHERS' REPRESENTATIONS OF EMOTION

In order to investigate children's responses to representations of emotion in faces which they had not made themselves, I monitored as many as possible of the children's reactions to the stimuli already described. These responses were extremely varied and suggested that they were probably influenced by several factors. The medium in which facial emotion was represented seemed to make a difference to the reactions expressed. In particular the masks, and any pictures or photographs of masks, appeared to stimulate the children's interest and attention more than any other of the art which I provided.

Another tendency was for the quality of the response to improve as the number of children involved decreased; that is, individual or small group responses were more illuminating than those of the whole class. Some children who were reluctant to speak in a large group and who could be dominated by more vocal children's comments were able to describe their own feelings in a one-to-one situation. Amy, for example, hardly ever talks voluntarily in a class discussion but when asked about her feelings when she looked at one of the African masks on her own said, 'He makes me feel very scary. My tummy feels all funny. His teeth make me frightened.'

I summarised the type of responses shown by the children in the categories which follow, recording examples of each type and suggesting possible explanations for them. In some cases there was considerable overlap in the type of reactions. The only spontaneous *physical response* which was recorded was Kelly's reaction to the black wooden mask – she lowered her head and covered her eyes with her arm saying it was 'too scary' to look at. Her twin brother Kane's response was to imitate the expression of the mask by gritting his teeth and squinting with his eyes. Both these physical responses support Angela Anning's view that 'children can feel art as well as learn about it' (Anning 1993: 21). I had certainly anticipated that there would be much more physical reaction from the children, which was why I asked them just to look at the masks without speaking at first. Perhaps some children are exposed to so many images that the mask did not produce the grimacing which I had expected.

The *verbal responses* of the children ranged from one-word comments to long and detailed monologues and from short, factual descriptions to imaginative reflections. Again, the children responded differently according to the type of stimulus, their mood, etc. I have sub-divided these verbal responses into the following six categories.

The children who gave what could be described as a *minimal* response fairly consistently were those who were usually quiet and shy or who had limited language and little self-confidence. However, Ryan, who is usually very imaginative and articulate was reluctant to say very much about the Picasso *Weeping Woman*. When asked if it looked like a real face he replied, 'No, it's a piece of paper.' I felt uncomfortably like an interrogator as I tried to elicit something more from him.

I was conscious that a few children were giving what I would describe as *artificial* responses to the pictures they were looking at. Although they did respond verbally, they spoke without enthusiasm or conviction and possibly, in some cases, without understanding. These children were mostly, but not exclusively, those with limited language. I sometimes felt that their answers were repeated using words they had heard other children use and which I had confirmed as appropriate either verbally or by my own facial expression. These responses were usually very short and said in a very flat tone of voice. Karl, who had been interrupted in the middle of a spirited game with bricks and cars, reluctantly sat down, looked at the mask and rattled off his reply before the question was asked: 'It's scary and sad and frightened.' My interpretation of his response was: 'I've heard those words before – one of them must be right!' These 'unconvincing' or unauthentic responses made me aware of the necessity (ideally) for sensitive and appropriate timing when talking with the children. I also felt that it was not clear to some of them that their own response, however short or hesitant, was valid and acceptable.

Instinctive/intuitive responses were usually made by the least inhibited children in the group – often they were called or blurted out as soon as the children saw the face in front of them, so they were made with little time to think first. I recorded numerous examples of this type of reaction, such as:

LEE-ANN [*looking at Cassatt's 'Child with a Red Hat'*] It's my mummy and she's happy. She's looking this way.

KELLY [*looking at 'My Uncle'*] That's my Dad. . . . It's a boy. . . . He's grumpy.

KANE [*looking at a collection of black and white prints of faces*] They're all soldiers. They're strong. And fierce.

Although there was no visible evidence that the faces were those of soldiers, Kane had instinctively made that assumption, possibly linking the harsh features and expressions with other images of soldiers' faces which he had seen.

The variety of responses recorded in this section seemed to depend on most of the factors discussed earlier: the children's own experiences, their ability to understand and use language, and their imagination. The extent of their perception of emotion in facial representations would presumably depend on their awareness of particular emotions in their own experiences. By introducing the children to a variety of artwork I felt I had begun to extend their own experiences and to stimulate their imagination. My research certainly showed evidence of the children's growing confidence both in their own use of descriptive language and in their understanding of vocabulary related to the expression of emotion. Some children seemed able to make definite connections between images and

feelings and to show signs of awareness of the way in which language can
be used to link or explain the relationship between images and feelings.
Those who lacked confidence and language reminded me of the need
to extend opportunities in appropriate circumstances, to pursue the work
I had begun.

FURTHER READING

Anning, A. (1993) 'An eye for art', *Child Education* 70 (12): 21.
Blizzard, G. S. (1990) *Come Look With Me: Enjoying Art With Children*,
    Charlottesville, Va: Thompson-Grant.
Bridges, D. and Kerry, T. (eds) (1993) *Developing Teachers Professionally:
    Reflections for Initial and In-Service Trainers*, London: Routledge.
Clement, R. and Page, S. (1992a) *Investigating and Making in Art*, Harlow: Oliver
    and Boyd.
—— (1992b) *Resources pack teacher's book*, Harlow: Oliver and Boyd.
Dean, J. (1971) *Art and Craft in the Primary School Today*, London: A. and C.
    Black.
Diehl, G. (1974) *Miro*, New York: Crown.
Hopkins, D. (1985) *A Teacher's Guide to Classroom Research*, Milton Keynes:
    Open University Press.
Kellaway, K. (1994) 'When every picture tells a poem', *Observer*, 6 March, page
    22.
McHugh, C. (1992) *Faces*, Hove: Wayland.
McKellar, S. and McKellar, S. (1980) *Sense and Nonsense – Touching: Poems for
    Younger Children*, London: Macdonald.
Measham, T. (1980) *Picasso and His World*, Morristown, NJ: Silver Burdett.
North Eastern Region of the Art Advisers' Association (1978) *Learning Through
    Drawing*, Yorkshire: NERAAA.
Parry, M. and Archer, H. (1975) *Two to Five: A Handbook for Students and
    Teachers*, London: Macmillan Education.
Whitford, F. (1987) *Expressionist Portraits*, London: Thames and Hudson.

Chapter 8

Reception for a wolf and a little dancer

Maggie Croft

As an art co-ordinator in a primary school, I am very interested in the expectation that even the youngest children should apply knowledge of the work of other artists to their own work. This study of reception children's responses to a visit to the Sainsbury Centre for Visual Arts focuses on the way children responded to the work of other artists. There is little evidence of young children (and their teachers) undertaking work of this kind. My findings were shared with colleagues in order to help them to develop this aspect of art education.

The lack of literature concerned with young children studying art, and especially with the issue of incorporating their understanding into their own work, was immediately apparent. I was not able to find any studies of Key Stage One children involved in gallery visits, but read Rod Taylor's (1986) *Educating for Art*; René Marcousé's (1974) *Using Objects*; and Michael Laxton's (1974) *Using Construction Materials*. These books were all published in pre-National Curriculum times, and concerned older children. Rod Taylor and Glennis Andrews' (1993) *The Arts in the Primary School* provided some general 'models' for using art objects and gallery visits. However, my feeling was that the work I would undertake would be exploratory, first-hand experience which I would need to record for the benefit of my school.

A brief description of my school, the children involved in the study, and also the other adults involved in the visit to the gallery, is provided as a setting for the work we did. The teaching aims and strategies I employed to prepare the children for the visit and the reasons behind the choice of particular objects are also described. The research aims are presented, with a description of the research methods chosen to study the teaching strategies and the children's responses to them. A report of the visit itself includes accounts of the responses made by the children during the visit. The following day's workshop in school, in which the children made further responses, completes the description of the practical work, and I conclude with my analysis of their responses.

Elm Tree Primary School, Oulton Broad, serves the south-western area of Lowestoft and has a roll of approximately 290 children. The school was built in 1969, with extensions provided in 1971. Originally of semi-open plan design, the teaching areas have since been modified to form traditional teaching spaces that can be opened on to large activity areas. The catchment area has predominantly private housing. Approximately one-third of the children will have had nursery school experience for two or three terms before entry to the Reception Class. There are parallel classes from Reception to Year 4. The Reception year group, with termly intakes, comprises thirty-four children with two teachers.

The whole Reception group took part in the visit and all the opportunities for follow-up work. For the purpose of the research I chose to focus on six children who began school in September, making it possible to gather data throughout the project. The particular six chosen were selected because they are articulate and reasonably confident children. I felt there would be plenty of response to monitor from those children, though I recognised that they might not be 'typical'.

In class the children are used to being photographed alongside their work, for displays I make. They are not used to being recorded on a tape machine. I introduced a tape recorder in language sessions in preparation for the research. It proved necessary to prepare the children, as their initial reaction was to put their mouths very close to the microphone and distort the sound reproduction. By the time of our visit to the gallery there was no problem with either of the tools – still camera and audio tape recorder – being used to record their responses.

There were 8 adults accompanying the 34 children on the visit: the two Reception Class teachers (of which I am one); an ancillary helper, a nursery nurse, and four students, of whom one worked as sound recordist and photographer. This ensured a ratio of one adult to four children (six in my case for the purposes of this study) whilst in the gallery. In order to try to offer all the groups a similar experience whilst in the gallery a booklet was made which offered background information for the chosen pieces. Time was spent in discussion with all the group leaders on approaches to employ when engaging the children in looking at objects. These approaches were also listed in the booklet as 'questions to ask'. During the visit, gallery guides worked alongside the adults and shared their expertise. I did not use their help as I wanted to study my own approaches.

The journey time from the school to the gallery is approximately fifty minutes. After setting aside time to eat, play and get over the journey, we formed our groups to walk across to the gallery. I felt that the children were refreshed and ready for their new experience.

SELECTIONS

Before any account of the visit itself is read, the methods I employed to introduce the children to their visit need to be recorded. The decisions I made, to introduce the children to a collection of such scale and diversity, and the particular objects I chose to focus their attention on, were not easy. My initial focus of animals for the chosen pieces to be used in the research arose because a topic of 'Animals' or 'Pets' would be running during the period of the visit. However, this focus was rejected as the animals portrayed in the collection are predominantly very small and are displayed in cases which would require the children to use the footstools that are provided for inaccessible objects. As a direct result of that problem, I thought of using the large sculptures in the collection, particularly those by John Davies, Henry Moore and Alberto Giacometti, but I could not decide which to select, and could not find a suitable approach to these sculptures for my young children.

My eventual decision came about after a teachers' workshop in the gallery on the artefacts from America's North West Coast and Arctic regions. We learned about the stories behind a variety of objects from the Inuit drill-bow to the bear frontlet from a head dress. This left me wanting to share this knowledge with my group. Objects from all over the world make up the Collection, and stories behind some of the objects, I thought, could make a starting point for me to introduce these artefacts to the children.

My strategy for preparing the children for our visit was based on the concept of a collection. I had chosen this approach so that I could start from a familiar standpoint. Their knowledge of collections spanned monsters, shells, My Little Ponies, and numerous other family experiences. My colleague introduced her collection of shells which was so special that no one was allowed to touch in case she lost any of them. I then told the children about the collection that Robert and Lisa Sainsbury had made of art objects. I followed on with the precious nature of all that would be on show in the gallery – but we could not touch.

I was particularly concerned with this aspect of taking 5 year olds to a gallery. My 5 year olds are normally encouraged to squeeze, push and feel objects they encounter, to aid their language development and extend their tactile experiences. A purely visual approach for study with this age group of children was a new experience for me to offer in the reception class, and I would need to learn how they responded.

I built on our shared experience of a 'collection' by talking in more detail of the Robert and Lisa Sainsbury Collection. I introduced the inflatable globe and shared the information that pieces within this Collection came from all over the world. My class's experiences of holidays abroad was related to our globe, and the two new class members from the Oman and Zambia were able to find their countries, as others found Great Britain.

RESEARCH AIMS AND METHODS

The research aims and the methods chosen to allow me to study the teaching strategies and the children's responses to them took some time to clarify, just as my puzzling about which objects to focus on had taken time. My research aims were:

- To investigate the children's response to particular objects;
- To discover how young children respond to the experience of a gallery visit;
- To look at the responses they make to the work of other artists in their own work.

The research methods were:

- To record what I did with the children to introduce them to art objects;
- To tape record their verbal responses;
- To use the camera and tape-recording for further evidence of responses.

The Inuit wolf mask

I introduced this piece through a general description of life and climate in the Arctic region. The class instantly related 'North Pole' to Father Christmas and lots of snow. We progressed with the idea of life in the Arctic with sunshine for only part of the year, and darkness for several months of the year. The idea of parties when it was possible to travel, and the use of masks to celebrate the gathering of people seemed to be acceptable to the children's understanding of this different place and the people who lived there. We discussed things they liked to wear to parties.

I showed a photograph I had taken of the wolf mask so it would be a familiar object for the children to seek out on the day of our visit. I employed this strategy for introducing chosen objects before the children actually visited the gallery in the hope that they would enjoy a 'find a friend' exploration through the wealth of sculptures and artefacts they would encounter. I had hoped that through selection we would end up with some definite focused responses, and not just fleeting glances at an enormous range of objects.

I was employing a strategy that I had discovered had worked for me on my first visit to the Collection. Initially I had felt overwhelmed by the range of cultures, countries of origin, works from different times, and methods used in the sculptures, paintings, ceramics, and other artefacts.

I had found the experience much more enjoyable when I had stopped trying to take it all in and had begun to focus on specific cultures and pieces.

The bear frontlet

In introducing the second of my chosen objects I employed a similar strategy to the one I had used for the wolf mask. I showed the children a photograph of this piece so that the object would be familiar. We looked at books with pictures depicting the life of the North West Coast Indians; we talked of their celebrations, particularly the potlatch ceremonies, likening them to our parties when many people could come together and share gifts in celebration of a wedding or the bestowing of a title. The children's familiarity with special clothes to be worn for parties made this bear frontlet and its place on a ceremonial head-dress very acceptable to them, and they spotted some similar head-dress frontlets in the books I had put on display. I felt that the bear frontlet, like the wolf mask, had become an object that they would be looking out for on our visit.

Mesoamerican hip-ball game players

My third object was introduced to the children in a different manner in preparation for their visit. My choice of this object came partly because of a child in the class who loves football, and partly through my fascination with all that I had learnt about the Mesoamerican hip-ball game. I did not feel that it was suitable, however, for 5 year olds to hear about the death of the losing players in this game, so I restricted the background information to a more practical description, of people playing ball using their hips for contact, not hands or feet. My colleague and I demonstrated a game of hip-ball and this certainly intrigued our classes (I intended to use physical play of this kind in some physical education sessions). I showed the children a photograph of the ball game players, and we discussed famous present day football ·players and the photographic pin-ups we use to commemorate our heroes in football.

Bucket Man

My introduction to this sculpture was to show a photograph of the *Bucket Man* alongside the other objects which we were going to find during the visit. He did not provoke a great response or interest from the children at this stage and I did not pursue this piece. My preconceived idea was that the model itself would have far more impact, and I certainly did not wish to impose my ideas on the children.

THE VISIT

The wolf mask was the first object I had wanted to visit with my group. The purpose with which the group followed me in search of the mask was apparent. No one was drawn to other artefacts *en route*. Arriving in front of the mask seemed to satisfy the group (my strategy of 'finding a friend' seemed to be successful for this first object) and the children looked closely and began to talk about all that they could see. Callan had noticed a piece of the mask that puzzled him.

CALLAN   Ain't got a horn on the other side.

Despite my earlier close observation of this piece on an evening in the gallery which focused on the work of the Inuit, I had not noticed that the mask had a piece of orange material on one side of its mouth. A conversation followed within the group and an interpretation of this feature was arrived at finally.

JESSIE   I think it's his tongue.
CALLAN   Tongue?
M.C.   So that's why there wouldn't be one on the other side, would there? His tongue is lolling out.
CALLAN   Mmm, because he saw something delicious to eat.
M.C.   Look, Jessie can make that face ... yes, that's just how he looks ... and Katie, and Ellie.

Here all the group practised making a face to mimic the mask with tongue lolling out. It seemed very pleasing to them to have solved the problem Callan had posed, of what the orange piece could be, and a very natural response to pull a similar face. One chose to sketch the mask and they all settled down, kneeling or squatting in front of the masks, engrossed in the study, and sketching (Figure 8.1). The children's concentration lasted far longer than I had anticipated. It was a very positive response, as so often the set task will be completed in minutes, and the interest may be equally short. They were able to observe some very fine detail, and recorded it in their sketches. All the members of the group also included a sketch of the walrus mask, as these two pieces were beside each other in the display stand. The wolf mask drawings show the feathers on the mask, and the tongue lolling out of the mouth. Even the white surface marking was noticed by three of the group. Katie and Ellie worked together and they were the only ones to draw a face shape to depict the mask; the rest showed the elongated face of the wolf and the wide jaw of the walrus quite clearly in their drawings.

Bucket Man was not the second object I had planned to visit with my group, but while the group was sketching the wolf mask he had been spotted by Curtis, who excitedly drew the rest of the group's attention to

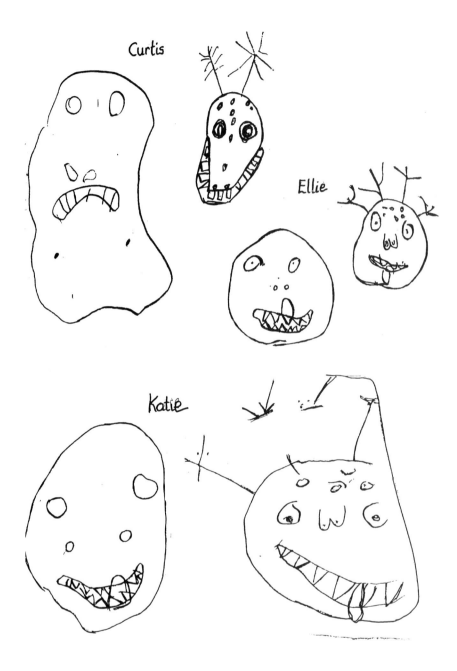

Figure 8.1 Sketches of the walrus and wolf masks

the sculpture. Their intention was very obviously to get closer to *Bucket Man*! He certainly provoked plenty of interest and a fairly heated discussion followed between Callan and David. There is a black ball on the head of this piece. After some preliminary discussion, Callan became adamant that the figure was a genie. The discussion continued for some time till Callan won his point. The Walt Disney film *Aladdin* had been on general release in the half-term holiday. It seemed to provide a secure answer in Callan's mind to the uncertainty of the sculpture. The argument about *Bucket Man* continued back at school in follow-up discussions to our visit, where Callan still managed to convince himself and others that this figure was a real genie despite the fact it was flesh coloured and not blue!

As we walked towards the bear frontlet, David went ahead and was very excited to have found the bear for the rest of the group. We gathered in front of the display stand for a better look. I was disappointed at how little of the bear my group could actually see. This piece is in the back right-hand corner of the display and the children could see the bear only from the left-hand side. We solved the problem by using a footstool, and after taking it in turns for a better look the group again settled to sketching. Then Curtis mentioned that he could see paintings. After the children's experience of finding it hard to view small artefacts, I decided to show them the Anthony Green painting of his bathroom, which I knew they would all be able to look at easily.

Having arrived in front of *The Bathroom at 29*, the group seated themselves comfortably and began to study it. Their responses in this case differed from those made to the other three pieces we had studied. Previously, the sketches made by the group had always been instigated by one member of the group, with the rest following suit:

JESSIE I think I can draw that.
CURTIS I want to draw it.

Similar requests had followed our initial discussion about each piece in turn. Now that we were sitting in front of Anthony Green's painting the group soon made it clear they did not want to attempt any recording.

CALLAN We can't draw this one.
CURTIS We can't do this.
M.C. We could if you'd like to.
CURTIS There's too much in it.

The group chose to look at and discuss this very detailed painting. They were most interested in the unfamiliar portrayal of objects within the picture, for example coat-hangers above the bath, where they were used to hold up washing lines. The group responded by close observation, apparent in all the detail to which each drew others' attention. This painting, given its size and hence ease of vision, was exactly the right thing to study at this point in our visit. The children were tired; one was complaining of being thirsty, another of being too hot. I realised then that a whole hour of very concentrated work had taken place without a break.

Going to the Reserve Collection provided an opportunity to see Anthony Green's *My Mother Alone in Her Dining Room*. On the way, the children seemed curious about the foggy, indistinct works by Yuri Kuper which are displayed alongside Anthony Green's vibrant colours. They seemed to be seeking as many differing experiences as they could fit into their visit, and hardly glanced at the dining room painting. I found this surprising as they had been so involved in *The Bathroom*. Perhaps the similarity of style in *My Mother* meant that it did not capture their interest when there was so much else to appreciate and discover.

On their return to the main viewing area, the children sat back and relaxed in the squashy chairs without any prompting. The point of these chairs, that the gallery should have the feel of a living room for all visitors, was not missed by these 5 year olds. They looked as if they had all returned home from a hard day's work and had collapsed in the most comfortable chair! Jessie spotted the Edgar Degas sculpture, *Petite danseuse de quatorze ans*, and excitely drew the other girls in the group to her find. She immediately put herself in the pose of the dancer, with the other girls, Katie and Ellie, following. Their mimicry was a very simple and natural action, and one they returned to time and again in our retrospective discussions about the visit. The act of standing in the pose of the dancer preceded any verbal description of the sculpture. It appears to me that this physical expression is easily remembered by the group and has left a lasting impression.

FOLLOWING UP

My strategies for follow-up work were made with the needs of the entire class in mind, not merely the research group of six. The children had opportunities to draw, paint, model and write about their experiences and memories of the visit. We began with discussion, and referred to sketches for aids as necessary. The children chose throughout the day whether to paint, model or draw objects they remembered. I made tape recordings of the six children's impressions of the visit and of the objects they had seen. A simple mask made from cardboard cartons with papier mâché and PVA glue was devised in discussion with the six.

The initial discussion was succeeded by a series of workshops on the following three Tuesday mornings. The science and technology workshops, in which we were studying a 'materials' topic, became science/technology/art sessions. The children had been engaged in a study of malleable materials – sand, soil, clay, mud, papier mâché. I wanted to introduce a less resistant material for the children to pare away and to gouge and scrape. This was offered in various forms – soap blocks; plasticine lumps; hard clay. The children were also offered the opportunity to make a frame and, at a subsequent workshop, to cover the frame. Art straws, pipe cleaners, and rolled paper were used to construct the frame. The materials for covering the frame or skeleton were wool, masking tape, fabric, and tissue paper.

I had planned these activities so that the children could work in a three dimensional way. Previously their 3D work had been based on experiences with construction toys such as *Quadro* and *Clixi* and *Clever-sticks*. Each activity, to cut away a form, to make a skeleton or frame, and to cover the framework, occupied one of the three workshops.

The discussion about our visit was lively and full of description of the images the children remembered. John Davies' sculpture was mentioned often. *Bucket Man* sounded like an old friend, but was not used by the children in any paintings or models. Callan chose to do a painting using the postcard of Anthony Green's *The Bathroom at 29* which I had put on the display about our visit. He applied brushstroke upon brushstroke within his painting, using the same colours as Anthony Green had. Callan also used a six-sided irregular shape to frame his work, including the flowing curtain. This was the only piece of work in response to the painting we had studied.

I was surprised that the simple idea of painting a familiar room from memory had not elicited any further response from other members of the group. Katie and Ellie chose to work together on a painting of a dancer, which followed the girls' posing in the style of Degas' *Petite danseuse de quatorze ans*. Their painting of the dancer, and the colour mix they used, left the finished picture almost bronze in colour, reminiscent of sculpture. Jessie also chose to draw, colour and paint a dancer in her work that morning, and also in the following workshop. Her pipe cleaner frame was a person, dressed up with net curtain to be a dancer.

Curtis painted a mask that he said was a wolf mask, before going to work on a papier mâché version of it. All the group had time to work in plasticine and many mask-like faces appeared. These were hard to capture on film as the children were used to changing their models and did not usually save their work in dough or plasticine.

The workshop sessions over the three weeks provided me with evidence of the short-term nature of the responses to our visit. After a week had elapsed the children were involved in the new experience, for them, of making a structure from rolled paper, bending pipe cleaners, joining art straws. They seemed too busy with the process to be concerned with the experiences of a visit of the week before. If I had wanted this work to be in response to our visit it probably should have taken place on the next three days of the same school week. It also should have been based on a practical activity that the children were familiar with, so that the technicalities of their medium (for example, how to bend a pipe cleaner) did not take over from the images they had encountered in the gallery. I was reminded that reception children, at the beginning of experimenting with many media (from charcoal to Mod-Roc), are likely to focus their concentration and energy on the manipulative and tactile problems and qualities associated with each medium until such time as the exploratory stage has been successfully accomplished. Here, with the immediacy of the visit now in the past, they were more interested in their own investigations of the materials than in being aware of other artists' work.

CONCLUSION

I began this study by contemplating a new approach to my teaching of art to young children, and looked forward to discovering evidence related to the questions I posed at the start of the project:

- What will the children's responses be to the artefacts we studied on our visit?
- What will these children do in the setting and formality of a gallery visit?
- Will they take account of these experiences in their own practical work?

Answers to the first question are very clear in the evidence I recorded of their physical responses, especially their gesturings, and the very close observation they afforded to the objects. Girls responded in a particularly lively way to the statue, *Petite danseuse de quartorze ans*, mimicking her stance and imitating her expression. Their memory of this piece continued into all our retrospective discussions.

Their verbal response is also clearly recorded in the taped evidence. Their ability to reflect to themselves and to discuss with each other, in their own terms, their perception of these objects, particularly the John Davies sculpture, *Bucket Man*, was very enlightening. They were quite at ease in their conversations and ready to share openly their impressions.

I was looking specifically at my teaching strategies for introducing a group of children to a gallery visit. My preparation session, through the concept of a collection, its value, and importance to the owners, may well have influenced their behaviour on the day. My methods of introducing the children to particular objects as 'friends' to find during their visit also proved very effective and was evidenced in the single-minded way the children approached the chosen objects.

The children's obvious ability to behave appropriately in the gallery was a great pleasure (and relief) to me. I had not anticipated that a trip with this age group could be so successful and enjoyable for staff and children. The children adapted readily to the conference room where they had lunch, and they were so at ease in the gallery itself that I realised that I had previously underestimated the ability of reception children to conduct themselves so well in unfamiliar surroundings.

For my third question there was less clear cut evidence to draw upon. The images seen during their visit mostly excited the children, and they indeed took account of them in their paintings, drawings and models, using the media they were familiar with, i.e. pencil, paint, plasticine and clay. In the series of workshops in subsequent weeks, in which I also wanted to extend the range of materials and experiences of technical processes, the children were fully engaged in the technicalities of the new media on offer to them. With straws to join, wire pipe cleaners to bend and join, and paper to roll, they were so engrossed in their exploration of the material that they did not take account of the artwork we had seen. I should not have expected them to react in any other way, perhaps. But their responses showed me that my plans for follow-up work to the gallery visit were inappropriate and did not meet my intention to exploit their use of the visit as a stimulus for their own artwork. The timing of these sessions was also wrong for these children. I should have used the remaining days in the week of the visit, not waited for Tuesdays spread over the next month.

FURTHER READING

Gardner, H. (1980) *Artful Scribbles*, London: Jill Norman.

Laxton, M. (1974) *Using Construction Materials*, London: Van Nostrand Reinhold.

Marcousé, R. (1974) *Using Objects: Visual Learning and Visual Awareness in the Museum and Classroom*, London: Van Nostrand Reinhold.

Taylor, R. (1986) *Educating for Art: Critical Response and Development*, Harlow: Longman.

Taylor, R. and Andrews, G. (1993) *The Arts in the Primary School*, London: Falmer Press.

Walker, R. (1985) *Doing Research: A Handbook for Teachers*, London: Methuen.

Chapter 9

Looking at faces

Sue Feather

A strong theme that runs through the objects in the Sainsbury Collection is the way in which the human figure is represented, and in particular the many ways in which the human face is portrayed. Some of the faces are very realistic and some are stylised, highly distorted, or have exaggerated features. This prompted me to consider the images of faces that children see in their daily lives and whether their perception of faces in life is affected by those images.

Children are surrounded with simplified images, from cartoons on TV to video games, comics and books. These contain simplified standardised faces designed to evoke sympathy (big eyes), fear (big teeth), stupidity (outward slanting features, open mouth), and other similar emotions and characteristics.

This study centred around the observations of a lively mixed ability group of 5 and 6 year olds. They were encouraged to examine each other's faces, their own drawings and models, and those of other artists. To find out how well children identify emotions and other human characteristics in faces, and how well they communicate what they see, I used a series of teaching techniques and recorded what I did and their responses to the teaching. Conversations showed how aware the children were about what a face conveys. Their images became more detailed and their observations more expansive as the study progressed. They showed abilities to make perceptive judgements on many aspects of the size, shape and position of the features of the faces represented in a variety of kinds of art. They also related these to varying characteristics and emotions. In many cases their own pictures showed an awareness of these factors.

At early stages of their development children usually draw the head as the most prominent and detailed part of the human figure. They already recognise its importance in conveying meaning. They produce a kind of visual shorthand of what they consider to be the important and meaningful parts. Research into the way in which children's representations of the face develops from the early scribbling stages onwards (for example Kellog 1970; Freeman 1980) relates to the intellectual and mental development of the child. There seems to be little research into the way children perceive and interpret facial characteristics and emotions in their own work, or in that of other artists. Lowenfield (1939) in his studies of creativity asked children to draw yawning, happy and sad faces and found that 'drawing facial expressions and gestures is not only not predominant during the schematic stages of development but seems almost impossible' (Lowenfield 1939: 35).

His explanation for this was the low flexibility of schematic symbols and a low capacity for co-ordination. He was, of course, interpreting children's ability to draw and not their ability to understand and react. The supposed difficulties in representing expressions accurately does not necessarily mean that children cannot understand and react to such expressions in life or in art. Thomas and Silk (1990) point out that 'almost without exception, children's drawing has been studied from an adult point of view. We know very little of what children themselves think about their own drawings and that of others' (1990: 154).

The same could be said of the study of art forms other than drawing. Given the prominence of the face in the children's own work, in the works in the Sainsbury Collection, and in other art and media images which the children encounter, there seemed to be both a teaching need (to help children to convey meanings) and a research question (to understand how they think about the portrayal of facial expression).

While working on a project investigating these questions I aimed to develop the children's:

● Powers of observation;
● Awareness of visual expression and its relationship to conveying characteristics and emotions;
● Powers of verbal communication.

Research questions which I considered during the teaching were:

● Do children recognise distortions/exaggerations/simplifications in faces?
● Can they identify where these occur?
● Can they identify any expressions that the faces may be conveying?
● Do they portray and interpret these in their own work as a result of these discussions, and if so how?
● How do my teaching strategies develop their observations and perceptions, and the capacity to portray and interpret facial expressions?

The children helped me to try to answer these questions. The research material was gathered mainly through recorded conversations and the children's drawings. I used questions and exercises to focus their attention on particular aspects I wanted to consider. I worked with six of the children more closely than the rest for data-gathering purposes. The group included lively conversationalists and quiet thinkers, within a wide range of general maturity and abilities. The data I gathered included:

- A record of my own teaching strategies and interactions and tasks set for the children;
- A record of children's observations and their verbal interpretations and analysis of expressions;
- A record of children's own facial reactions to the objects encountered;
- Children's own artwork showing their interpretations and portrayals of expression using visual language.

The data were collected, and recorded in the form of audio-tapes, photographs, notes and the children's own work.

Most of the data were generated as a consequence of the teaching project, for example:

- Using mirrors and photographs to identify what they see as important elements in their faces;
- Making distorted faces in mirrors and at each other to see if they can identify the emotions conveyed;
- Looking at distorting surfaces to see the effect they have on the face;
- Making a visit to the Sainsbury Centre for Visual Arts to study specific pieces to try to identify the ways distortions and simplifications are used to convey emotions;
- Making drawings and/or models of a face to convey expressions of emotions;
- General questions and interactions by me to encourage observation and expression of ideas.

Field notes of the events were taken by me throughout the project, which was presented to the children as an interesting investigation. I hoped that the children would produce their own ideas to help the inquiry as they came to know what it was about. My guidance mainly involved focusing, through posing questions and providing chosen stimuli, and talking to them about what I was interested in finding out.

LOOKING AT EACH OTHER

As the first stage of establishing what the children actually look at when they draw faces, I chose one child, Thomas, who I felt had strong facial features. The children were asked to identify what they felt made his face particularly interesting. I expected them to give me a list of the features of the face and maybe more specific details, such as 'his eyes are brown', but their comments were more perceptive than I had anticipated:

S.F.   What can you tell me about his face?

SAM   He's really smiley.

S.F.   What do you do when you smile? Where do you smile from?

SAM   His eyes are always smiling.

S.F.   How do you mean?

SAM   They're wide open.

S.F.   Can you tell when he's not happy, then, when you look into his eyes?

SAM   Yes.

S.F.   How?

SAM   His mouth doesn't smile?

S.F.   That's not his eyes.

They were stumped. I covered Thomas's face so we could see just his eyes.

SARAH   When he smiles his eyes get wider.

We uncovered his face and looked again.

HARRY   When he smiles his cheeks go up.

S.F.   Just up?

HARRY   Up and that way [*showing out*].

TOM   His nose goes out a bit too.

SEAN   His ears are red and like a curly 'c' and they have a curly 'c' inside.

S.F.   Where do they go on the head?

OLIVER   Beside the eyes.

We looked at the pupils in the eyes – Sean knew how they worked. He also suggested a way of planning to draw the face.

SEAN   It has a kind of 'n' at the top and a 'u' underneath. His nostrils are like 'o's, with a line in the middle. His mouth is like an 'm'. [*He had already described the ears.*]

The children identified the features that made Thomas individual, and also a characteristic expression, associated with emotions that the features conveyed and the way the face changed as the emotions changed. Sean's suggestions on how to draw the face were interesting. They suggested that he saw the head in terms of identifiable 'coded' shapes. We continued to discuss the other less striking features of Thomas's face to form a detailed observational and verbal study of how Thomas looked. The children then set about drawing each other's faces trying to show what was special about each one.

Almost none of the children drew in their usual manner, which was to draw the outline of the face first. They started with either the eyes or the mouth (Plate 9.1). This would seem to indicate that our conversation had focused their concentration strongly. One or two used their hands to work out the position of the features on the face. They all established that the eyes and ears were about on a level. Elizabeth drew the sides of the face opened out on the page, as she apparently thought this was an important part of her subject even though she could not see it.

Several drew elements of their sitter's face that they could not see at the time, such as hairs in the nostrils or the uvula! Harry's drawings are usually rather sketchy. Here his concentration was intense. His subject, Venetia, was hardly allowed to breathe and he obviously felt that her mouth was the most important part of her face (Plate 9.2). The drawing is very large and detailed with large teeth – he spent more than two-thirds of his time on this feature. He also seemed to see each feature of the face in complete isolation. We reviewed the pictures afterwards and some interesting observations were heard:

SARA   Harry looked much harder than he usually does on his pictures. He's looked hard at the mouth.

SEAN   Well, she does make a lot of noise.

HARRY   There's the tongue and the other thing at the back [*uvula*].

SAM   The mouth is big. She looks like she's shouting.

S.F.   How? Loud, soft?

SAM   Like this – Ahhhhhhh [*puts his hands up to his face and yells*]! Like Kevin on *Home Alone* – Ahhh!

S.F.   When?

SAM   He puts shaving cream on his cheeks and goes like that – Ahhhhh! [*General amusement and agreement.*]

S.F.   Why does it make you feel like that? Is it just the open mouth?

SAM   No – the nose.

S.F.   What about it?

SAM   The nose is open wide. You can see right up.

S.F.   What about the eyes?

SAM   Titchy.

S.F.   So they are not important?

SAM   No, not here.

SARA   Eyes can get big when you shout – like this – Ahh!

Sam identified the power of the mouth in Harry's picture and also that it was not the only important factor. They seemed to understand that the exaggerated size of the mouth and nose was emphasised by the smallness of the eyes and these helped to give the full effect of the scream. Sara was also quick to point out that this is not the only way to draw someone screaming or shouting.

SARA   That face looks cross. The eyebrows are closer together.

ELIZABETH   Sometimes they go zig-zag when you're angry.

Plate 9.1 Thomas's portrait of Tom (photograph: Sue Feather)

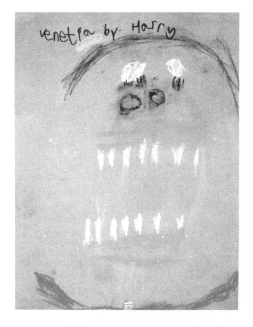

Plate 9.2 Harry's portrait of Venetia (photograph: Sue Feather)

S.F.   Really? Zig-zag?

ELIZABETH   No, but when you draw them they do.

Elizabeth had established that there is sometimes exaggeration when we draw things to emphasise a characteristic.

SARA   That face is sad, its mouth goes down.

ELIZABETH   The mouth doesn't always go down.

S.F.   Well, what else can happen?

ELIZABETH   I don't know.

S.F.   Can you do that face?

ELIZABETH   Yes. [*She does.*]

S.F.   So what is she doing to look sad?

SAM   I can see – her eyes go thinner [*makes a narrowing action with his hands*].

Elizabeth was already aware that sometimes more than one feature can be involved in showing an expression but help was needed to identify which other features were involved.

IDENTIFYING EXPRESSIONS AND EMOTIONS

In order to develop their awareness of different expressions and also to see whether they could name more subtle expressions than happiness or sadness, we watched a mime artist on television. In a clip lasting approximately two minutes, the following characteristics were identified by the children while watching the sequence: crossness, happiness, boredom, amazement, relief, disgust, sadness, tiredness, concentration, surprise, laughter, eagerness, thought, and pleasure.

The only prop the mime artist used was his hands. Sam, who had done the *Home Alone* extract, pointed out that hands helped to tell you how you felt. We all agreed the mimes would have been harder to guess without the hands.

Having established that the children could recognise a wide range of feelings and characteristics when looking specifically for them, I now needed to encourage them to look at their faces even more closely – to discover ways of emphasising features in order to produce notable and noticeable facial expressions. I made a collection of shiny curved surfaces and asked the children to look at their faces in them. This caused great excitement and hilarity – so much so that I decided to let them just look and talk about what they saw for fifteen minutes. They moved their faces around in the objects and identified with ease what was happening to their faces. Conversations were full of sharp observations.

The next day the children recorded some aspects of what they could see in the surfaces. They reverted to drawing the outlines of their faces first, followed by the features. They used only drawing pens or pencils as I wanted them to concentrate on looking at features and not to worry about colours. A very wide range of pictures were produced showing what I regarded as an excellent standard of observation and producing a wide range of facial expressions and characteristics. They had already identified distortion and its effects on the face in Harry's picture, and I asked my smaller group what they thought about some of the pictures they produced. Venetia's face was the first focus of discussion:

VENETIA   When I put my head like this [*head on one side*] one bit went shorter and one longer so it's gone oo-oop [*waggles hands in a wobbly jelly action*].
HARRY   It looks like it's slipped off.
S.F.   So she doesn't look like that normally?
VENETIA   It's thinner longways with a bendy nose.
S.F.   The right size?
ELIZABETH   It's all the same amount of long [*in proportion?*] – the eyes have got closer together.
HARRY   A bit cross-eyed.
VENETIA   She looks surprised because her mouth's open.
HARRY   Singing maybe.

Venetia's portrayal of her face showed the bendy motion she observed very well. The position of the mouth could well have conveyed surprise or singing. The children were not interested in the fact that several features were missing. The simplification was not referred to. As many of the pictures they normally drew were simplified, this really was not surprising. Sam's face was discussed next:

S.F.   Can you see any differences?
SAM   The face is fatter.
S.F.   Fatter all over?
SAM   No. Round the chin and cheeks are fatter.
S.F.   How does it make him look?
SARA   Like Frankenstein – he did actually have a big chin.
S.F.   What do you think he is thinking?
SAM   He's really a horrible person.
SARA   Yes, he looks tricky but he's really a horrible person.
S.F.   So you wouldn't trust him?
ALL   No.
SAM   He's sad.
S.F.   But he's smiling.
SAM   He's still sad and he's got small eyes. They look tricky.
S.F.   Is your face fatter at the bottom?
ALL   No.

SAM   The other way round.

S.F.   So you think this would be a good way to make a frightening or tricky face, do you?

ALL   Yes.

HARRY   Like Frankenstein – with a bolt in his neck!

In this conversation Sam's identity was soon lost as Sara mentioned Frankenstein. Sam established that even though he was smiling he was still sad and Sara said he was still horrible, the small eyes being identified as the real indicator of his character. The influences of films also were evident in their analyses of the faces. We discussed Elizabeth's face.

HARRY   She looks like a robot – robots have straight shoulders like that.

SARA   She's lost her mouth.

HARRY   It's gone into her chin.

The popular images of robot culture are referred to here and Harry is very definite about how they do and should look. Finally, we discussed Claire's face.

S.F.   What would you say about Claire's face in this picture?

VENETIA   She looks stupid.

S.F.   Why?

VENETIA   She stuck her tongue out.

S.F.   Why did you do that?

CLAIRE   It was already funny so I did it to make it more funny.

S.F.   What would you do if you met that face?

CLAIRE   I'd laugh.

S.F.   Look at the eyes.

VENETIA   They're big.

SARA   They go like – 'oh'.

S.F.   What does that do?

SARA   Look out.

S.F.   What would you call this face?

CLAIRE   Stupid.

SARA   Surprised.

HARRY   Sleepy.

SAM   Scared.

S.F.   A sudden scare or a slow scare that creeps up on you?

SAM   Sudden – oh!

S.F.   Could you change that picture to make it more scared?

CLAIRE   Make its hair stick up.

Making the hair stick up is a common practice in cartoons to show scared faces. This conversation also showed Claire's attempts to exaggerate a characteristic that she had already identified, though the final face had more than one interpretation – stupid, sleepy, surprised and scared were all considered as possibilities.

So far the children had drawn pictures and only thought about the characteristics they produced afterwards. I wanted to establish whether they could deliberately emphasise or simplify features in order to produce a desired characteristic or emotion. Rather than give the children a completely new exercise, I placed the distorted drawings around the room and asked them to choose one that they could identify as showing particularly obvious characteristics or emotion, and to draw another version that emphasised them. If, for instance, they found a face that was cross, how would they draw it to make it more cross? As a class we considered several pictures, identifying the effects of various features – something the children were getting very confident at by now – and discussed how we could improve the effect. One discussion involved a face with slanted eyes, Molly's face.

SARA   Its eyes go down.
S.F.   How do you feel about it?
SARA   I think it's an evil face.
S.F.   Why?
SARA   Because its eyes are slanty.
S.F.   Have you ever seen a face like that?
TOM   A devil.
ELIZABETH   It's a cross face.
S.F.   How could you make it more cross or devilish?
SAM   I'd give it horns and pointed ears.
VENETIA   And pointed teeth.
S.F.   Would you change its nose?
SAM   Make it long and sharp.

The features they have described are very much the standard stereotyped image of how a devil is perceived and portrayed in their culture. The influence of cartoons was evident in several of the pictures, especially Harry's. He had recently been to see the new *Aladdin* animated film and his evil face was reminiscent of the wicked magician Abenazer in the film. When asked whether he had had anyone in mind when he drew the picture he said not, but on asking him what was in his face's ears he said, 'Earrings, like in *Aladdin*'. He refused to talk about any bad or evil characters in the story.

Sara's picture had some interesting features. She exaggerated the eyes by drawing dark rings around the outer edge. They had almost an hypnotic quality about them, I thought. Several cartoon characters over the years have used moving concentric circles around the eyes to indicate an attempt at hypnotism, for example the snake in *Jungle Book* and the magician in

Aladdin. She used and exaggerated the freckles from Molly's picture, had sharpened the nose as suggested in the conversation, and had twisted the mouth to the side. She added frown lines above the nose. How much was deliberate? These are her comments:

SARA   I put the dark rings round his eyes because vampires have eyes like that and anyway the shark in *Popeye* had rings round his eyes too. He was really bad. He is thinking something really bad and his face is thinking like this [*she screws her face up – mouth on one side, frown lines between eyes and eyebrows down*].
S.F.   Have you left anything out that you did not need?
SARA   Oh, ears, they're under his hat.

I think the last statement was a spot of quick thinking. She may have thought that I was disapproving of the fact that she had forgotten them – they were obviously irrelevant in this picture. However, the effect she achieved and her conversation show an awareness of how to manipulate and in some cases emphasise or enlarge the features in order to produce the desired characteristics in her face. This was evident in about half of the new drawings. The other half showed that the children understood how to change the features of the face to show characteristics or feelings but in very simplified forms, often changing only one feature to produce a different effect. This was evident in Emma's pictures of a sleepy and a happy face. Both figures had the original stance with the hands up, the only changes being a differently shaped mouth and the addition of a nose in the sleepy picture. These changes seemed to serve well as a kind of visual shorthand to convey different moods.

Other feelings chosen to be illustrated were sadness, crossness, surprise and fright. These were fairly simple, straightforward emotions to illustrate as far as the children were concerned. They all used felt tip pens to draw with although other materials were available. Some coloured their drawings with crayon or chalk but I felt that the use of the pens tended to emphasise the symbolic nature of their pictures and reduced their opportunity to make subtler statements.

OTHER ARTISTS' WORK

So far the children had worked from their own ideas or from each other's pictures. The visit to the Sainsbury Centre for Visual Arts was designed to widen their awareness of the way other artists portrayed the face and to discover their reactions to these portrayals. Most of them had never experienced an art gallery before. Their initial reaction to the exhibits was an excited curiosity, as they looked and asked questions of themselves and each other, and they seemed desperate to sit down and draw the items. Questions such as 'How did they make that?' or 'What's it

made from?' were frequent, but also they were making observations
on the features of many of the pieces. Three pieces produced intense
observation amongst the members of my group. First, French Palaeolithic
Man (Plate 9.3):

ELIZABETH   His face is sad.
SAM   Its a bit like one of those faces I drew in the shiny things [distorted
    images].
S.F.   What do you mean?
SAM   It's sort of bendy and long.
S.F.   Have you looked at his eyes?
SARA   They've got spots in. I drew spots.
HARRY   His nose is funny.
S.F.   I think it's been broken.
ELIZABETH   Yes, it's all bumpy. He's got a line round his head.
S.F.   What do you think it could be?
HARRY   A helmet.
ELIZABETH   Hair.

The children related this head to their own work twice in the conversation,
and this happened on several other occasions. They obviously found
comparison interesting and felt some empathy with the artist. Sam
recognised that the face was distorted. Two were willing to interpret a
line as a simplification for adornment. Next they saw a Cycladic marble
head:

ELIZABETH   I like this head.
S.F.   How do you know it's a head?
HARRY   Well, it's got a nose.
S.F.   Anything else?
HARRY   You can just see the eyebrows.
ELIZABETH   He's got ears, they're just circles – no holes in. I like them.
HARRY   He's a bit like a robot – sort of squarish.
S.F.   Why do you think there are no eyes? [*Silence.*]
S.F.   Would it look better with eyes? [*Pause.*]
ELIZABETH   You can nearly see the eyes anyway. He looks sad.
S.F.   Well, that's not because of his mouth. He hasn't got one.
ELIZABETH   Well, he's still sad.

Elizabeth's opinion was confirmed by several other children who wrote
'sad' or 'glum' next to their drawings of this head later on. It is difficult
to identify what gives this head an air of sadness even for an adult – the
curved plane of the head and the angle of the eyebrows perhaps, but
the children were able to use the simplified features and interpret them.
Elizabeth was also appreciating the simplified design of the ears and

the fact that even when familiar objects are not there (the ultimate simplification!), we can still see them in our mind's eye.

The third incident was as we looked at *Bucket Man*. I had not intended to spend time for the purposes of this research in looking at him, because I felt the children would find him difficult to interpret as far as emotions were concerned. How wrong can one be? Most had opinions about what he was doing and some about why he was doing them. Felicity had temporarily joined our group:

FELICITY   He's a builder or decorator but he doesn't like doing it any more, he's had enough – he's thinking about something else.

S.F.   What does he have on his head?

FELICITY   A ball. That's what he wants to be next – a juggler.

Felicity could not label the feelings she identified, which I interpreted as 'detachment' or 'indifference', but she was able to explain how the figure felt through telling a story about him. Again these seemed very sophisticated emotions for a 5 year old to be able to identify.

There were many distractions away from my research focus while looking at the objects at the Centre, so there were not as many in-depth conversations as I had hoped. However, the children were highly stimulated by the objects and this was particularly evident in their drawings. One brief that I gave them was to record a face from an object of their own choice and to use the images they had collected in the visit, adding their own ideas to produce their own work of art. I wanted them to create a face which would produce a reaction from the people who were going to look at it, and which would help people to identify what the face was feeling or the characteristics it was showing, just as the children had done on their visit. By this time we had several masks and models in the classroom, which had been supplied by parents and friends, as well as a large number of pictures and books on faces. We looked at the use of colour on some Japanese face masks, at how the use of different lines produced different expressions. We also examined the picture *Weeping Woman* by Picasso, which Sara had found:

SARA   She's sad – her eyebrows are stripy and zig-zag and go down very strong.

TOM   She's crying.

SAM   Those lines bits on her face – she's crying lots.

ELIZABETH   I can see her teeth – she's really worried.

SARA   She's holding a hanky in her teeth. She has a big mouth and teeth. She looks horrible.

TOM   She's looking at something bad in the sky.

HARRY   She could be in disguise.

Plate 9.3 Palaeolithic head (stone, pigment) France, 3rd century BC (Robert and Lisa Sainsbury Collection; photograph: James Austin)

s.f.   What about the parts of her face? Are they the right size?

SARA   Her head's long.

SAM   Her mouth's big.

SARA   Her chin has got lines on it – in and then down.

s.f.   What was the artist trying to do or to make her say?

HARRY   Make a puzzle.

SAM   It's to make people cry and feel worse.

s.f.   Do you think the colours make a difference?

PUPIL   They're bright.

SARA   And kind of stripy.

s.f.   They are very strong colours and she is feeling something very strongly. Do you think that was a good idea?

ALL   Yes.

It was noticeable that I was now contributing less often points on how to look at faces for the information needed. In this conversation the children recognised distortions and exaggerations, and where they occurred. They were strongly affected by the emotions in the portrait and Sam recognised that the picture was designed to have that effect on others. The use of colour is yet another aspect of the ways in which artists convey emotions and characteristics and I was adding my own opinions here. The children were going to be using colour if they wished and so some consideration was necessary to start them thinking about that. Some of the children decided to draw faces, using water-soluble crayons and wax crayons. Others chose to make clay masks, putting far more detail and decoration on the faces than was usual in their previous work (Plate 9.4).

INITIAL ANALYSIS: TEACHING AIMS

Observation skills

The children's powers of observation were surprisingly (to me) acute from the beginning of this project. They made observations about faces with confidence and, with the guidance of my tasks and questions, they examined them in detail. During the course of the study my questions became less frequent as the children learned to focus on the features themselves. They began to make statements about how a person was feeling as well as appearing – a greater degree of empathy with the subjects had developed. (Compare the first conversation with the last two conversations.) Their drawings generally showed an improvement in observation and recording. In Emma's case, for example, there are several more features included in her final picture as well as some attempt at decoration.

Awareness of visual expression

The initial conversation showed that these 5 year olds already made astute observations about what a face was telling them. At times I felt I had influenced them by asking badly worded questions. However, there are enough data from the conversations to show that the children were very much aware of the relationship between visual codes or devices and the conveying of meaning. By the end of the conversation on p. 148, for example, we had established that Venetia's face gave the appearance of a loud scream, not just because of the large mouth, but because of its relationship to the other features. Sara also gave another interpretation of how to make a shouting face.

Verbal communication

Studying and following through conversations in detail has emphasised the value that discussion had in developing ideas. Whilst the children were able to give their own replies to my questions a more complete picture of how a face appeared was given by several children building

Plate 9.4 Elizabeth decorating a clay mask (photograph: Sue Feather)

on or giving alternatives to each other's opinions. The conversation on Picasso's *Weeping Woman* was an example of this.

Here the children built on each other's ideas as well as giving alternatives. They observed colour, shape, proportion, line, and the way in which these were used to portray appearance and emotion. The discussion enhanced their observation, and vice versa. The final conversation also showed that the children had begun to look at faces in greater detail for themselves. I had given no guiding questions throughout this part of the conversation. At the beginning of the study my questions alternated with their single statements.

INITIAL ANALYSIS: RESEARCH AIMS

Awareness of distortion

In the initial pictures and throughout the whole investigation no child recognised that the position of the eyes is approximately half way down the head. They consistently drew the eyes at a higher level and did not point out that anyone else's were 'too high'. Nor did they recognise the change when the eyes were drawn in the 'correct' position. For their first drawing, once I had focused their attention on the features, they did not draw the outline of the head until almost the end (ears or hair generally being last). This often affected the position of the other features but, provided that the size and alignment were not changed, the position of the other features was not commented on. This indicated that the children did not use the outline of the head as a reference point when drawing the features. It would seem possible that the children were concerned with recognising emotions in the features, with looking for the most obvious signals, that is, the scale, shape, proportions and relationship between the features. Research by Bassili (1978) showed that adult observers can identify faces in darkness from a moving configuration of lights placed only on the main facial features and showing no head outline. They could also identify some emotions from the way these highlighted features moved in relation to each other.

Although the outline of the head did not seem important, when this was changed or distorted the children not only recognised the change and described it but also were able to draw it quite accurately and recognise it in three dimensional faces.

Exaggeration

The conversations identifying exaggerations in the features tended to be mainly concerned with the relative size of the mouth or the eyes. The eyebrows were not considered as often, even though they would seem to be an important part of the information one would look for in an expression. They were alluded to three times in conversations, by two children who recognised that exaggerating the shape of an eyebrow can make an expression more powerful. The nose was not regarded in general as being particularly important, although changes in size and shape were often noticed and drawn. The one time that the nose was recognised as being an important part of an expression was when Sam observed that the large, open nostrils added to the effect of a person screaming. It does emphasise the tension of the picture and Sam's portrayal of how the image would appear in real life was very effective. The perceptiveness of his comments was underlined a few days later, following the theft of *The Scream* (Edvard Munch) from a gallery in Oslo. A critic was reported as saying that this picture looked like MacCaulay Culkin on acid. The critic was obviously affected by the acting on *Home Alone* as much as Sam was!

Both the eyes and mouth were constantly referred to as being affected by the characteristics and expressions that the children identified and the children often recognised changes in their size or shape and the effect it had on the face. Harry's drawing of the extra large mouth and teeth was recognised as making the shout louder. The oversized mouth and the teeth of the *Weeping Woman* added to the children's feeling that she was in despair. Large round eyes together with a large open mouth and tongue were identified as being sleepy, scared, surprised or stupid. The children offered alternative emotions and characteristics most often when discussing each other's pictures. This would seem due to the fact that these pictures, which often employed a fairly simple range of shapes, did not always contain all the indicators which might give a narrower range of possibilities.

The size and shape of teeth had a strong influence on the way the children interpreted faces. The teeth in both Harry's picture and the *Weeping Woman* were referred to by the children as intensifying the strong emotions in each case. Pointed teeth were used in several ways. Fangs were used to emphasise evil in several pictures, and pointed or zig-zag teeth were used or recognised as being threatening or fierce.

Simplification

The identification of the technique of simplifying the features was much more difficult. In their pictures the children were constantly simplifying what they saw, often using the minimum amount of lines to portray the information that they wanted to convey. They seldom referred to the lack of features present on a face, and, provided the shape used to represent a feature was recognisable as such, made no comment on it. One exception to this was when Elizabeth admired the shape of the ears on the Cyclades head and actually made a profile drawing to show them. In the conversation about the face the children saw nothing wrong with the lack of features, and Elizabeth implied that I really should not be worried about this because one could see them in one's mind's eye. The simplicity was important in this face and they seemed to feel this and were unable to answer my question.

Occurrence of distortion, exaggeration and simplification

The children identified the features that were distorted without difficulty. They were also able to recognise the nature of changes to the features (from the natural life-like characteristics of a face) that conveyed a particular expression, such as in the *Weeping Woman* discussion. They noted the artist's use of line, shape and proportion in the head, mouth, eyebrows and chin, and made comments on how the expression was affected. They were also aware of the effects the strong lines had in making the statements more powerful, and the intention behind that. Sam said, 'It's to make people cry and feel worse.'

In conversation about one picture Elizabeth observed that in the distorted face the features had been made longer and thinner but were still 'all the same amount of long'. She would seem to have observed that the features were still in proportion even though stretched and that the dynamics of lengthening the face had brought the eyes closer together. This appears to indicate how sophisticated her judgements of the effects of distortions can be, and also, perhaps, reveals a sense of understanding artistic intention.

Identifying expressions

Most of the emotions and characteristics which the children identified in their own work were fairly straightforward: happy, sad, cross, tired, surprised, for example. Others, such as pain, evil, and untrustworthiness, were slightly more complex expressions and required more discussion. In three conversations the children referred to films or other media images from popular culture as references for their ideas. The influence of popular culture was evident throughout the study. Harry often compared distorted or angular faces to robots, and often mentioned cartoons in association with faces he saw, as did several other children. Sara went as far as to discuss the techniques animators used to make eyes seem evil, and related this to her own work.

When studying adult artists' work the children were able to identify subtler expressions. The mime artist, Picasso, John Davies, and the Cyclades head produced observations involving more complex ideas and associated language. I felt that this was because there were different kinds of visual information to analyse. In the case of the Cyclades head it was the relative lack of information that provided stimulation. Sometimes the expressions the children recognised were so complex and subtle that they used story telling as an aid to identifying them.

Some of the phrases they used implied an interconnection of the features and inferences of meaning to express a feeling, for instance: smiling eyes (as when describing Thomas). 'Cheeky smile' occurred several times when describing a mouth smiling at an angle.

There were also occasions when the children decided to ignore one feature and to take note of another that was implying a different expression. A conversation on Frankenstein was an example of this. Both Sam and Sara ignored the fact that the face was smiling and chose other indicators on the face – small eyes and distorted chin – to emphasise what they felt was the expression. This selection of signals is complex and is obviously important when reading people's expressions. If a person were 'tricky' one could be in a lot of trouble if one chose to trust a smiling mouth! The inferences seemed to be as important as any literal interpretations.

Portraying and interpreting in their own art

There were several factors affecting the way the children interpreted expressions in their own work. Their skill in drawing and observing is at an early stage of development. Their concentration span was short. They switched off very quickly, losing track of their original intentions and ideas on occasions. For this reason I chose materials that would make marks quickly with minimal organisation. The more factors the children had to keep in mind, the more difficult it was to concentrate on the matter in hand. For instance, some children became interested in the decorations on the faces we studied in the Sainsbury Centre and forgot about the expressions. This also happened when handling materials that they did not use frequently, such as clay. They were having to control the material as well as keep their mind on trying to produce a face with a particular expression.

The children showed an ability both to convey and to interpret expressions in their pictures. The faces in the bent shiny surfaces produced simple but highly accurate pictures. In many of them the features drawn were closely observed and recorded. The pictures showing the most detail were produced from studies at the Sainsbury Centre. The beaded mask was observed particularly closely and stimulated much conversation as to why the mouth was covered. It was drawn with extensive detail.

The skill of the interpretation was variable and the meaning was perhaps not always what the artist intended. Harry was really only trying to show Venetia talking. He was so intent on showing the detail that he was not aware that he was enlarging the features to produce a powerful screaming effect. The features included what he could not see but knew was there – the nostril hair and the uvula. These also added to the effect. He was rather put out to begin with when the others started discussing his picture in an unexpected way, but did later concede that they had a point.

At other times the children were very much aware of the techniques they were using to create particular expressions and the medium was referred to as an influencing factor on several occasions. Sara discussed her drawing of eyes as a technique that she had seen used on faces on television, and a similar technique was used by Emma for a fierce face. Many of the children added the kind of extras necessary to complete a stereotyped character, such as hair sticking up to convey fright, or fangs, horns and trident for a devil. I found that whenever stereotyped images were discussed and then drawn, the facial features became almost irrelevant and the stereotyped 'extras' took over. The discussion about the devil and the features of Molly's picture was used as a basis for a drawing by six children altogether. Of these, half included slanty eyes, two exaggerated the eye deliberately, all included pointed teeth and five included horns and the sticking out tongue, although the latter had not been alluded to in the conversation about the face originally discussed or drawn.

The effects of teaching techniques

I deployed the use of questions as a guide to how to look at images as a common form of teaching technique. The children required a large amount of prompting, with questions initially serving to focus their attention on analysing the faces before them (my questions alternated with their answers). It was clear early on that they were able to identify the effects of some changes in the features of the face. In the first conversation, the children already had used phrases such as 'smiling eyes' but were more concerned with the shapes of the features than with their effects on expression. As the study went on, my questions seemed to provoke deeper thought and more complex ideas. The questions acted as a focus which was then enhanced by the children drawing themselves. Towards the end of the study, the children were taking the ideas suggested in conversations a step further in the pictures, drawing from their personal experience. For instance, in the discussion on Molly's picture mention is made about how evil the face looks and reference is made to devils. Sara then drew an evil face, developing the themes mentioned and her conversation shows a strong empathy with her drawing as she discusses why she drew it, what influences she used, and what the character is thinking.

On listening to the early taped conversations I felt that the main barrier to discussion was the children's lack of vocabulary, and this was confirmed by the language they used to describe the actions of the mime artist. They would have benefited from specific lessons on words relating to feelings and characteristics. The use of story telling to overcome their problems with language was very useful and emphasised a feeling of empathy with the observed faces. However, as a result of listening to the taped conversations I was made aware of how loaded questions can influence answers and so I tried to avoid using them.

I set exercises to heighten the children's awareness of the range of different expressions the face could make. The work on distorting faces was particularly exciting for them and produced the largest amount of vocabulary and excellent observation. By the time the children visited the Sainsbury Centre to examine the collection of faces and heads there, they were making occasional comments about people's faces wherever people were encountered, both in and out of the class. There was no sense of reticence or awe when viewing the artefacts in the gallery. They interpreted visual expressions enthusiastically and made hypotheses confidently.

The drawing of quick impressions (not necessarily completing them as a whole picture), in the way that some artist might use a sketchbook, was valuable in two ways. I was able to assess very quickly how stimulating the input was. The children were able to make a record of what they saw while they were concentrating, at a very fast rate, matching a 5 year old's fairly short concentration span. We were then able to use these impressions as a reference point for discussion and further work.

When undertaking final models and drawings time was also short, so choices in materials were limited to those with which the children were familiar.

FURTHER READING

Bassili, J. (1978) 'Facial motion in the perception of faces and of emotional expression', *Journal of Experimental Psychology* Vol. 4, pages 373–9.
Bruce, V. and Green, P. (1984) *Visual Perception: Physiology, Psychology and Ecology*, London: Inner London Education Authority.
Clement, R. and Page, S. (1992) *Investigating and Making in Art*, London: Oliver and Boyd.
Freeman, N. (1980) *Strategies of Representation in Young Children*, London: Academic Press.
Hopkins, D. (1985) *A Teacher's Guide to Classroom Research*, Milton Keynes: Open University Press.
Kellog, R. (1970) *Analysing Children's Art*, Palo Alto, Calif: National Press Books.
Lowenfeld, V. (1939) *The Nature of Creative Activity*, New York: Macmillan.
McHugh, C. (1992) *Faces*, Hove: Wayland.
North Eastern Region Art Advisers Association (1978) *Learning Through Drawing*, Yorkshire: NERAAA.
Piaget, J. (1973) *The Child's Conception of the World*, London: Paladin.
Taylor, R. (1986) *Educating for Art: Critical Response and Development*, Harlow: Longman.

Taylor, R. and Andrews, G. (1993) *The Arts in the Primary School*, London: Falmer Press.

Thomas, G. and Silk, V. (1990) *An Introduction to the Psychology of Children's Drawings*, London: Harvester Wheatsheaf.

Chapter 10

First responses to sculpture

Helen Grogutt

Although I had used reproductions of works of art (generally paintings) in school with children, I had not previously visited a gallery with them. I was interested in observing the reactions of Year 2 and Year 3 children to original works of art. I feel that it is important to analyse their responses to works of art, their perceptions and ideas, if we are to enable them to come to some kind of understanding about them. We cannot really begin to help children to express their feelings about art and question its nature if we do not observe their initial responses to it. The main focus of my research, therefore, was to observe the children's initial responses to works of art, to analyse the types of questions they asked and the feelings that they expressed. I looked at how their perceptions and ideas changed after teaching lessons which involved them in working with a variety of 3D material and learning about the sculptures that they had seen. I chose four sculptures to focus upon with the children for the teaching and research: *Bucket Man* by John Davies; *Femme* by Alberto Giacometti; *Mother and Child* by Henry Moore; and *Petite danseuse de quartorze ans* by Edgar Degas.

I chose to focus on large sculpture because I wanted to take full advantage of the opportunity to use a type of art that the children had not previously explored and which they would not usually have the opportunity to study in a school situation (paintings are, physically, relatively easy to work with in the classroom). Although the children had engaged in some practical three dimensional work in art I had not introduced them to other artists' sculpture: 'Working with three dimensional materials is important for children as it develops their knowledge of form and enhances their understanding of spatial concepts' (Graham and Jeffs 1993: 27). To do so might help them to develop their own work, but initially my concern was to study the children's response to the work and how it changed over time. It seemed important to begin with unfamiliar works of art, so that none of the children would have preconceived ideas, and their initial reactions and questions would be less affected by previous experience of the particular art form. I thought that the large scale of the selected sculptures would appeal to the children and that they would be able to relate to the familiar image of the human form. Furthermore, I like these four sculptures myself, and hoped that my enthusiasm for them would enrich the work with the children.

The teaching aims I adopted were:

- To develop the children's ability to question the nature of unfamiliar work, to think about its purpose, the materials it is made from, who might have made it, and so on;
- To give the children opportunities to express their views about the sculpture both verbally and practically through their own two dimensional and three dimensional artwork;
- To give the children the opportunity to work with modelling materials which are new to them, such as clay, wire and Mod-Roc and thus develop their knowledge and understanding of the possibilities and limitations of using certain materials and their effects;
- To give them the opportunity to return to the works of art and discuss them further.

The research aims were:

- To understand children's initial responses to large scale sculptures of the human form;
- To observe and attempt to come to some understanding of the children's ability to analyse, reflect upon and judge the sculptures;
- To understand the effects that the sculptures have on the children's own feelings and on their own artwork;
- To observe whether or not the children's perceptions and ideas about the sculptures change over time.

The work was done in a first school of approximately 180 children. There were thirty-one children in the class. The school was built in the 1950s and occupies a central position on one side of the green on a council housing estate. Many of the houses are now privately owned, and the children come from a variety of social backgrounds. The children had been exposed to many different forms of art and had worked at a variety of practical tasks, mainly two dimensional. In the Autumn term we watched the TV programme *Art Show*, which introduced the children to the idea that art includes videos, photographs, advertisements, large sculptures using 'junk' materials, paper sculpture, and so on. We had spent a lot of time looking carefully at and describing various objects and artefacts as well as paintings and prints. Therefore, the children were used to expressing their feelings, describing what they see and also sketching. However, only three of the children in the class had previously visited the Sainsbury Centre for Visual Arts, although some had visited the local museum and perhaps seen works of art exhibited there.

Because of the size of the class I decided to focus my research on a group of six children, two boys and four girls. Jody, Cheryl and Anna are Year 3 and Thomas, Brydie and Kimberley are Year 2. None of these children had visited the Sainsbury Centre before. All of them are intelligent, articulate and confident children who I felt would not be inhibited by being photographed or recorded on audio tape. They agreed to take part in the research after I described what I wanted to do.

During the week before the first visit I explained that the gallery visit was an opportunity for them to see a wide range of artwork, and that from it I hoped to learn more about how best to teach art. I told the children that I would be writing about the visit and that I would be photographing the research group and recording them with a dictaphone both at the gallery and in the classroom.

I asked the children in advance what they thought they would see during the visit (having already told them that it was an art gallery). They suggested paintings, clay pots (many of the children had made clay pots in school the previous week), people and art. During the first hour, the children were free to explore the main gallery looking for objects that they particularly liked or found interesting. All the children had paper and pencils and were encouraged to sketch (Plate 10.1). Jody and Thomas found some of the masks and knives interesting, whilst some of the girls particularly liked Lucie Rie's ceramics. All the children found the Anthony Green paintings fascinating. After lunch I gave my group pictures of the four selected sculptures. They recognised them immediately and had no difficulty in locating them.

Bucket Man (John Davies)

During the morning session Thomas, Kimberley and Brydie had already noticed *Bucket Man* and we had had a conversation about him. I had encouraged the children to think about the materials which artists use. Thomas thought *Bucket Man* was made from clay. He then noticed his feet and said that he thought the sculpture was made quite some time ago. Kimberley noticed the ball on his head and that his clothes appear to be ripped and old. She then asked how his clothes could have been put on over the buckets and Thomas said that the buckets must have been put on last. The children then returned to the subject of the ball on his head. Thomas said that it was his hair and that people in Japan have hair like that. Kimberley, however, thought that it was a hat.

I asked the children how they thought the man was feeling. They thought that he was sad, perhaps grumpy. The conversation returned to the state of his dress, and interest in the fact that he has no shoes. Perhaps he is too poor to have shoes? The children were obviously interested in *Bucket Man*, particularly his appearance and how he was made. They

Plate 10.1 Kimberley, Cheryl, Anna and Brydie sketching their chosen object (photograph: Helen Grogutt)

continued their conversation for some time with little intervention and were able to express themselves well. When we returned to *Bucket Man* as a whole group in the afternoon the children talked a lot about how the sculpture made them feel. Most of them found him quite scary. Brydie was very aware of his staring, life-like eyes. The children were unable to decide how he was made, and what from. Most still thought he was made of clay but Jody was unsure, although he could not offer an alternative. They were all certain that the clothes are real. Anna said that one can see where the head is fixed on and that his head must have been made separately. I asked the children what they thought the object behind *Bucket Man*'s head is. Jody and Thomas said it is to keep the sun off as he works in a hot country.

When I later compared the children's responses to all four of the sculptures it was clear that *Bucket Man* promoted the most response from them although they were not sure that they actually liked him. Most found his size and pose quite intimidating. Only Thomas chose him as his favourite of the four sculptures. His reason was that *Bucket Man* looks real.

Femme (Alberto Giacometti)

The children initially had little to say although they were not uninterested. They looked closely, but did not converse as they had with *Bucket Man*. In order to promote conversation I asked them what they thought the sculpture represented. Thomas said that it was roughly the shape of a lady and Jody asked if the artist copied a lady. The children noticed her big feet. Initially there was some feeling that this might have been a mistake, but when they looked carefully they decided they were made like that so that the lady did not fall over.

Anna liked the sculpture and felt that she was real. She was the first to notice the drawing of *Femme* on the wall, saying that she knew the lady was sad because she looked sad in the picture. All of the children then looked at the drawing and decided that this was produced before the sculpture. They were sure that the sculpture was made from clay. They liked the texture and had hoped that they would be able to touch it.

Mother and Child (Henry Moore)

Most of our conversation about this sculpture was concerned with relative size and scale. The children could see that the proportions were wrong in their eyes and seemed to dislike the sculpture because of this. Jody immediately noticed that the mother's head did not look right, that it was too small, and Kimberley noticed the large shoulder. Thomas then noticed that the baby's head was proportionally correct for its body, but that in comparison it was about the same size as the mother's. He then exclaimed at the size of the baby's feet and legs and all the children laughed.

They did not like this sculpture although they were interested in the aspects of it mentioned above. However they could see no reason for the large shoulder and small head. I made a note that it would be interesting to explore this issue with them and see how much they are capable of understanding. Perhaps the concepts of the mother's strength and dependability portrayed in this way are too complex for young children to understand? When we went outside the children immediately noticed the similarity in style between *Mother and Child* and the *Reclining Figure*, and Thomas also pointed out that they were both made from the same type of stone.

Petite danseuse de quatorze ans (Edgar Degas)

It appeared that this sculpture appealed to the children least of all and they were not particularly interested in looking at it. However, I thought that they might have been getting tired by this point in the day, and that I would need to observe their reactions on our follow-up visit. Perhaps these were the first clear signs of the limits of their capacity for sustained, concentrated observation, analysis and articulation of ideas. It took a long while to extract from the children that this sculpture is of a ballet dancer, and I suspected that none of them had seen ballet performed in real life or even on television. After much discussion about her skirt and what it is made from and the style of shoes she is wearing, Anna eventually said that she was a ballet person.

The children were interested in what she is made from, discussing this amongst themselves, rejecting clay and stone and deciding upon copper. I told them that she is made from bronze (some children still wrote 'ballet dancer made from clay' on the drawings that they produced in school the next day). They were interested in her pose, particularly the way she is holding her hands behind her back, and all tried to stand like her. However, the children did not find her appealing or attractive. Brydie even said that she was ugly, although she could not explain why she thought that.

ANALYSIS OF OBSERVATIONS

I was pleased and excited by the amount of interest and response that the visit provoked. The dictaphone proved to be invaluable as I was able to join in the conversation normally without having to try to write everything down. When I listened to the recording I was surprised by how much the children had said, how carefully they had listened to each other and how clearly they expressed themselves. Analysis of the children's reactions and comments in relation to my teaching and research aims showed that some of my assumptions seemed to be right and many aims had been met but that some of the children's reactions were surprising. For example, I had thought that in choosing works of art that were unfamiliar to the children they would have no preconceived ideas about them. However, I had not taken into account the fact that the children had recently used clay to make pots and decorated tiles in school, but had not had equally recent experience of working with other materials. They therefore initially thought that all the sculptures we looked at were made from clay. The only sculpture that the children themselves realised was not made from clay as soon as they saw it was *Mother and Child*. Thomas pointed out soon after we began to look at it that it was made from the same type of stone as the sculpture we had seen outside. I had to persuade the children to look very closely at the other sculptures and to think about whether the texture, colour, and so on could really be produced with clay before they suggested other materials that could be used. Even then the children had little idea of what materials could be used and made lots of guesses.

Before the visit I had not considered the fact that the children would bring with them their own ideas about what is normal or right in relation to the works of art that they would be looking at. However, I realised that children of this age (7 and 8 years old) are often very concerned with trying to copy things accurately when they are drawing, and with making things look real. They found *Femme* very strange because she did not look like a real lady and disliked *Mother and Child* because of her unusual proportions. They could not see why Henry Moore would want his sculpture to look like that and thought that he had 'gone wrong' or made a mistake. Most of the children preferred *Bucket Man* because he looks like a real man.

One of the teaching aims was to give the children opportunities to express their feelings about the sculptures. One of my research aims was to understand the effects that the sculptures had on the children's feelings. I found this a difficult area to explore with the children during our first visit. Whilst the children were willing and able to describe the sculptures in terms of texture, colour, size, subject matter, and so on, they found it difficult to express how the sculptures made them feel. All of the children preferred some sculptures to others but found it very difficult to explain why they liked or disliked a particular one. It was from their comments that I inferred that realism was an important factor, though that seemed to be compromised by their rather negative response to the little dancer. In terms of invoking feelings, *Bucket Man* had the most profound effect, with children exclaiming that it frightened them or that they did not like looking at it. However, I think that the children had not yet had enough experience of observing and talking about works of art actually to be able to put into words any effect that they might have on their own feelings. It would be interesting to see if the children began to talk more about their personal feelings in relation to the sculptures on their return visit. Perhaps once the children became more familiar with the sculptures they would begin to feel an emotional involvement with them, or think about their own response to them.

FOLLOW-UP WORK

On the morning after the visit the class discussed what they had enjoyed and found interesting about the gallery. They had a lot to say about what they had seen and done. Most found the four sculptures that we had focused on particularly interesting. They were able to describe them in detail and remembered a lot about them. Several talked about the Anthony Green paintings and also Lucie Rie's ceramics. They had all made sketches of objects that particularly interested them and later used them to make drawings to display in the classroom. Most drew one or more of the four sculptures. Some made accurate and detailed drawings whilst others were not so interested in the detail and made a sketch that conveyed the general image of the sculpture.

Plate 10.2 Brydie drawing Giacometti's *Femme* (photograph: Helen Grogutt)

Plate 10.3 Anna using a modelling tool to make patterns on a clay tile (photograph: Helen Grogutt)

During the period between the two visits the children had the opportunity to work with clay and also had a brief introduction to using Mod-Roc and wire. Working with my research group on one such occasion, using clay, we discussed the four sculptures that we had studied at the gallery. We discussed the different textures of the sculptures and how smooth, bumpy or jagged textures could be achieved using the clay. Anna decided that she would like to make a model of a ballet dancer like the Degas. The other children pointed out that she was made from bronze not clay, and that it would be very difficult to make something like her in clay. Jody then commented on the fact that he had liked the ballet dancer, but not *Femme*. Anna said that the latter was 'the one where you could see all the bones', and Kimberley described her as 'bumpy'. Thomas said that she was made from clay, and that it would be easy to make something like *Femme* 'because you could use something like a fork or your fingers to press out all the bumpy bits'. Kimberley then remembered *Mother and Child* and Jody pointed out the contrast to *Femme*, in that the Henry Moore sculpture was very smooth. Brydie commented on the big shoulder and relatively small head of *Mother and Child*. Jody said that this was because Henry Moore wanted to make his sculpture look interesting rather than real. We went on to discuss further the contrasts in textures and what they thought might have been the artists' intentions. The children all experimented with the clay, trying to achieve different textures, and puzzled over how the sculptures we had looked at had been made. They said they found working with the clay on a particular task quite difficult, and began to appreciate the talent of the artists whose work they had seen. Having attempted to make small figures that stood up, the children wondered how the sculptures they had seen had been made so stable. Jody and Thomas remembered the large feet and solid bases of the *Femme* and the *Mother and Child* and decided that making the feet larger than they actually are and moulding them into a base was a possible answer. They were not sure how this could be achieved in stone or bronze, though.

Three or four weeks after our first visit I had the photographs which I had taken developed and displayed in the classroom. These prompted a renewed interest and further discussion and reminiscence about the visit. At about the same time I displayed several books about John Davies, Henry Moore, and Edgar Degas. The children enjoyed looking at these, and were particularly keen to find photographs of the sculptures that they had seen. I used three of these books as the basis of discussion and learning about the sculptures and their artists with my research group before we returned to the gallery. Earlier in the year the class had spent several sessions looking carefully at, describing, and making detailed drawings of pieces of driftwood, bark, shells and stones. Having undertaken this activity themselves they were interested in the fact that Henry

Moore used sketches of wood, stones, shells and bones as inspiration for some of his sculptures. They were also interested in comparing the different mother and child sculptures which Moore made. The children were evidently beginning to be aware of the particular style of Henry Moore's work.

The children also spent some time looking at the John Davies book and were pleased to be able to find photographs of all of the sculptures of acrobatic figures which we had seen in the gallery. They were disappointed that there was not a photograph of the *Bucket Man* in this particular book. They were interested in the way in which *Bucket Man* was made and puzzled over why the contents of the buckets he is holding had been 'thrown over him'. The children found the fact that John Davies rarely talks about his work and does not have a story to explain the questions which *Bucket Man* poses quite strange. Their own artwork is planned and they know the purpose of what they do, so they found sculptural devices such as the ball and the collar difficult to understand. They seemed to need concrete answers as to why something is as it is. However, *Bucket Man* was the one sculpture which the children talked about in terms of how they thought he felt and how he made them feel. They seemed to think that he was trying to communicate with them and talked a lot about the fact that he seemed real. I hoped that if the children return to John Davies' work as they become older they might ask themselves what it is that the artist is actually trying to tell us about ourselves and our fellow human beings through his sculptures.

ANALYSIS OF TEACHING

When I looked at my original teaching aims I thought that I had actually worked through these satisfactorily, and felt that the children were quite well prepared for their return visit. I had intended to develop the children's ability to question the nature of unknown works of art. Without any prompting they had questioned many things about the sculptures during our first visit. Through the practical work undertaken in school and through looking at books about the artists and learning a little about them they had also begun to question more. The children's questions generally remained on a very practical level: 'How could that be made?'; 'What tools would the artist have used?'; 'What is it made from?' and so on. Perhaps I had hoped that they would begin to question on a deeper level. On reflection I wondered if that could be achieved, and how.

My aim to give the children opportunities to express their views about the sculptures had been achieved even before the second visit. There had been many opportunities for discussion. The children had sketched what they had seen whilst at the gallery, made drawings in school using pencils, charcoal and pastels, and modelled and sculpted with play dough, clay, wire and Mod-Roc.

Through the practical activities the children had developed their knowledge and understanding of the possibilities and limitations of using certain materials, particularly clay. They had spent a long time exploring what could be done using just hands, before discovering the different uses of tools. They had also tried to achieve particular effects with the clay which they had seen in the sculptures at the gallery. I had tried to explore with the children their feelings about the sculptures, although this aspect was quite difficult. They did not seem to have become involved with the sculptures yet in a way which evoked emotional responses, other than perhaps with *Bucket Man*. I was now looking forward to returning with the children and observing their reactions to see if their perceptions and ideas had changed, and if perhaps they would begin to engage with the sculptures on a more affective level.

THE SECOND VISIT

One of the first questions the children asked was whether *Bucket Man*, *Mother and Child*, *Ballet Dancer* and *Femme* would still be there. They were very enthusiastic about going back and keen to see if anything had changed. When we arrived they remembered exactly where everything they wanted to look at was. Jody and Thomas went to look at the masks and knives that they had sketched on their first visit, whilst Kimberley showed me a pot by Gabriele Koch that she liked because of the interesting patterns and colours. Brydie, Cheryl and Anna looked at *Bucket Man*. This was definitely the sculpture that the children were most keen to see again. His life-like qualities, the fact that he looks as if he is about to move and speak, appealed to the children. Although he is mysterious in some ways, even disconcerting, there was no doubt in the children's minds about what they were looking at, and they liked that. They seemed to appreciate less those works of art that they did not understand. The children talked again about the fact that his clothes are real and that John Davies would have 'built' him first, then added the clothes and buckets and then poured the contents of the buckets over him. Kimberley, who had found him very frightening on our first visit and did not like to look at him, now said that he was less scary, and that she quite liked him. The other children agreed that he was definitely one of their favourites, that they liked him because he seemed to be real.

During the time since our first visit many of the children had begun to express more of an interest in *Mother and Child* and in Henry Moore's style of sculpture. We had probably spent more time looking at photographs of Henry Moore's work than that of the other artists, and the children were becoming familiar with his style. Thomas and Jody were quick to find another Henry Moore sculpture, a Half Figure, of which they said they had seen a photograph in a book. Jody noticed that this sculpture had a big shoulder like *Mother and Child*, and Thomas said that the fingers on the two sculptures were similar, like 'lumps with lines'.

When I questioned the children they said that they thought that they would immediately recognise a Henry Moore sculpture now if they saw one. Cheryl said that she would not confuse a Henry Moore sculpture with a John Davies because 'John Davies makes sculptures that are real, Henry Moore doesn't.' Jody thought that he would recognise a Henry Moore because of its 'funny shape' with big shoulders and legs and small arms and head. Kimberley thought (mistakenly) that all the Moore sculptures they had seen were made from stone.

A little while later Cheryl stood looking at *Mother and Child* on her own. She told me that it looked good, that when they came on the first visit she had not known anything about it but now she knew more she liked it better. It was interesting to find that on our second visit all of the children spent a considerable time looking at this sculpture. All except for Anna said that it was the one that they now liked best and found the most interesting. This was the sculpture that we had talked about most in school and which I had taught the children most about.

This seemed to indicate that their perceptions of individual sculptures did change as their knowledge and understanding increased. Having spent some considerable time looking at photographs of Henry Moore's work in school, discussing his style and the things that inspired him, the children now observed more closely, noticed more features, and seemed to be comfortable with the characteristics which had previously seemed disconcerting. The children did seem more able to analyse and reflect upon the sculpture once they knew more about it, and certainly seemed more ready to accept the unusual proportions that they had found so strange at first.

Further evidence of a capacity to express their feelings about sculptures which they knew something about came from Anna. She told me that her favourite was now the ballet dancer because she could see what it was, whereas she was not so sure what the other sculptures were supposed to be.

Although it is not possible to know exactly what the children are thinking or feeling, it is clear from what they said during the second visit that many of their perceptions and ideas had changed, in that they were able to relate differently to the sculptures that they felt they now knew more about or understood. I am not sure that the children were analysing or judging the sculptures in greater depth, but they were able to express their views more clearly and seemed more confident in engaging with and talking about most of the sculptures. Perhaps the Giacometti, which we had not really focused on during the time in school, would need rather more attention in order to formulate and extend their responses.

FINAL ANALYSIS

Making a final summary is extremely difficult. On the one hand there is so much evidence to base it on. On the other, in a study such as this one, in which the children's relationship with sculptures is only just beginning, I find my ideas in a state of flux, and my sense of what I have learned rather tentative. I find it virtually impossible to come to any conclusive understanding of children's responses to sculpture, partly because one cannot know exactly what they are thinking and feeling. It seems obvious that the children's initial responses were determined to a large extent by their previous experiences; their perceptions and ideas were based on what they already knew and understood about art, particularly that art should be 'realistic'. On our initial visit the children knew whether or not they liked something, and were able to talk about their initial reactions, but further reflection or analysis appeared to be limited by a lack of knowledge or understanding about artists' intentions and the visual devices which they use to convey ideas or generate responses.

My observations of the children's reactions and my conversations with them led me to believe that, on the second visit, the sculptures had a greater effect on the children, and, perhaps more importantly, that they were able to express their feelings more clearly and confidently. I believe that this was due to the opportunities to look, think, discuss, compare, sketch, and reflect in ways which helped to build a repertoire of ideas in relation to selected objects which shared certain features in common, but which also contrasted with each other in certain aspects. Therefore, I would conclude by saying that the children's perceptions, ideas and ability to express their views about the sculptures did change over time, and that the teaching programme had some impact on their understanding. The strategy will be tested further by continuing work related to these artists as a resource for developing the children's ability to analyse, reflect upon and judge the many works of art held in the Sainsbury Collection and others. In particular I will try to extend their thinking about the feelings which art invokes.

FURTHER READING

Barnes, R. (1987) *Teaching Art to Young Children 4–9*, London: Allen and Unwin.
Bowness, A. (ed.) (1988) *Henry Moore: Sculpture Vol. 6 1981–1986*, London: Percy Lund, Humphries.
Elliott, J. (1991) *Action Research for Educational Change*, Milton Keynes: Open University Press.

Graham, J. and Jeffs, H. (1993) *Practical Guides Art, Teaching Within the National Curriculum*, London: Scholastic Publications.
Hopkins, D. (1985) *A Teacher's Guide to Classroom Research*, Milton Keynes: Open University Press.
Marlborough Fine Art (undated) *John Davies*, London: Marlborough Fine Art.
Mitchinson, D. and Stallabrass, J. (1992) *Henry Moore*, London: Academy Editions.

Chapter 11

Art and communication

Alex Henderson

This is a description of the first stages of an action research project aimed at developing teaching strategies with Year 4 pupils, in order to develop their understanding and awareness of art as communication. My class was working on a communications project and we began to consider what artists might be communicating in their work. Learning that ideas, feelings, and meaning are communicated through art, and how this is done, was intended to complement the study and use of other means of communication. To this end, I chose to test out some new teaching strategies that might help my class to learn about the content and meaning of art. To assess the effectiveness of the strategies for conveying that idea I recorded what we did, and my impressions of the children's responses.

I intended the children to begin to make connections between what they studied in other subjects of the curriculum, their own artwork, and original works of art. However, I was all too aware of Morgan's statement that 'We may have much to learn ourselves first, for until we become visually sensitive, we cannot help the children to any depth of experience' (Morgan 1992: 20). I had very little knowledge or understanding of works of art or of artists. Any teaching of art I had previously done was non-specialist and untrained. Therefore, before challenging the children with the question, 'What does art communicate?', I felt the need to improve my own knowledge and to challenge my own ideas on what and how artists might be trying to communicate.

Having realised that my knowledge of works of art was restricted by lack of development and training I wanted to work with the children on developing questioning and observational skills centred on our theme. For my own learning and as a base for the teaching project, the aims I adopted were:

- To develop my way of looking at works of art, towards a more informed understanding and awareness of art as a means of communication;
- To develop my teaching in such a way as to guide the children to a more informed understanding and awareness of art as a means of communication;

- To develop the children's way of looking at works of art by helping them:
  - (a) to consider what the work of art is communicating through its content;
  - (b) to consider the methods artists use to communicate through the work;
  - (c) to form constructive opinions of art as a means of communication by questioning its appearance and function;
- To develop the children's own artistic expression through gaining an understanding of art as a means of communication.

As I gradually introduced the idea of art as a means of communication, and as the teaching of skills and ideas progressed, I discovered that the children worked in a more informed way, appearing to study the works of art in greater depth. These were impressions I gained as I tried to implement the following research aims:

- To describe and interpret the effectiveness of my teaching of art as a means of communication by observing and analysing the children's responses, with regard to content and methods of art and the development of constructive opinions;
- To understand and become aware of any development of the children's responses;
- To be able to advise colleagues about the teaching approaches used and the children's responses.

The teaching consisted of nineteen lessons leading up to and including a visit to the Sainsbury Centre for Visual Arts. These lessons were linked together in phases as outlined below:

- Looking at and sketching original works of art in the classroom and using them to inspire the children's own ideas in practical work. This was for me to observe and analyse their responses at the beginning of the project;
- Looking at, discussing and creating works of art to begin an understanding and awareness of art as a means of communication;
- Developing the idea that works of art might communicate, then guiding the children's emerging ideas of what might be communicated. The children then used these ideas in producing their own artwork;
- Forming judgements about art as communication by devising questionnaires and setting up group art galleries;
- Direct preparation for the visit, introducing photographs and background information on selected art objects;
- The visit and follow-up work in school.

The description of each phase which follows is in the form of a diary presentation, analysis of the children's responses, and my reactions to them. Preliminary impressions are drawn with reference to my own learning, the development of teaching strategies, and the children's understanding in relation to the teaching aims. In creating this presentation I am aware of the impressionistic status of the evidence, which is based on selection from an extensive amount of data.

PHASE 1: UNTUTORED RESPONSES

I showed the children some representational bronze African statues. I explained that I had no information about them. I asked the children why the artist might have made the statues. They responded: it was a hobby, they enjoy making things; to give as a present; to sell; for people to look at. Asking questions and thinking about their answers led them to consider an artist making a statue representing something which he or she saw regularly. When asked what might be an equivalent subject from their lives they responded quickly with examples such as teacher, footballer and shopkeeper. When asked how we would recognise the subject in the statue, an ensuing discussion led to seeking out clues such as clothes, accompanying objects, and the idea of body positions, or posture.

They produced many excited responses when I showed them a mask, explained that it too came from Africa, but gave no more information. I wrote the following on the board: What does it communicate to you? What would you like to know about it? Tell me any thoughts you have about it. We discussed each question to ensure that the children understood. I gave no further suggestions or guidance. Although there was much excited whispering, not many children gave a public answer. I gave guidance when they began story writing, making the suggestions: you can be yourself in the story; you could be the person who made it; you could be the person it was made for. The class was quieter than usual and appeared to lack confidence in generating ideas. This was unusual as the children normally have many ideas for story writing, and I puzzled about the reasons.

The children made sketches of all, and part of, the African statues and then drew a subject from their lives that was represented in a similar way: a single figure, with dress and relevant posture. I intended that they should consider both the subject and the artist's relationship to it. After answering my questions, and comparing the ideas from the statues to something similar in their lives, their awareness of the representation of subject matter became the focus of discussion.

The children sketched the African mask. Some finished very quickly, showing little attention to detail. I then set them the task of studying the decoration closely and designing a pattern using the mask for ideas. They seemed to have difficulty considering its subject or function. This, and the fact that little had been said about the purpose of works of art, may have been why they lacked confidence with their subsequent creative writing. A few children showed some detail in their design work.

During this phase I learned that using the African art in the way I had engendered some enthusiasm, but also engendered a rather muted response to the related tasks. Through questioning the children I discovered that, like myself, they lacked confidence when first considering art as communicating something. Linking it to their own lives seemed a successful strategy, in terms of representing a familiar subject. However, when they began to do that in drawings the children were restricted in their practical artistic expression, wanting to produce facsimiles of their subject, which resulted in much disappointment and rubbing out. The use of story writing after looking at the mask might have been more successful if I had prompted discussion beforehand and helped to develop some ideas. Wanting to observe, hear and read their untutored responses at this stage, I had not done that prompting.

PHASE 2: LOOKING, DISCUSSING AND CREATING

We looked at ink blots and previous random pencil sketch exercises, introducing the idea of looking more closely into a picture to discover what may be seen. In a practical lesson the children experimented with paints and paper, producing random work to study with friends. I hoped they would begin to see beyond the shape on the page, to read any images which might be detectable.

When asked what these drawings might convey to them they responded tentatively with simple ideas. Later, lively enthusiasm extended to energetically pointing out images they could see. This development seemed to be enhanced by my participation, encouraging the children to look more closely, attempting to spot what their classmates saw. Most suggestions were reasonable interpretations of random shapes, not simply imagination: sun, boot, blue whale, and elephant wearing a hat. Following this, some children worked in pairs recording their ideas on to audio tape.

In talking about their random work, one pair gave one-word descriptions. The ideas of the other four pairs' were highly detailed, to the extent of seeing a complete scene within the random, 'abstract' work, and describing its features verbally. In their practical art the children were confident and relaxed when the only expectation was experimental, and the outcome random. This led to some attractive works of art, as well as increasing their knowledge of the results they could obtain by inventive use of materials. The strategy of looking closely at their abstract work appeared to have been successful, increasing motivation and developing ideas of what can be seen. In considering what an 'abstract' could convey most children quickly displayed confidence in describing their interpretations of shapes.

PHASE 3: CONTENT AND METHOD

I described my lack of knowledge to the children, sharing the idea of working together to discover how to appreciate art as a means of communication. I drew their attention to our wall display of cave paintings, which they had already worked on. Previously they had learned the possible reasons for cave paintings as being 'bringers-of-good-luck' or records of what the hunters had achieved. We recalled these reasons and I asked what is meant by calling something a work of art. In friendship groups the children discussed the questions: what do you think art is? what do you think art is for? what might it communicate?

The discussion groups did not respond well to the questions, and the children soon began to be distracted. In a report-back session the only idea, although expressed in different ways, was that art is something to look at. Following this I gave suggestions to the children to extend their ideas about what art may communicate. These were that art might help us to think about people from history as well as now and to think about people from other countries. We made a list of the ideas the children had. These were: to put on the wall; to enjoy and look at [their original idea]; to tell us something; to decorate something; to display a sequence of colours; to communicate if a person is happy or sad; to tell us about history.

I distributed picture packs of ten reproductions of works of art organised around themes such as faces or fruit. I challenged the children to consider what the pictures communicated, using their ideas as discussion aids, and working in established friendship groups. The children worked enthusiastically, keeping on target. Some were beginning to form opinions about the content of the works of art. This was evident from their questioning of each other's reasons for liking the pictures, rather than their proffering of comments. At this stage we had considered communication as a broad concept, rather than looking for subject content and method of representation. In the remainder of Phase Three I used the sub-divisions of my teaching aims, more explicitly and selectively related to content, method and opinions. These lessons were planned around a list of purposes of art which the children had formed through discussion. Briefly, the list included art which: tells a story or records an event; is attractive to look at; is from the artist's imagination; is useful; may be used to decorate; is to do with myths. The focus and methods used for each group, and the children's responses are summarised briefly from extensive data.

Recording a scene or telling a story

The strategies adopted were to ask the children to sketch an event from their lives; writing and illustrating stories; looking at *The Physicians' Duel*

(Aqa Mirah); and listening to the accompanying *Story of a Deadly Rose* (Kennet and Measham 1978). The practical work, sketching an event, was completed quickly with little attention to detail as they wanted to write all their ideas, or tell me about them, rather than select one incident to draw. There appeared to be a difference here between the potentials of pictorial narrative and those of linear-time narrative of oral and written traditions. This seemed to be confirmed when the children were captivated by the *Story of a Deadly Rose*. The stories they wrote after this, selecting their own work of art as the basis, seemed imaginative and were created with great enthusiasm. When I suggested writing their own stories and illustrating them they were more motivated than when asked to sketch an event, and seemed more pleased with the results. The relationship to pictorial realism seems to be a crucial factor here, too, but I still had in mind the nature of the task of 'capturing' a single event pictorially. This would need more thought.

I had decided to base the next lesson around the content of works of art, the idea that a work can communicate the recording of a scene, a part of daily life, or an everyday object, as a camera would. I read extracts from *Facts at Your Fingertips* (Marshall 1993) and we looked at *A Winter Scene with Skaters* by Hendrick Avercamp. I asked the children what the picture communicates and some typical answers included: 'It shows a picture of what is happening'; 'It shows lots of people'; 'It shows some houses'.

The children found it easy to answer, which may be because of the action within this painting. Having had their attention drawn to all the activity, they broadened their answers to include such examples as: 'The artist is clever to put in so much'; 'It makes me want to join in'; 'I'd like to write a story about it; it would be more fun than the mask story because there's more to think about.' The last statement seemed to confirm my thoughts on why the class struggled with the African mask story. In friendship pairs the children selected, from the resources available in school, examples which told a story or recorded a scene. Some children discussed this on audio tape and all the children were tasked to write a story or a detailed description about one of the works of art selected.

Something attractive to look at

This lesson focused on the content of the work of art and the name of the artist. Using the picture packs I asked each child to select their favourite picture and to read the title and artist. I wanted them to become more aware of the person who is responsible for producing a work of art so that they could begin considering how and why that person was working in a particular way. I asked them to think of reasons why it was their favourite, so working towards forming and expressing judgements.

The children were all keen to say which was their favourite, though the reasons given for their choice were brief: 'It looks pretty'; 'I like the house'; 'It's exciting'. When I suggested that they tried to involve other children and get them to enjoy the painting, the ways in which they expressed their ideas became more involved. They described the content in more detail and began to talk about colour and arrangement, and to make comparisons to other images they knew. I also suggested at this point that noticing what other artists were doing and why could give them ideas in their own artwork.

From the artist's imagination

These lessons introduced how artists may represent imagined ideas in their work and included looking at and discussing reproductions, with the children then attempting to record their dreams or thoughts by painting. I read extracts from *Facts at Your Fingertips*, which suggests that artists use different styles to express themselves. I also read extracts, and showed pictures, from *Just Imagine: Ideas in Painting* (Cumming 1982), which suggest that artists may use their imagination or dreams, referring to Max Ernst, Picasso, Matisse and Bronzino. I showed a large reproduction of Picasso's *Ladies on the bank of the Seine*. As an introduction to a painting lesson we also looked at *Weeping Woman* (Picasso); *Girl's Adventure* (Paul Klee); *Children's Swimming Pool, 11 o'clock Saturday Morning August 1969* (Leon Kossoff). I asked the children to consider how, and later why, the paintings were different from photographs. I suggested that they take an ordinary event and attempt to create imaginative pictures based on how they thought or felt about it.

Studying works of art communicating dreams or expressing the artist's own ideas excited the children, who seemed intrigued by the works I showed them. They were very keen to look at and discuss each one, offering their own interpretations when considering what the artwork represented. For example, 'a woman with a strange face' was offered as a description when looking at Picasso's *Weeping Woman*. During the painting lesson the children appeared confused and when I asked individuals what they were trying to paint, their answers included: 'I don't really know', 'I think I'll do a fuzzy one' and an uncertain, 'girl behind a tree'. Although I gave more instructions, most children remained unsure and I found myself confused in what I was saying. This could be because the number and variety of the examples I chose, and the complexity of ideas involved, was too great at this stage for me and for the children. It might have been more successful had I built on one kind of possibility for the time being, recognising that 'imagination' covers a range of forms. My reflections on this would, I hoped, help me to analyse more fully what the communication of imagination might hold within its range of possibilities for art.

Something useful which may be decorated

These lessons considered function and appearance and also the influence of culture on works of art. Firstly, I showed the children two jugs, one plain brown, the other shaped and decorated by Liz Beckenham, and asked why some useful objects were decorated. Their responses included: to make them more special; to give as presents; to have as an ornament; to give to someone important, like the ancient Egyptians used to give things to the Pharaoh, or bury them. I extended their task, suggesting that they look around to identify pattern or decoration. I asked them to consider if either function or appearance was more important than the other, or if it did not matter. Every child discovered something to talk about, which indicated to me that they had understood the meaning of an every day object being considered as a work of art. I expanded this by recalling artefacts we had looked at in our work on ancient Egypt. In this context the Egyptians' every day objects may be considered by us as works of art which can communicate to us about their culture. I told the children that many of the artefacts which they would see in the gallery are also from other cultures and times. This new dimension of the notion of communication would be followed up later.

Myths and magic

These lessons focused on subject content and artistic method, and I presented that distinction explicitly to the pupils. Sessions included listening to readings from Davidson's *What is Art?* (1993) and searching for, and sketching details of, examples in other books on mythology. Using Davidson I read the chapter on magic and making things happen. Subsections were about cave paintings of animals (recall of an earlier lesson); and the use of magic (recall of an ancient Egyptian scarab). Examples of good luck charms helped most children to understand the issues, with suggestions about St Christopher pendants, horse shoes and lucky mascots flowing freely in discussion.

I used a story, 'a dead man's luggage', from Davidson and again I questioned the children about information learned in the ancient Egyptian project. One remembered that they buried a boat with someone important; others that they buried beautiful things with important people. They all knew that the ancient Egyptians buried animals as mummies, because they were sometimes special. Images of gods and spirits – again, the link with ancient Egypt – were also considered. I encouraged suggestions of any such images from the Christian religion. The children had drawn symbols of some of the religions the previous week. Totems and masks were also discussed, and most of the children responded with enthusiasm, especially on seeing illustrations in a North American mythology book.

They all claimed to have seen or heard about totem poles. I distributed the mythology books which all contain many images of works of art. The children were encouraged to look for items from what we had just been discussing. A list was written on the board. I asked them to read the caption or find information in the text about the artefact they chose. The next activity was to sketch something of their choice and give it a title. They were then asked to select a small detail from something to sketch.

I found that previous knowledge in the context of ancient Egypt made this section easier for the children to understand than I had expected. I was pleased that they were so enthusiastic. The books helped their understanding of the information we had been discussing. Several groups called me to show what they had found. Finding examples increased their enthusiasm and awareness of the task.

The teaching in this third phase involved me and the children in several learning situations. I had become more than usually aware that expressing my enthusiasm added to the success of a teaching strategy. Linking stories to paintings by listening, writing and illustrating also seemed to encourage their responses beyond that which they made by discussing the purpose of art objects. The response, 'I'd like to write a story about it; it would be more fun than the mask story because there's more to think about', indicated a possible reason for their earlier lack of ideas. Pairing or grouping the children, to share and challenge their opinions, was successful in getting them to look closely and to think about their responses to the works of art, especially when they had a 'story' context to consider. Also, by attempting to interest other children they had to look closely and consider their opinions of what the works of art represented.

The strategy I followed in the lesson on the artist's imagination, that of looking at selected works of art, questioning and discussing, seemed less successful. The works of art I selected could have caused the difficulty. Using artefacts appeared to gain interest when looking at decoration, and relating this to their own lives encouraged confidence in their opinions. The children responded well to a small amount of information with pictures in the mythology books. The activities of finding examples and sketching detail focused them on a task, leading to interest and involvement. Requesting detailed sketches seemed to encourage them to look closely.

At the beginning of this phase the children seemed unsure and lacking in confidence, apparently because of the abstract nature of the concept of communication. In group discussions and specific tasks they were beginning to learn that art may communicate different things, in different ways. They were learning to form and justify opinions by considering each other's ideas, and responding with their own. This ability was further developed when trying to interest their peers in a reproduction and to explain what, and in what way, they thought it communicated. Within the last group of lessons based on mythology, the children showed themselves to be aware of communication through the content of some works of art, and their awareness and understanding appeared to be developing. They were also beginning to consider the relative importance of function and appearance. However, I judged that the idea of artists communicating through their work would need further teaching, building on the earlier responses at the beginning of this phase.

PHASE 4: FORMING AND EXPRESSING JUDGEMENTS

The aim of this phase was for the children to apply what they had learned about what art may communicate in content and method, in ways which would involve the use of analytical skills and judgements. I planned to note any evidence of their learning and to consider the effectiveness of the teaching up until the visit to the gallery. I suggested that we were discovering a lot in forming judgements and using analytical skills, and beginning to understand works of art. Questioning ourselves and each other seemed to make us look closely and think carefully about what the art might communicate. The children agreed and we devised class and individual questionnaires to be used at an art gallery. I also asked for their ideas on further activities which could be undertaken to help children think about what art may be communicating and how the artist may achieve this. Using the resources available and working in groups the children set up art galleries in the classroom. I borrowed some more works of art, and the children were encouraged to include their own work. I told them to select art which communicated something defined by the categories they had decided on in Phase 3. They were then to invite other groups, members of staff and the other Year 4 class to visit their galleries and use the questionnaires to guide their viewing. I explained that visitors from outside our class might be inexperienced in looking at works of art and that we might need to use the skills we had developed to help them.

The children appeared to enjoy the activity and to think carefully while writing their questionnaires, especially when considering how they could help other children. When preparing their galleries they became very engrossed. I observed a buzz of excited, involved activity. From questioning the children I detected confidence in the explanations of what the chosen artwork communicated to them. When the other Year 4 class was invited into the art galleries my class showed their developing skill in looking at art by sharing their ideas with inexperienced visitors. They were completely engrossed, explaining what was in their gallery and talking about what and how art communicated different kinds of things.

The activity of devising the questionnaires seemed to have developed the skills of questioning and thinking about works of art. Their lively dialogue with visitors showed them to have become confident in their judgements. I noted, by observing how they guided their visitors, that their observation skills seemed to have improved compared with the earlier lessons.

PHASE 5: PREPARATION FOR THE VISIT

I showed the class photographs of four items from the Sainsbury Collection and gave them information from *Starting Points* (Sekules and Tickle 1993). This was the first time I had self-consciously told the children about works of art rather than generating and sharing ideas jointly. Most of them were fascinated and began asking for more information about who made the artefact and why and when. Reading information to them about the four selected objects which they would see appeared to be successful as an additional way of generating questions which, in turn, could lead to more detailed understanding of some of the principles and purposes of art.

I gave each group a photograph of a different artefact at the gallery, intending them to begin the visit by finding that item. They were tasked with interesting others in this artefact by making a presentation to the class. When the children delivered their presentations to the class any reticent ones were soon keen to join in. Those speaking seemed very proud of 'their' artefact. The children chose the following approaches: carefully describing; drawing attention to detail and pattern, by pointing to the photograph or painting; describing what they thought was being conveyed; expressing their judgements about how they thought it conveyed particular ideas or images; expressing their opinions about whether they liked it or not and also saying why.

The earlier strategy of involving the children in interesting each other, in directing their own and each other's learning, seemed to have contributed to this preparation for the visit. Their verbal and practical responses showed evidence of careful consideration of the work in the photographs they had seen. The quality and content of their presentations appeared to show that they were considering the objects in terms of the ideas which had emerged in class, regarding different categories of communication.

PHASE 6: THE GALLERY AND LATER

The morning session was spent looking for and responding to the objects we had studied in photographs at school. The children were very keen to record their responses to the real object. They spent the afternoon selecting one or more works of art and responding to it (or them) guided by the class questionnaire. They appeared particularly interested in the works of art they had seen in photographs. They studied their choice in depth and carried out as many tasks as possible. The children were so enthralled at the gallery that it was difficult to get them to leave; many of them wanted to repeat their tasks by looking for and selecting objects which fitted a different one of their categories of 'communicating'.

After the visit I concluded the teaching project by allowing the children to express their ideas in practical artwork. They initially painted using their sketches from the visit for inspiration. I explained that they did not have to make copies and suggested that they develop their own ideas. In the following art lesson I used a theme of art communicating magic through some form of good luck charm. In another practical lesson we repeated the activity of recording an event.

CONCLUSIONS

My overall impression was that after the project the children showed confidence in their judgements and some understanding of art as communication. This meant that, although only one visit to the gallery was possible, they were able to enjoy and benefit from the experience, improving their knowledge of art available locally, by way of the extensive preparatory work which was done at school. During the project I developed my own way of looking at works of art. My visits to and information received from the Sainsbury Centre and other sources played an important part in this, enabling me to realise how children could also benefit from the combined experience of classroom learning and gallery visit. Previously I had thought of art as a practical activity involved only with natural ability and skill development. I now realise that through observing, thinking and gathering ideas, it can also be a learning activity in which the constructive development of analytical skills, and understanding of the principles of art, play an important complementary role in practical art.

As the teaching project progressed I realised that from my position as a non-specialist I had mostly considered communication through content which I had found more interesting and easier to form my own judgements about. It became apparent while observing the children, and noticing the development of their responses, that my teaching must also have been biased this way. They were paying less attention to the methods used by artists. Having observed the children and their work and listened to their developing ideas and opinions, I was able to consider the value of the teaching before the visit and, in interpreting its effectiveness, was able to develop my own knowledge of how to present visual art to children. I now feel I can advise colleagues on strategies for teaching visual art and using the resources available in the community.

FURTHER READING

Baker, E. (1992) *Modern Artists*, London: Folens Primary Art.
Bell, J. (1992) *Doing Your Research Project*, Milton Keynes: Open University Press.
Bernard, B. (1992) *Eyewitness Art: Van Gogh*, London: Dorling Kindersley.
Clement, R. and Page, S. (1992) *Primary Art*, Harlow: Oliver and Boyd.
Cross, J. (1977) *For Art's Sake*, London: George Allen and Unwin.
Cumming, R. (1979) *Just Look: A Book About Paintings*, Harmondsworth: Kestrel.
—— (1982) *Just Imagine: Ideas in Painting*, Harmondsworth: Kestrel.
Davidson, R. (1993) *What is Art?* Oxford: Oxford University Press.
Department for Education (1995) *Art in the National Curriculum*, London: Her Majesty's Stationery Office.
Eisner, E. W. (1972) *Educating Artistic Vision*, London: Macmillan.
Field, D. and Newick, J. (ed.) (1973) *The Study of Education and Art*, London: Routledge and Kegan Paul.
Gardner, H. (1980) *Artful Scribbles*, London: Jill Norman.
Grigson, G. and Grigson J. (1967) *Shapes and Adventures*, London: Marshbank.
Janson, H. W. (1991) *History of Art*, London: Thames and Hudson.
Kennet, F. and Measham, T. (1978) *A Child's Guide to Looking at Paintings*, London: Marshall Cavendish.
Luka, M. and Kent, R. (1968) *Art Education: Strategies of Teaching*, Englewood Cliffs, NJ: Prentice-Hall.
Marshall, D. (1993) *Facts at Your Fingertips*, Hemel Hempstead: Simon and Schuster.
Monk, C. H. (1975) *Leonardo Da Vinci*, London: Hamlyn.
Morgan, M. (1992) *Art 4–11: Art in the Early Years of Schooling*, Hemel Hempstead: Simon and Schuster.
Richardson, W. and Richardson, J. (1985) *The World of Art: Entertainers Through the Eyes of Artists*, London: Macmillan.
Schools Council (1974) *Children's Growth through Creative Experience: Art and Craft Education 8–13*, London: Van Nostrand Reinhold.
Sekules, V. and Tickle, L. (eds) (1993) *Starting Points: Approaches to Art Objects Selected from the Sainsbury Centre for Visual Arts*, University of East Anglia, Norwich: Centre for Applied Research in Visual Arts Education.
Taylor, R. (1986) *Educating for Art: Critical Response and Development*, Harlow: Longman.
Tickle, L. (1987) *Learning Teaching, Teaching Teaching*, Lewes: Falmer Press.

APPENDIX

Other teaching resources used

Books

Mythology, London: Hamlyn
   Burland, C. (1973) *North American Indian*
   Christie, A. (1968) *Chinese*
   Ellis-Davidson, H. R. (1969) *Scandinavian*
   Ions, V. (1965) *Egyptian*

MacCanna, P. (1969) *Celtic*
Nicholson, I. (1975) *Mexican and Central American*
Parinder, G. (1967) *African*
Perowne, S. (1975) *Roman*
Piggott, J. (1969) *Japanese*

Encyclopaedia Britannica, *Great Artists Collection*, London: Phaedon Press
Fry, R. (1971) *Seurat*
Gaunt, W. (1971) *Turner*
Kitson, M. (1969) *Rembrandt*
Uhde, W. (1970) *Van Gogh*

Raboff, E. (1980) *Art for Children*, London: Ernest Benn
Marc Chagall
Leonardo Da Vinci
Paul Klee
Pablo Picasso
Vincent Van Gogh

Venezia, M. *Getting to Know the World's Great Artists*, Chicago: Children's Press
Da Vinci (1988)
Michelangelo (1991)
Picasso (1988)
Rembrandt (1988)

Art packs and pictures

Clement, R. and Page, S. (1992) *Primary Art Pack*, Harlow: Oliver and Boyd.
Philip Green Picture Packs (n.d.) Studley, War: Philip Green Educational
Animals
Buildings and Townscapes
Faces
Families
Flowers
Seasons and Weather
Shape and Pattern
Water

Shorewood Fine Art Reproductions (1983) *Shorewood Collection*, Norfolk: Mainstone Publications
Autumn Landscape Alfred Sisley
Birth of Venus Sandro Botticelli
Blue Nude Henri Matisse
Broadway 1936 Mark Tobey
Flowers and Parrots Henri Matisse
Haymaking Pieter Brueghel
Improvisation Vasily Kandinsky
Jane Avril Henri Toulouse-Lautrec
Justice, Faith, Hope and Peace Joe Overstreet
Ladies on the Banks of the Seine Pablo Picasso
Queen Elizabeth I Nicholas Hilliard
Rockets and Blue Lights J.M.W.Turner
Seine at the Grande-Jatte Georges Seurat
Starry Night Vincent Van Gogh

The Brook   Paul Cézanne
The Haywain   John Constable
The Swans   Maurice Prendergast
The Swing   Pierre Renoir
Water of the Flowery Mill   Arshile Gorky
Zebegen   Viktor Vasarely

Chapter 12

Art is . . . extending the concept of art with six year olds

Jennifer Ladusans

AWAKENINGS

The underlying theme of my research was to discover the verbal responses of my Year 2 children when asked what art is. I particularly wanted to find out what their response and reaction would be when encouraged to look at, discuss, relate to and understand objects from different times and cultures.

Art, to me, is many things in many forms; the problem I encountered with my class of 6 year old children was that to them art meant only painting and drawing. I wanted to show them that art need not be just those things. We began by discussing what they thought art was, and it quickly became evident that 'good neat drawings with no scribbles or rubbings out' and 'paintings that look like what they are meant to be, not smudged or messy' were the order of the day. The children were confident that what they had described was 'good art' and would be the only acceptable images to be chosen for exhibition either in the classroom or by Mr and Mrs Sainsbury in their Visual Arts Centre.

Further questioning revealed that not one child among thirty had ever visited an art gallery or any kind of art exhibition. We therefore went on to try to imagine what the Sainsbury Centre might look like. It was speedily decided that it must be big! I wondered why, and the children became eager to explain that it must be a big place because inside there would be lots of rooms and housed within these rooms would be very large, dark paintings in thick gold frames. Obviously the children had some preconceived ideas of what an art gallery might look like, and what it might contain. This became an important issue for me. How would I research the children's responses and their understanding of the objects I was going to present to them if they had narrow preconceived or limited knowledge of art and art galleries to begin with?

Our school is not within easy reach of an art gallery. There is a small gallery in the town, but even if we could have managed to visit it, the current exhibition was not suitable. I thus began by showing the children a videoed series of television programmes called *Art Show*. This series shows a variety of artists at work: a painter, a sculptor, a potter, a photographer, a video artist and an artist who worked with textiles. One of the programmes was about different kinds of studios and exhibition centres, ranging from the Tate to a small exhibition in a local library. The children enjoyed the videos immensely and immediately their perception of 'art' began to change. Alongside the good drawing and neat painting we could now include photographs, videos, ceramics, sculpture, textiles, prints and kinetic art. Although their knowledge of the various areas of art was still limited, and did not extend beyond what they had seen on video, it was broader than simply painting and drawing, and was therefore a great improvement.

During the time spent working with the videos (about three weeks in late November and early December), the children would often appear at my desk in the mornings and proudly present various items, announcing, 'That's art, isn't it?' We would then have a class discussion in order to decide. Usually the conclusion was 'yes', if we could find something that we valued about it. For example, beautiful patterns on shells and stones, little things the children had made themselves, pictures torn from colour supplements, and so on. The children were awakening to a totally new outlook when they thought art; their ideas were changing! I now had the impression that the children had extended their view of art to include several other aspects. I could hear little clusters of children talking in earnest about why they liked this pattern more than that one; how they preferred the big one to the small one; how when you put something on dark paper it looked better than on light. Small beginnings, but something to build on. All our thoughts and energies then went into preparing for the visit to the Sainsbury Centre for Visual Arts around which the bulk of my research would begin.

THE SCENE

Our school was built in the 1950s. We have 300 children on roll. Many have social and educational 'problems' of one sort or another. Most are from financially deprived backgrounds, and their language is deemed to be very impoverished. The school and its setting do not convey any sense of environmental deficiencies. To the front of the building is a busy road along which can be found many different styles of architecture, including a beautiful old church. The grounds of the school are lovely; there is a large meadow with a variety of shrubs and trees surrounding it. To one side is a riding stables where horses and ponies graze all year round in small grassy paddocks. On the right of the meadow is a wooded area that leads to a small park to which the children, when accompanied, can gain easy access. In the park, besides the usual playground apparatus, is a very large pond which is home to a variety of ducks and geese.

However, the classroom environment in more challenging. Nearly all the research took place in my classroom, in which, by the time the tables, chairs and children are installed, there is not room to swing a cat! I finally decided on 'dance' as a topic to extend the children's conception of art, and to explore their response and reaction to the visit to the Sainsbury Centre. The project and associated research took place during the winter months when it was impossible to use the grounds or surrounding area. I wanted a topic that would interest me, excite and stimulate the children and take place mostly within the classroom. I felt that the topic should also allow the children to express themselves in as many ways as possible and so I decided to incorporate music and drama into the theme.

THE BEGINNING

'Dance' provided a context to explore the children's responses, reactions, and understandings when presented with artefacts other than painting and drawing. A teaching theme that the children could work through, and identification of teaching aims, needed to be more specific. I wanted to develop an awareness and understanding about different kinds of art, craft and design. Having visited the Sainsbury Centre myself several times, I had become fascinated by the masks and other paraphernalia associated with tribal rituals and dancing, especially the idea of dancing which tells a story, for instance, in times of celebration. I liked the use of natural materials in some objects, especially, for example, the use of found items such as driftwood, feathers and shells, as part of 'dance' objects. By focusing on these my intention was that the children would be more observant, articulate, expressive and knowledgeable at the end of the project about the range of possible sources of ideas and materials for their own art. From the research perspective I wanted to know what the children thought about the particular forms of art chosen for their consideration, and whether looking at the many and varied images would affect the way they responded to artefacts within the chosen theme. I chose particular objects in the Collection on which to focus.

From the North West Pacific coast of America I chose the raven rattle, the Chilkat blanket (Plate 12.1), and the head-dress frontlet. We would make a study of the head-dresses the people wore, how they made them, what they made them for, and the significance of the animals depicted. We would look closely at pattern and design. Finally we would consider the stories they told and the way they expressed them through dance and celebration.

From among Inuit objects I chose the wolf mask and the walrus mask, to be used for considering the way in which animals played a part in the lives of the people and which were often represented in artefacts.

Plate 12.1 Shoulder blanket (mountain goat wool, wood fibres) Chilkat Alaska
(Robert and Lisa Sainsbury Collection; photograph: James Austin)

I used the *Little Dancer* (*Petite danseuse de quatorze ans*) as a contrast to
the other objects, for looking at the way Degas represented a ballet dancer,
the way she dressed to dance, the kind of music she would dance to, and the
stories she would tell through dance. This provided an opportunity to
compare dance-related art from the cultures of distinct groups of people.

From sources other than the Sainsbury Collection I was also able to
use Solomon Islands artefacts, including dance sticks from North Malaita,
Santa Ysabel and Santa Ana; musical instruments of the percussion kind,
log-like drums slit down the middle and beaten with a stick; ankle bracelets
made from nuts, and dance fans made from coconut tree fibres and
feathers.

We would look at the reasons for dancing as well as 'story' – ritual,
aesthetic, fighting, celebration. I would focus on the way in which animals,
fish and birds are represented and the patterns used, in some cultures,
and the reasons why they are often included in art.

My teaching aims were:

• To build up the children's confidence to make sense of the objects
  under consideration;

- To develop their visual and language vocabularies in order to help them to look at and respond effectively to their own work, to other children's work, and to artists' work.

Certain characteristics of my teaching were kept at the forefront of my mind as I thought about the project from an action-research perspective. I was conscious of my own part in:

- Creating and managing a framework for the children to work within, so that they would know what was expected of them, what they needed to produce, and how it would be used or viewed when completed;
- Paying a good deal of attention to the creative process and to the conversations, interactions and self-evaluation made by the children;
- Using a combined approach of attention to planning and directing the detail of each part of the project, with an openness of mind and willingness to be flexible about how these were interpreted by the children.

I read what I could acquire about the chosen objects, and looked at slides, artefacts, catalogues, postcards and photographs, and began to share some of my understanding with the children. I had thought that hearing about 'Indians' and the like would be very exciting to them, but although they seemed to listen attentively nothing stirred inside them and they did not show very much interest or reaction. I was disappointed. Was it the way in which I had sought to put it across? Was it because times had changed and the children of today do not watch the films I did in my childhood? I knew something of American native cultures from watching television, but at the age of six these children seemed to know nothing except how to do a war cry.

I also introduced stories from the Arctic and the Solomons, and spoke about Edgar Degas' life, his work with ballet dancers, and about ballet itself. Some of the girls went to dancing classes and took a mild interest in Degas' paintings. The general reaction, though, was still a disappointment. Although I did not know it at the time, I need not have worried, because when we later visited the Sainsbury Centre the children reacted quite differently. Even though the focus related to much of what we had discussed in class, this time the children were a lot more interested. They became excited with the objects. Was their reaction better than it would have been had they visited the Centre with no previous knowledge? I could not be sure, and realised that I could not tell what impact the preparations had had.

The framework of lessons which I decided on for these 6–7 year olds to work within was as follows:

- The objects from 'other' cultures (nineteenth Paris was deemed 'our' culture in my mind) which we looked at are all to do with dance and/or

ceremony. When the dancers wore or held these artefacts they sometimes told a story, or stories were associated with the activities and
celebrations. For example, the North West Coast native Americans
would tell the story of Raven the Trickster, hence the raven rattle.
(Stories told in dance form were not entirely new to the children as
we had worked with the story of Coppelia the previous term.)

- Often the dancers would 'change' into animals (hence the masks). The
animals they became were the ones that lived around the same place
as the dancers. Mostly the artists who made the objects, such as masks,
frontlets, rattles, blankets, dance sticks, fans and musical instruments,
made them from natural materials or objects. (I dealt with the idea
that natural objects are those which grow or were made a part of the
Earth, and which we find, for instance, on the beach or in a wood, or
get from an animal or a bird; they are not materials that people have
invented, such as plastic, or machine-made things.)

- In groups the children wrote a story together that could be acted out
in a dance without words. They were asked to think about the natural
materials or objects they might find locally, and consider which animals
or birds are common in their area. Each designed his or her own mask
and/or frontlet to wear during the dance after being reminded that they
would be dancing as a group and telling the group's story.

- Patterns seen on things such as the Chilkat blanket and the dance sticks
were used as a stimulus to work out a pattern of their own that could
be printed on fabric to make into a dancing costume.

- Musical instruments seen in books about the Solomon Islands, the
dance sticks, fans, and the raven rattle were also used to generate the
idea of something of their 'own' to accompany a dance. The instruments
were to be used after writing their own music to accompany the group
while dancing.

- When we had made all these things, the dances were performed to
show off our art to the rest of the school and to parents.

I wanted to introduce the children to the use of the following media and
techniques for practical work:

- Observational work with natural objects;
- Use of sketchbooks;
- Pattern designing for textile work;
- Pastels and Brusho to supplement pencils and paint;
- Fabric printing;
- Some drawing and painting;
- Mod-Roc techniques;
- Clay.

I also planned to use some music by other composers to stimulate and
inspire the children's dances, as I was not at all sure that the music they

composed for themselves would do so. I chose music, entitled 'Rainforest', composed by the Lowestoft Sixth Form Consortium for a group of dancers performing at the Seagull Theatre. I also used 'Waltz' from *Coppelia*, composed by Delibes, reinforcing previous work. I did not talk to the children about the practical work that they would be doing to produce their own artefacts until after the visit to the Sainsbury Centre.

THE RESEARCH

One of my main concerns was that I should be a teacher first and a researcher second, and I wondered how far my research activities would impinge upon my teaching time. David Hopkins suggests that one of the principles we might adopt as teacher researchers is: 'that the teacher's primary job is to teach, and that any research method should not interfere with or disrupt the teaching commitment' (Hopkins 1985: 41).

I did feel that within the framework I created it would be possible for me to do just that, and that I should also be able to use the classroom research as a means of reflecting critically on my teaching. But just what did that mean? Richard Pring says:

> Such systematic and critical examination will involve philosophising, appealing to evidence, reference to . . . theories. But there is no reason for saying that it will add up to a theory. [Classroom research is about] helping the practitioner to theorise, i.e. think more systematically, critically and intelligently about his or her practice.
>
> (Pring 1978: 244–5)

My research hinged on recording what I did, the children's written and visual responses, audio-taped interviews conducted on a one-to-one basis, and observation. I recorded the group at the Sainsbury Centre by means of a video, and in the classroom whenever I got the chance during their practical work. It also hinged on maintaining a disciplined search for evidence *only* about my teaching aims (extending awareness/understanding about different kinds of art, and developing their responses to these).

THE VISIT

The thought of taking the children to the Sainsbury Centre was a worrying experience. I knew the children well enough to feel concerned about their behaviour. For the majority of them, the visit would represent their first experience of learning in a gallery. I did not want it to be either traumatic for me or boring for them. Anticipating the gallery tour conjured up a picture of children trailing behind their guide, feeling restless and unin-terested, in at most a passive learning situation which might fill their minds with irrelevant information. The idea that children learn best through participation, discovery and the stimulation of their natural curiosity was the procedure that I preferred to adopt. I have long been aware of John Holt's indictment, that children 'are bored because the things they are given and told to do in school are so trivial, so dull and make such limited demands on the wide spectrum of their intelligence, capabilities and talents' (Holt 1964: 98).

The guided tour could so easily fall into this trap unless I could alleviate the problem through activities where the children would be able to take some control over their surroundings and to sense a feeling of purpose and belonging. I divided my class into groups to work with me and with parents guided by prepared materials. For my research purposes I selected a group of four boys and four girls, with the ability to make articulate verbal responses and to write down some of their thoughts, ideas and opinions about the visit, and later about their practical work. They were Sam, Ashley, Harry and Samuel; Hannah, Nikita, Katie and Rosanna. Before the visit I spent some time with my 'team' exposing them to as much of my knowledge as I felt they could cope with concerning my five chosen objects. I provided them with photographs of the objects, some basic questions to use and the order that their group should follow (so as to avoid congestion).

The children were extremely excited at the prospect of seeing the Sainsbury Centre and now at last we had arrived. They were truly amazed at the enormity of the building, and such exclamations as 'wow', 'massive', and 'gigantic' were heard. Once inside the building, things got even better! I had wondered if the strategies I had chosen would hold the children 'with' the work of art – I was concerned with the act of looking and responding. I need not have feared. My group quickly homed in on objects even as the groups dispersed. Instantly, out came their sketchbooks, and they wanted to draw. Even with the promise of plenty of time to sketch the chosen objects, and time for free choice at the end of the visit, some children were very reluctant to follow me to the Inuit wolf mask which was the first item on my agenda.

The children gathered themselves into a group on the floor in front of the wolf mask. I began to use questions to evoke responses and reactions. The following transcript of parts of a conversation, to which I have added a few of my thoughts, was taken from a video recording of the visit.

J.L.   What can you tell me about this?
HANNAH   It's a reindeer.
J.L.   What makes you think it's a reindeer?
HANNAH   It's got antlers [*Pointing to the feathers*]!
J.L.   What about you, Rosanna?
ROSANNA   It's got white spots on, it looks like a reindeer.

J.L.   What do you think it's made of?

ALL   Wood!

J.L.   What do you think it's for?

HARRY   For a mask.

J.L.   Good. You all said wood and you all think it's a mask, but, do you know, it's not meant to be a reindeer, it's meant to be a wolf. [*They all show surprise.*] Do you think it would be comfortable to wear?

HARRY   No, scratchy.

J.L.   Why do you think the Inuit person who made it did a wolf mask and not a zebra or an elephant?

HARRY   They used to shoot wolves with bows and arrows then look at them and draw the pictures and make masks 'cos they liked them and thought they were good.

J.L.   What about these feathers, what are they for?

ASHLEY   To represent fur.

HANNAH   Do you think it's fur, Mrs Ladusans?

J.L.   I don't really know, I'll have to think about it too. What do you think?

HANNAH   Well, I think Harry is right because feathers are soft like fur.

At this point the children were sitting quietly on the floor. Later, as I watched the video, I could remember thinking to myself, 'they're listening, but are they interested?' They were all drawing busily and did not seem to want to bother with questions. Perhaps, for them, just being there and sketching was enough. I realised that I was desperately trying to draw them all into conversation, with the exception of Harry, who was already overtly enthusiastic and making all the verbal responses. Suddenly Harry spotted the wolf's tongue hanging out.

J.L.   Why do you think his tongue is hanging out like that?

HARRY   I think he has been running.

J.L.   What's he running from? [On reflection, it might have been 'towards'.]

HARRY   I think he's being hunted and he's doing a hunting dance and people see a wolf and they think, wow, it's a wolf. But it's not really, it's the Inuits.

The rest of the children were still engrossed in their drawings but were now beginning to look more closely at the mask by getting up and peering into the glass case. Katie especially spent her time equally between the case and her sketch pad. Everyone appeared to be working hard.

HANNAH   Look! I can see *Little Dancer*!

Hannah was very excited that she had found a 'friend' and called Harry to come and look too. She tried to entice him away, but he was not sure which interested him more at that moment, *Little Dancer* or the wolf mask. Eventually we all went to look at the statue. The children did not want to talk again. They preferred to draw. I was becoming increasingly aware that I had to offer the children more stimulating questions in order to receive a verbal response.

J.L.   What do you think she's thinking about?
HARRY   I think she's at a ballet dance and she's thinking like this: 'Oh, I wonder if it will be scary? Look at all those people out there!'
J.L.   How do you think M. Degas made the little dancer?
HANNAH   I think he made it and then he put the clothes on, first the top, then the skirt, then the ribbon.
J.L.   Why do you think he made it? What for?
HARRY   Well, he's done it because she's dead and other people want to remember what she looks like.
J.L.   Yes, that could be true. After all, here we are still remembering her today.

The other children were still drawing and seemed totally absorbed in their work.

HANNAH   It was made in 1880 so it's quite old.

The girls in the group started to show an interest and speculate about the original colour of the skirt. Pink was decided upon. I suggested that I should do some sketching and the children gathered round to watch me. They helped by counting the number of buttons on the bodice and pointed out other aspects of the work. They eventually started to wander off, so we went downstairs to look at the Chilkat blanket.

The group were fairly quiet and seemed interested, but still wanted to draw. I was finding it extremely difficult to get any verbal responses, except from Harry, who was flowing with ideas. The others seemed to need direct questioning.

HARRY   I never knew blankets were art.
KATIE   Well, it might not be a blanket, it might be for over a door or curtains.
HARRY   I don't think so, Katie. you wear those to dance in and that long bit goes up and down.
ROSANNA   No, you wrap it around to keep warm and those long bits are to go round your ankles.

After some time we went back upstairs to look at the raven rattle.

KATIE   I think it's a rattle and it's got beads or balls inside to make a noise.
HANNAH   Yes, and when you shake it it can make a lot of noise.
J.L.   Where do you hold it?

HANNAH   On the plastic bit there.

SAMUEL   It looks like birds.

SAM   It could be a wolf or a bear.

NIKITA   It looks like birds.

HANNAH   That bit wrapped round the handle isn't plastic, it's leather. I just read it.

J.L.   Why do the Indians need a rattle?

ROSANNA   So they can make the music to dance to.

This time the children were very restless, wanting to go off by themselves. I felt myself losing some control of the situation and I desperately wanted them to look at my last object, the frontlet. Perhaps a new object would hold their attention.

J.L.   What could this be?

ASHLEY   A hedgehog.

SAMUEL   All those blue things make it look like a hedgehog. [*All nod in agreement.*]

J.L.   What about those 'blue things', what do you think they are?

SAMUEL   Gold.

SEVERAL   Silver ... diamonds ... jewels.

J.L.   The Indians had to use something they could find, maybe on a beach.

SAMUEL   Stones or glass?

J.L.   Shells!.

They reacted as if they did not believe me. I explained that they did not look like shells now because they had been cut into shape and that some shells are such a lovely blue colour inside, but that we do not usually see them like that in this country.

   With further questioning the group went on to tell me that the frontlet was made of wood, was carved and could be worn either on one's head or one's face.

KATIE   There are holes to put elastic through.

J.L.   What else could the holes be for?

KATIE   The feathers.

J.L.   What feathers?

SAM   Well, I think it's a hedgehog and it goes on your face and you put elastic through the holes.

HARRY   No it doesn't, it goes on your head like this. [*He does a war dance holding an imaginary frontlet on his head.*]

KATIE   It's beautiful.

J.L.   Does it frighten you?

KATIE   No, it doesn't frighten me ... maybe in the dark. It would be scary then, if the firelight got on it.

HARRY   It must be for a war dance.

The children by now could see all the other groups wandering around and they were more than ready for some free choice. Two hours had passed. I had not noticed the time. I reflected that if we had been in the classroom for two hours of continuous discussion I would most certainly not have held the children's attention, nor would I have expected it of them. I decided that, under these circumstances, the children had reacted well. It would be more interesting if I were able to bring them again. Perhaps they would say more. I still felt disappointed that their verbal responses were not immediate, or as curious as I had hoped they would be. Could this have been through boredom? Because I had talked too much? Or simply because they are not used to discussion? I have found 'asking questions' a problem in other areas of the curriculum and I thought it worthwhile noting to myself that in the future 'asking questions' might be on my priority list for curriculum planning.

I recalled that Rudolph Arnheim had reproached educational practices as being too biased towards verbal abstractions and pointed out that: 'Visual form is not recognised as a medium of productive thinking' (Arnheim, 1970: 279). I disagree so far as I am concerned. I have always recognised that visual forms can provoke productive thinking, and verbal abstractions, as indeed the objects did with Harry, at least. I should perhaps be satisfied with the other kinds of responses made, the way the group were absorbed in their drawings, the way they seemed to listen to what was being said, quietly. When they did speak it was either about their work or the objects. They said that they enjoyed the visit and definitely wanted to go back again. Harry even said he was going to try to persuade his mum to take him!

FURTHER RESPONSES

Over the following weeks I conducted interviews with the eight children in my group. I had decided that the interview method would be the most appropriate way of finding out how these children reacted to the visit, in terms of what they most remembered and any thoughts that they had formulated. There is always the danger of bias creeping into interviews, of course. As the teacher and the only interviewer I was also aware of other pitfalls too. Borg draws attention to a few of the problems that may occur:

> Eagerness of the respondent to please the interviewer, a vague antagonism that sometimes arises between the interviewer and the respondent, or the tendency of the interviewer to seek out the answers that support his preconceived notions, are but a few of the factors that may contribute to biasing of data obtained from the interview. These factors are called 'response effect' by survey researchers.
>
> (Borg 1981: 87)

My interviews were fairly unstructured. The initial question was normally one which asked them to recall their memories of the gallery. The second question was usually influenced by their first answer, so the interview was essentially free-flowing. The interviews might be classed as conversations, except that my contribution in terms of talking is very small indeed. Each of the interviews lasted about twenty minutes (the length of an average assembly). The interviews took place in our classroom on a one-to-one basis. The children were all used to the procedure as I often keep them with me for a 'chat' and I have always scribbled down what they say whilst working. Between their responses I encouraged them to go on, by interposing with such phrases as: 'Why was that? Anything else? What can you tell me about it?' and 'What was it made of?'

After asking Rosanna what she remembered about the visit, the 'conversation' unfolded as follows:

> I thought it would have loads of windows, but it didn't. I especially liked all those pretty ornaments in it . . . but I really did like the ballet dancer. That looked poorly [ill] because not enough air was in it for her to breathe and it was very dusty. She looked so real but they didn't take care of her, they let her die and get dirty. Edgar Degas made her, . . . I think. There's about twenty of them made out of metal. I liked drawing all the different things. I was pleased with my drawings. I did the ballet dancer . . . the rattle. . . . There was a lot of different colours in that, and it's made of wood and you hold it in your hand and shake it when you dance and you dance very fast. I also liked the hippopotamus. I looked at that by myself, it is very colourful and not too much dusty. I've only been to the zoo when I was a baby, I don't really know what a real one looks like, but I don't think the one in the Sainsbury Centre looked like a real one. I think in the olden days somebody made it for the church as an ornament . . . then the people who came to church would have something to look at and to talk about. When we went downstairs we saw a lovely blanket. Indian women wove them. My mummy is going to teach me to knit. I might make a blanket. Do you remember those drawings down there [Giacometti]? Well, they were scribbled, weren't they? I don't think they should be in there, he should do them again more carefully next time. I would like to go there again because I didn't have enough time to draw all the things I wanted to draw.

I have found Rosanna to be more responsive when interviewed alone (whatever the subject), and I was delighted to hear her thoughts as she had clearly made several observations, as well as showing some knowledge and understanding. Her lack of self-confidence within the group at the gallery had been apparent and she made little or no comment while there. Yet when she recalled the visit her response in terms of description and understanding of the artefacts is extensive and, I thought, perceptive.

Nikita also lacked the confidence to contribute to the conversation during the visit. Her response to the same question was different to Rosanna's:

> I saw a great big head [by John Davies]. I thought it was a bit odd. It had all lines over it. We went into where all pictures were and we saw this mask that looked like a deer with all white spots on it. It was made of wood, I think. It was really a wolf and they used the mask for dancing in just before a war. I saw a little hippopotamus at the end and drew a picture of it. I think it looked like a real one. I chose it as my favourite thing because it's all white and it's from a different country. I think the artist is French. I think it's just something to look at. I think it's really good there. I would like to look at some more pictures. I liked all the colours in the pictures. I saw this naked woman, not the one in the bath, a different one.

Nikita's thoughts were difficult to elicit; I received these brief answers to a multitude of questions, and have combined them here. She seemed unable to respond without the support of the group. Perhaps she had been dependent on their responses for her ideas. She seemed used to forming and expressing judgements in short, simple terms, and had a less extensive vocabulary than others with which to talk more fluently about her reactions. I am becoming increasingly aware that an extended vocabulary is an essential part of responding to art and of acquiring information and understanding about it. Nikita had some rather idiosyncratic ideas, I thought, which would need working on. The other children in the group had a varied range of responses. All interviews, including Nikita's, provided evidence of a favourable reaction to the artefacts, coupled with some knowledge and understanding (see Appendix, p. 215). Most importantly, they provided a basis from which I could seek to extend that.

A BROAD CURRICULUM EXPERIENCE

Initially, the class listened to some more myths and legends, which could be connected with the objects that we had looked at, as a way of remembering the objects. I included in my stories a version of the story of the Raven, while the children watched the soundless video of their observation of the raven rattle. I hoped that this would inspire them in their own story writing. They had as their starting point the idea that they belonged to a tribe that lived long ago in Lowestoft. They thought of a seagull as being a bird representative of the seaside and a herring as being part of Lowestoft's fishing industry. During the time that they were writing,

I played the two pieces of music: 'Rainforest' and the 'Waltz' from *Coppelia*. The children were asked to decide which music they preferred and what kind of tribe they wanted to belong to. (They had earlier thought of a warrior type or a ballerina type.) The research group divided into two, the boys opted to be warriors, while the girls were set on becoming ballerinas. The rest of the class also danced according to gender – boys warriors, girls ballerinas.

The Mermaids and the little girls

A long time ago there lived four little dancers. They used to dance from morning till night but they never thought that they were any good. One day while walking by the sea they spotted some lovely silver fish. They watched them swim in and out of the waves. They wished they could dance like the fish. Every day the girls looked longingly at the fish. They wanted to dance like them so much. They even tried to copy their movements. One day the girls just walked right into the sea to be nearer the fish. The Herrings took pity on the drowning girls and they took them deep into the cold dark icy water to the place where the Mermaids lived. The Mermaids all had beautiful silver tails just like the Herring fish. Now that the Queen of the Mermaids had turned them into Mermaids they could at last dance like little silver Herring fish.

(Written by Katie Jewson, Hannah Taylor,
Rosanna Nash and Nikita Grant)

Warriors and Seagulls

Once upon a time there was a tribe of boys called the Meadow Warriors. They were very brave. In their town everybody used to eat the silver Herrings but one day all the Herrings disappeared. The boy warriors looked everywhere for those Herrings. Luckily the boys found the Herrings, however they were found in an unusual place – not the sea as you would expect, but in the seagulls' nest. The seagulls flew around and around the nest flapping their wings in panic because they wanted to keep the Herrings for themselves. The warrior boys kept trying to kill the seagulls. The Herrings suddenly spoke: 'Please put us back into the sea. If you do we will forever make sure that there is enough food for everyone to eat ... for we are magic Herrings.' But the seagulls and the warriors said 'no', and so the Herrings changed themselves into flying fish. Just before they flew away they turned the seagulls and the warrior boys into pebbles on the beach.

(Written by Harry Hoodless, Sam Merrell,
Ashley Mitchell and Samuel Betts)

Once the story was written, the children began to design their masks. A uniformity of a kind was imposed upon them as I decided that we would use Mod-Roc to make a mould of the children's faces. They found this very exciting. A variety of patterns and colours emerged, along with lengthy discussions about how to keep the mask on, and how it could be made more comfortable to wear. The boys' group wondered if the Inuit had had the same thoughts when they made their masks. They asked questions among themselves, and made observations such as: 'The wolf mask would be heavy to wear because it was made of wood'; 'Mod-Roc is much lighter . . . but wood would last longer because it was stronger', and 'Which would rot first, the wood or the Mod-Roc'?

The children also made frontlets (Plate 12.2). They seemed to derive great pleasure from this activity, decorating creatively with a mixture of natural objects, paper, beads, ribbons and junk. Some of the children in the group were clearly influenced by the frontlets they had seen. When they were finished, some of the frontlets were very heavy and tipped forwards. They pondered over the weight of the 'real' ones made of wood, and the colossal size of some head-dresses on slides we had seen of dancers from New Guinea. The children found it hard to move in theirs, and the girls wondered if the reason that men always seemed to be the dancers in the North West Coast of America was because one needed to be quite strong to hold the weight of a head-dress.

After studying the patterns they found in books about the North West Coast and the Solomon Islands, the children were left to devise their own patterns, and to transfer them using printing techniques on to strips of calico, each of which was then sewn into a skirt shape and worn at the performance of their dances (Plate 12.3).

The task of making dance sticks and musical instruments to accompany them whilst dancing was eagerly received and executed. By now these children had their own thoughts and ideas concerning the kind of sound and patterns they wanted to make, and the influences they wanted to use. I was impressed by their ingenuity and expertise. I noticed the boys busily incorporating birds, shells, animals, feathers and patterns into their work. Meanwhile the girls' group had started making bracelets and ankle instruments, which I had only briefly mentioned.

The performances impressed parents and colleagues, who were surprised that the inspiration for the dances had come through responses to artefacts. One middle school colleague suggested to me that I had wasted a lot of teaching time whilst doing the research. My reply was unrelenting: that I had in fact covered most areas of the curriculum well. My class is a Year 2 group and from this topic I am now able to make some well informed end of key stage statements in not only art but also PE (dance) and music (we also composed some accompanying music ourselves). Several aspects of history and geography have been covered, and it has

Plate 12.2 David, Harry and Samuel working on ideas for masks and head-dress frontlets (photograph: Jennifer Ladusans)

Plate 12.3 Nikita working on a decorative pattern for a dance dress, using fabric crayons (photograph: Jennifer Ladusans)

been an extremely useful time for the assessment of speaking, listening and writing. Aspects of technology, maths and science were focused on also. For RE we were able to compare myths and legends from stories told by the Inuit, the North West Coast American Indians and the peoples of the Solomon Islands, with our own legends of the Creation.

DISCOVERIES

The class was willing and eager to co-operate in this adventure, but visiting an art centre was for them an unfamiliar experience. Their first verbal responses were, I felt, commonplace and conventional. There were sparks of personal pleasure, likes and dislikes, starting points for further discussion. I rather assumed that seeing the objects would be sufficient in itself to stimulate extensive verbal responses. Perhaps, faced with many unfamiliar things in an unfamiliar setting, most needed time to look and think. They looked with sustained concentration, often without comment or question. They seemed at times to see many things concurrently, unfamiliar things. Perhaps they were on occasion at a loss as to what to think or say. Perhaps I was too committed to hearing their responses because of the research – thoughts unspoken make rather elusive data.

I noticed that it seemed helpful to compare responses to those of their friends. Seeing through other children's eyes and learning about their reactions led some children to have fresh ideas, to think about objects that could be looked at from a different point of view. Discussions that began in this way at the gallery continued in the classroom where visual memory was helped by the photographs and books I had collected. I particularly noticed this when listening to conversations in the classroom. If I asked the children a direct question a few were initially unresponsive. Yet, whilst talking with others, details were recalled by reference to a description, a photograph, or a drawing from their sketchbooks. The unstructured nature of this evidence made it hard to capture it, but clearly my interviews were not necessarily revealing all the data. That was confirmed by another event. During the visit what appealed to one child did not necessarily seem to appeal to another. At school the children collected data for a class survey entitled 'My Favourite Object'. The outcome gave Degas' *Little Dancer* 21 out of 30 votes. I really had had no idea which object the children would hold in the highest regard, but if I had been asked to guess the outcome, *Little Dancer* would have been near the bottom of my list.

An important issue for me at the beginning of my project had been how I was going to research the children's responses to, and understanding of, the objects that I was going to present them with, when they had such limited and preconceived ideas of what art was, as shown by Harry's initial thoughts: 'I think that Art is about when you have to do good neat drawings with no scribbles or rubbing out and paintings that look like they are real and mustn't be messy or smudgy.' By taking them to the gallery and using objects to stimulate practical work in the classroom I wanted to extend such perceptions of art. I wanted to discover what the children thought about the particular forms of art that I chose for them to consider, and the many wide and varied images. Would these evoke discussion and affect the way the children respond to art? Harry's response to the question 'what is art?' after our visit showed that his perceptions of art had been 'extended' quite radically:

> Art is about anything you like; videos, carving wood, clay things, and it could be making blankets in beautiful patterns, making head-dresses that have loads of things on them like birds, seaweed and other stuff. Art is drawing and sculpture like the *Little Dancer*. Mr Degas made her from a real little girl so that we can remember her when she is dead. Trees is art and that's because art is making things out of things and you can use the trees for all sorts of art things like masks and frontlets and carvings and statues. When I grow up I'm going to be an artist, a drawing one and I might do some carving too.
>
> (Taken from Harry's written work)

The other members of the group showed similar extended responses and reactions. They include knowledge and understanding of other times and people of other places, of the work of artists and the materials they use, and of the variety of 'users' of artefacts. The detailed nature of that new knowledge is a matter for further analysis of individual responses, for further research which might capture the more elusive data which began to emerge.

Such evidence as I have already from my discoveries will make a very different starting point for our next project. Further analysis, and more evidence, will help me to plan for the development of these Year 2 children's art education in ways which really do extend what they have recently gained.

FURTHER READING

Arnheim, R. (1970) *Visual Thinking*, London: Faber and Faber.
Bell, J. (1987) *Doing Your Research Project*, Milton Keynes: Open University Press.
Borg, W. R. (1981) *Applying Educational Research*, Harlow: Longman.
Department for Education (1995) *Art in the National Curriculum*, London: Her Majesty's Stationery Office.
Feest, F. (1980) *Native Arts of North America*, London: Thames and Hudson.
Gardner, H. (1980) *Artful Scribbles*, London: Jill Norman.
Hadley, E. (1983) *Legends of the Sun and Moon*, Cambridge: Cambridge University Press.

Holt, J. (1964) *How Children Fail*, Harmondsworth: Penguin.
Hopkins, D. (1985) *A Teacher's Guide to Classroom Research*, Milton Keynes: Open University Press.
Jeffers, S. (1991) *Brother Eagle Sister Sky*, London: Puffin.
Kendall, R. (1987) *Degas by Himself*, London: Macdonald.
Marcousé, R. (1974) *Using Objects: Visual Awareness and Visual Learning in the Museum and Classroom*, London: Van Nostrand Reinhold.
Morgan, M. (1989) *Art 4–11; Art in the Early Years of Schooling*, London: Basil Blackwell.
Pring, R. (1978) *Teacher as Researcher*, London: Routledge and Kegan Paul.
Stewart, H. (1979) *Looking at Indian Art of the North West Coast*, Washington DC: University of Washington Press.
Taylor, C. (1993) *What Do We Know About the Plains Indians?*, New York: Simon and Schuster Young Books.
Thistlewood, D. (1989) *Critical Studies in Art and Design Education*, Harlow: Longman.
Walker, R. (1985) *Doing Research: A Handbook for Teachers*, London: Routledge.
Wilson, E. (1984) *North American Indian Designs*, London: British Museum Publications.

APPENDIX

The children's responses in interview

Interviews with all eight children took place on a one-to-one basis in the classroom. The interviews began with the basic question, 'What can you tell me about our visit to the Sainsbury Centre, what do you remember?' The questions that followed were determined by the answers given. Some of the children needed very little interaction but others only managed to answer questions with a few words before needing another question. The responses of Rosanna and Nikita have already been given (pp. 208 and 209); below are those of the other six children.

Sam

That was big and had lots of squares and lights and air things. It was so big that even the statues seemed tiny. It was grey and black and it did remind me of an airport. I thought it would have lots of different floors. That looked even bigger 'cos there were twisty stairs and loads of statues of people. I liked the *Little Dancer* a lot because she is really a little girl. I don't know what they wanted to put her in the coffin [glass case] for, it might be because she is dead. I liked everything really . . . but we didn't see it all, did we? I would like to go there again and this time I would do some more drawings of different things like *Bucket Man* and the spears.

Samuel

The building, that was much different to ours. It had quite a lot of windows and it was a little bigger. I remember that head with a lot of lines on it was bald with no hair. The hedgehog thing, no, the bear thing with those pretty things, shells, were greeny blue. Well, I liked that mainly because it was so shiny. A man made it, not a woman, a long time ago in America . . . so that people could look at it because you couldn't really wear it, it would fall off. The man made it just for the Sainsbury Centre. My one that I made is different, I made it to wear on my head for the dancing and when we do the display but the man who made the one in the Sainsbury Centre didn't, he made it just to look at. [I then reminded him about the 'Potlatch' and stories.]

Well, he probably just used it for that once then after that everyone was only allowed to look at it. It is art, though, because it's in there, so it must be, and mine is art too because if he's done a frontlet and it's art then mine must be too. Only mine would fall to bits after a while because it's mostly paper and his is wood and shells. I was impressed by the *Little Dancer*. It was very good and that is art. Making things is always art and that's why I liked her because he had to make her and make her look really like a little girl. I know I couldn't do it as good. I would go again to the Sainsbury Centre and I would explore all the different parts because it was really big and we didn't see all the parts.

Katie

I liked the *Little Dancer*. She had a pink ribbon in her hair and she was brown because she is very old and made of metal. Edgar Degas made her, I should think for a competition, a statue competition. I think he would win because it was ever such a good cast, but he would put the real one in the competition because that's got real hair made from horses and I know what horses' hair looks like because my best friend goes horse riding every Tuesday. And I did like *Bucket Man* and you showed him to us quickly. He looked so real, I think he is a real person only made of a carved wood shape, or it might be the man's real shape done in Mod-Roc. I liked him because he looked so real. When I looked at him I thought he was going to come to life. That ball thing on his head must be to stop his hat going into his eyes. His hat was round his neck. I quite liked the Chilkat blanket. It must be hard to make all them patterns come into weaving. I liked the patterns, they looked like eyes. You wear it to dance in or you could keep it on your bed if you want. I liked the Sainsbury Centre because it was fun and you could look at things and draw and I like drawing a lot.

Harry

I remember that big head . . . it had funny little lines on it and pink and red lips. I liked the *Little Dancer* best. She was very beautiful, and I liked her the best because she had material on her and that made her look real. I like things that look real. I think the North West Coast Americans were real people and *Bucket Man* was real too. The things they used were real like the rattle shaker . . . I liked that, that was good. It had good patterns. What happened was, these men found them on the floor after a war dance and then they took them to the art gallery and copied them and painted them. They could be the real thing in the art gallery but I think that they are copies. To me they don't really look old enough to be like what the Indians have. Mr and Mrs Sainsbury when they made their art gallery, well, first they had paintings and there was plenty of room left so they had statues and there was still plenty of room so they thought, 'why not have these other things as art like Indian stuff and all that'. I think they are art because you can clean them up and make them look new and people will come and look at them. They don't have to be new. I wouldn't mind them being dirty and dusty, I would go and look at them anyway, but some people would not. I think that going to the Sainsbury Centre has changed my art because I can draw better now because you said we should really look hard and now I do. I want to go there again and this time I want to stop in front of everything and draw it, the whole thing. When I had finished the drawings I would add words and make a quiz and have a competition for people to try and find things out. I learned that you can look at the things there for ideas in your work, you can do lots of patterns and I liked those scribbly ones [Giacometti] that really looked like something, and you know that masks looked like animals now. *Bucket Man* and the *Dancer* have real clothes on and I never knew you could put real clothes on models. I really like art galleries now.

Hannah

Well, when we were there I liked going down the tunnel bit and I thought I was going to fall over. When we were looking at the *Little Dancer* I tried to draw her and I done it all wrong. Well, because at first I didn't look properly and when I looked again I could notice her legs were different and they were hard to do and I think Katie copied me. When me and Nikita were looking at *Bucket Man* we thought his eyes were moving. I thought he was real. He was quite big and ever so dirty, and he had real clothes on. Did you notice that he had a black ball on his head? I think you shoot at that with a rifle at a fairground, or he could be a waxwork. I liked the blanket because it had nice patterns on it. The face in the middle looked angry. The blanket is symmetrical. You were not allowed to touch the glass because if you do the alarms will go off. The blanket is in that under the ground bit and it is made of goat's hair for the Red Indians to wear when they have their Potlash. That's what they wear when they do their dancing too. The blankets ripple up and down, and on their head is a frontlet and in their hand is a raven rattle what you shake. You can wear a mask on your face if you want and that can change you into an animal like a wolf or something, it might be a deer. I liked going to the Sainsbury Centre. I told my mum all about it and she said it sounded really good and perhaps she will take me again one day.

Ashley

I remember that it was big, it was so big I nearly fainted when I saw it. Inside I loved it. I wanted to draw all those things but we didn't have time. The first thing that we looked at was a mask. It was made out of wood and feathers and at first I thought it was a reindeer. Next to it was a walrus one and I thought that one was a ghost! People used to wear masks when they did dancing about a story. I like the *Little Dancer* a lot. She was really nice and once she was a real girl at a ballet show and she could dance a story like *Coppelia* or something. There was a big head with a lot of lines over it and a statue called *Bucket Man* and they were made by the same man and he made some more things as well. You could go downstairs through a tunnel thing and the doors moved by themselves like at the supermarket. I saw the Chilkat blanket and it has a symmetrical pattern and the North West Coast American Indian women made it to wear at Potlashes. It's a dance. I would like to go again to draw some more things what I like. I don't know what I'm going to draw because first you have to look and then you decide.

Chapter 13

Understanding sculptors and sculpting

Pauline Orsgood

Working in a small rural primary school with Year 2 children, I wanted to see if they changed their initial observations of and/or views about sculpture, after work spread over a period of five months. I hoped to develop the children's appreciation of sculpture and to promote a greater understanding of three dimensional forms. By the end of the project there was some evidence (from conversations and sketches) to suggest that all the children were looking more closely at particular sculptures than they had done initially.

When the project began I especially had in mind the following expectations (aims) for the art curriculum which I was trying to implement:

- Work from what has been experienced, observed and imagined;
- Learn to gather information and use it;
- Record what is seen in a variety of ways, and use the records to stimulate and develop ideas;
- Develop the ability to form judgements about art;
- Express ideas and feelings provoked by what is observed, remembered and imagined.

I wanted to help pupils to question the nature of an art form previously unknown to them: what is its purpose? who made it? what is it made of? where does it come from? A critical factor in implementing this work included the provision of the widest possible range of other artists' work, in order to help pupils develop the ability to analyse and reflect upon it. My intention was to see if and how young children change their initial observations and/or opinions of works of art after repeated contact with the same pieces of sculpture. I did this through a series of three visits to the gallery, related to work in the classroom. I wanted to begin to develop the children's appreciation of sculpture and their knowledge of sculptors and to promote a greater understanding of 3D forms. Activities included:

- Observing and sketching selected large sculptures;
- Identifying the work of artists and developing understanding of it;

- Responding to ideas, methods and approaches used for making art;
- Showing that some sculptors, e.g. Degas and Moore, plan their work first;
- Looking at the different types of materials that sculptors use;
- Seeing a sculptor at work;
- Planning and producing 3D forms.

All the literature I could find relating to looking at and observing various art forms related to children in Key Stages Two to Four. It emphasised the need to visit galleries and the value of first hand experiences:

> If you give only a quick glance you will surely miss the experience. But if you stop, look carefully, walk around the sculpture and watch it change as you see it from different angles, you will be able to make some astonishing discoveries.
>
> (Finn 1989: 11)

> The requirement that 'they look carefully' is not only the most important, but is also the most difficult to achieve. In our experience this is best done by sketching. The children are required to choose from among the objects related to their theme any that they prefer and to make notes about them in the form of charcoal or pencil sketches.
>
> (Marcousé 1983, cited in Taylor 1986: 137)

The class is a Key Stage One group of twenty-two children in a school with forty children on roll. There are two full time and one part time teachers. The building is very small with both KS1 and KS2 children in the one teaching area. The children are from mixed social backgrounds, some travelling from outside the village. For the research I worked with five Year 2 pupils Michael, Emmalene, Luke, Charlotte and Christine, chosen as being the least likely to feel inhibited by the use of a tape recorder and/or video camera. We discussed the reasons for having video and tape recordings made of the visits to the gallery, and the work in class (in order to provide me with evidence to help improve my teaching). We discussed the access that I should have to their individual work, and, whilst the majority said that I could use it as I wished, Charlotte and Emmalene wanted the opportunity to take their work home to share with their families before I used it.

I personally had had very little experience of art in any form. I had never studied sculpture, either as part of my own education, or with children.

WHERE ARE THE SCULPTURES?

I explained that we would be visiting an art gallery. None of the children had previously visited one. When I asked them what they thought they would see, they replied 'paintings, drawings and people painting'. I asked if they knew anything about sculptures and they said they were models. One child thought we were discussing vultures, and pictures had to be produced to correct that.

The first visit was quite informal, the children free to choose what interested them, to sketch these objects, and to gain some idea of what an art gallery might contain (Figure 13.1). They moved around the gallery quite slowly, asking questions and making observations about various exhibits. Michael was intrigued by Giacometti's sculpture entitled *Femme*, wondering if it had been dug up. He also pointed to the picture hanging nearby and said, 'It's a picture of the model,' whilst Luke remarked, 'It could be a plan for the sculpture.' John Davies' *Bucket Man* also provoked much discussion. Charlotte pointed out the string around his mouth and suggested that it was to stop his head from falling off, whilst Emmalene thought, 'It's holding that thing behind his neck on.' There were many suggestions for the spherical object on his head. Charlotte thought it was a bomb. Emmalene thought this was a silly suggestion and said, 'It's one of those things that comes out of a cannon.' Luke disagreed and said, 'No, I think they've been playing a game and someone's trying to shoot an apple off his head.' It appeared that he did not know the story of William Tell, which I thought might have led to this opinion. Michael remarked, 'He's very dirty. Is there a real man in there?'

Their interest was sustained for far longer than I had anticipated. As we left the gallery I presented each child with a letter for their parents. This requested that their parents discuss the visit with their children and record any comments they might make. One reason for doing this was that in the group there are twin girls who are selective mutes and I knew that they would not talk to me about the visit. In order that they did not feel singled out I gave the task to everyone. Within a few days all the children brought in a reply, ranging from a list of the exhibits seen to the children's thoughts on various exhibits. These were encouraging, especially those returned by Emmalene whose mother commented, 'Emmalene enjoyed the trip and seemed stimulated and interested when she came home.' Luke told his mother that 'he enjoyed the visit and would like to go to other art galleries'. A number of parents also indicated to me that they would be interested in accompanying us on the follow-up visits.

The children also commented on their visit to Year 6 children, who helped with the research by using a tape recorder. This was again because of the twins, who would make comments to other children but not to me. In retrospect this was probably not a very good idea as one Year 6 pupil put words into their mouths and made assumptions, especially about *Bucket Man*. As a result, some of the children think he represents a poor person from the Victorian era. Claire (Year 6) asked Charlotte what a bucket man is and received the reply that he carries ash around:

a) *Bucket Man*

b) *Femme*

c) *Mother and Child*

Figure 13.1 Luke's first-visit sketches

CLAIRE   Oh. Do you think he's a rich or a poor person?

CHARLOTTE   Poor.

CLAIRE   You think he's a poor. I think he's a poor 'cos rich people would have servants to take their ash out, wouldn't they?

CHARLOTTE   Mmmmmmmm.

CLAIRE   Yeah. Was he in Victorian age . . . or was he in this age?

CHARLOTTE   Victorian.

The children showed common interest in just a few objects. I decided for the follow-up visits to concentrate on four pieces, in order to make comparisons between the children's responses over the period of the project (Figure 13.2). I also knew that similar projects were under way in other schools, and that the evidence could be compared. The focus was on: John Davies' *Bucket Man*; Edgar Degas' *Petite danseuse de quatorze ans*; Alberto Giacometti's *Femme*; Henry Moore's *Mother and Child*.

The children were happy with these choices as long as they had some time to look at other exhibits which also interested them. In preparation for our second visit we looked at pictures of the sculptures that were to be studied in more detail and tried to link them to the names of their sculptors. At this stage the only name that appeared to register was that of Henry Moore. They had looked at two large bronzes and the *Mother and Child*, and some had made the observation that 'Henry Moore made models with small heads'. We also discussed what materials a sculptor might use and they suggested wood, stone, bronze, clay and ice. Someone had seen ice sculptures of a shoe, bear, bird and head on television.

THE SECOND VISIT

The purpose of the second visit was to look in much more detail at the chosen sculptures, to get the children to make their own observations, and to produce sketches from these. The visit was video-recorded by a parent. The children were able to give their own views of the pieces after being encouraged by a guide to look at the sculptures from different directions:

GUIDE   I would like you to go and perhaps sit on that side of it and then this side of it and look round it, always look round it. So go and have a little stare from that way. Have a little stare from various different directions.

Looking at *Femme* the following comments were made:

GUIDE   We look at it and we say is it a . . .? What is it?

PUPIL   A skeleton.

a) *Bucket Man*

b) *Little Dancer*

c) *Mother and Child*

d) *Femme*

Figure 13.2 Christine's first- and second-visit sketches

GUIDE   You think of it as a skeleton. What do *you* think?
EMMALENE   A person.
CHARLOTTE   A lady.
GUIDE   A lady? You [*to each*] see a skeleton, a person, a lady. Anybody, any other things?

[*Leoni giggles and makes a comment.*]

GUIDE   You think she hasn't any clothes on.
ROBERT   She has!
GUIDE   You see clothes on her, *you* don't. Right, that's very interesting.

After the visit the children were given a picture of each sculpture. They were asked to talk about the sculptures with their parents. The parents were asked to record their children's comments and observations. Responses were received in the next few days, more detailed than the first set. Some children chose to write their own comments, and the child who had merely given a list of exhibits the first time had this time chosen to give her opinion of the Degas bronze.

The children were also able to watch the video with some of their parents in class. Each time the tape was paused at one of the sculptures the comments came flowing. The biggest clamour at the end of the session was to be allowed to take the video home to show to the rest of the family. It was particularly noticeable that now, after revisiting the sculptures and talking about them in detail, the names of the sculptors seemed like second nature to the children. Comments such as 'That's by Giacometti, there was a head of his wife there too,' and 'Degas made the ballerina, he made her out of wax first,' were commonplace.

Books showing works of Degas, Moore and Giacometti were introduced for the children to use during reading times and free choice sessions. They were seized by eager hands, the Year 2 children imparting some of the knowledge they had gained to Year 1 and Reception children. Comments such as 'This book has Giacometti's sculptures in it'; 'See, I told you Henry Moore made things with little heads'; 'Oh look, there's a picture plan of that sculpture,' were heard coming from small groups clustered around the teaching area.

Younger children found several books with identical sculptures in each one. Comments were made on the fact that Degas had painted pictures as well as producing sculptures, that he produced horses and lots of other ballerinas too. The Year 2 children used the books to find works they had actually seen. They were able to identify the *Little Dancer* and told the younger children about the skirt: 'It's the original. . . . She's got another one to take away with her. . . . That one's too fragile. . . . It's the only original one.' They identified *Femme* correctly, and the drawing by Giacometti which is in the gallery. They could not find the specific

Mother and Child by Moore, but they did find many more sculptures on the same theme and they started to point out the differences between those in the books and the one they had actually seen. 'She's not on a stool. . . . The baby's in a different position. . . . Her arms aren't the same' were some of the comments heard.

A MASTER AT WORK

Seeing the sculptor Jack Gillespie at work modelling a head was the next stage. Starting with an armature and a piece of clay he demonstrated the processes involved in creating the head of a young man about 17 years of age. Having created the head, he then set about gradually ageing it until he finished with the head of a man about 70 years of age. He explained every stage to the children and emphasised the need to know about bone structure and to observe faces carefully. He held their attention for the whole time as they watched the clay being transformed, showing that it is a medium which can be altered at various stages of modelling. Their own work with clay immediately after the visit produced some detailed observational models.

The children were still very interested in the art books and picked them up at odd moments. Kay found the ballerina: 'There's lots of her – she hasn't got any clothes on here.' She soon had a group clustered around the book looking at the different wax models. Luke found some paintings by Degas. He commented on *At the Races*: 'I like the way the shadows have been done. They look as though they're actually moving.' One group was looking at different types of work by Giacometti and they found a copy of the original sketch they had seen in the gallery. Leoni remarked: 'The head on that one is like a ball, but the one on the sculpture is more like an egg.' The children made comments that show their close observation of the subject, the kind of observations I would not have imagined possible before we started this work.

THE THIRD VISIT

On the third visit I wanted the children to observe the four sculptures closely and to make any sketches of them that they wished. They now started to look at the pieces in much greater detail. Michael started to make observations about the ballerina's fingers and observed that some have the nails shown and some do not:

MICHAEL   Some haven't even got one.
P.O.   Some haven't got a nail and some have. That one has, hasn't it? And that one hasn't.
MICHAEL   Yeah. If you can see that little . . . that one has.

P.O.   Yes. Why do you think some of them have got them? Why has he given some of them nails and some not, do you think?

MICHAEL   I think he didn't have time and when he came back from work or something it was all dried out.

P.O.   Ah, the wax had dried out and he couldn't actually change it then?

MICHAEL   Yeah.

Michael appeared to be trying to understand the properties of certain media. With this remark he seems to have thought that wax has similar properties to clay and that once it has dried it cannot be altered. That is not true of either clay or wax and clearly there was a need for further work here, but inquisitiveness might be a good basis for that. He also observed her hair carefully, and tried to see under the ribbon to find out how the hair was tied. He liked the wrinkles in her tights and the 'way her shoe and foot turned over'. Referring to her expression he said:

> I think she's tired because if she goes to school first and she does all that work, then I think she's tired. It's a fairly painful thing to be a ballet dancer. It's like doing PE every day, all day, including Sundays, and you get very stiff and you get very tired and you think, 'I'd love to do French, I'd love to do something else.' But they have to do ballet all the time to become a famous ballerina.

Michael was again at the forefront of the discussion on *Mother and Child*. He pointed out how the fingers and toes were represented, and he liked the way in which the fingers were foreshortened. He also pointed out the almost imperceptible line of the spine:

MICHAEL   It's not straight but it's got a little line down here.

P.O.   Yes it has, hasn't it? It's not absolutely straight, it's got that curve to give the bit where the back goes in, in between, like your spine goes down and your shoulders sticking out.

He did not think that the baby's legs were out of proportion:

P.O.   Look at the size of the baby and look at the leg.

MICHAEL   No, that's a bit, a bit of the muscle.

P.O.   Oh, you think that's the muscle?

CHARLOTTE   It's got a ponytail.

MICHAEL   Yeah, you see there's a muscle down here when you bend your leg [*demonstrates*].

He was on his hands and knees to look at the feet of *Bucket Man*. He decided that the sculptor had intended to put shoes on him, because no toes are marked on the feet as they are with the *Mother and Child*.

MICHAEL   I think he's just barefoot.

P.O.   He's just got bare feet.

MICHAEL   No. I actually think he's got shoes on, because the way he hasn't got lines down there. I think he's got shoes on.

He also started to compare the hands and the feet and how the hands prove to be very detailed.

Emmalene thought the ballet dancer was tired: 'She's happy because in ballet you have to look kind of sad but you are happy really.' Compare this with her initial reaction reported by her mother: 'Emmalene thinks she looked sad and fed up with ballet.'

Giacometti's *Femme* this time provoked the following conversation:

P.O.   Do you like this, then?

ALL   Yes.

P.O.   Did you like it the first time you saw it?

LUKE   No, it looked like a skeleton.

P.O.   Luke thought it looked like a skeleton the first time you saw it. Why do you like it now, then, Luke? What's made you like it now?

LUKE   Because now that I know it's *not* a skeleton, that's why I like it.

P.O.   Is that the only reason you like it now, because it's not a skeleton or is there anything else?

CHARLOTTE   And he knows it's a girl.

Luke, after more detailed observation of the piece and gaining some background knowledge of the sculptor, was now able to appreciate the work and changed his mind completely from his initial visit. Here is evidence of a response based on feelings which his initial interpretation of the work had invoked. Other changed responses seemed to be based on reflections about their initial ideas. Some appeared to reject their theory about the spherical object on *Bucket Man*'s head being a bomb and now referred to it as a ball. Charlotte asked what the thing around his neck was. Michael thought it might hold the ball if it fell back. Emmalene thought it was 'just because if there's coldness coming to it, it might, the coldness might just bounce back off it and go back to where it came from.' Luke thought it could be a form of protection 'for his head if he fell backwards'. Talk about the feelings provoked by what was observed is shown in the following extract, in which Luke also volunteers a reason for his observation:

P.O.   How do you think he's feeling, this man?

EMMALENE   Angry.

LUKE   Sad, because he has to work all the time and he doesn't get much time to break.

P.O.   How do you think he feels, Charlotte?

CHARLOTTE   Sad, crying.

The children spent a great deal of time during this visit sketching the sculptures. I thought the sketches showed an improvement from their work on the initial visit, in their attention to detail (Figures 13.3a, and 13.4b). Some of them were shaded to give more sense of form and depth. Some children sketched the same piece from different directions. They also all appeared to be much more confident about attempting to sketch, the later sketches being much bolder. Some of them, especially Emmalene, were starting to alter their sketches when they realised that they were not a satisfactory portrayal of what they wanted to record.

PRACTICAL WORK

The fact that there is only one teaching area for the whole school and that this area is of a very limited size meant that there was nowhere to set up an area for the children to be able to pursue artwork exclusively. They did, however, make the best use of their time that they could, given the circumstances. Emmalene asked if she could draw and then make a sculpture of her drawing. She was joined by Robert, Charlotte and Kay. They drew a plan and then used the Plasticine. Emmalene's head worked according to plan and she plaited some Plasticine together to make the hair, saying, 'I know how to plait this and this is what I want, but I couldn't draw it like this.' She continued to make her model but eventually came to me in tears, 'because it won't all stay together and stand up!'

Robert made a version of *Bucket Man*, which he made to stand by attaching the feet directly to the body. Kay produced a very realistic elephant eating an apple. It had a solid support shape with the legs marked out, but not separated. Charlotte produced a lady, but it did not resemble her sketch. Talking about their work later, Emmalene said hers was now a 'lying down girl'. Robert said his would not stand up when he put legs on, so his solution had been to put the feet straight onto the body. After further discussion Luke remarked, 'The legs are too thin and the body's too heavy. If you made stronger legs they'd stand.' I asked the children why they had drawn a sketch first. The reply was that they had seen sketches of the sculptures by Henry Moore and Degas in the books and had thought they would try to do one of their own.

The children had the opportunity to work with clay again and this time they were asked to produce a sketch of their intended piece of work before they began. Emmalene again attempted a person with plaits and this time she succeeded in getting it to stand by using Robert's method of attaching the feet directly on to the body. Kay drew a girl taking a dog for a walk (Figure 13.5). The attention to detail in her sketch was then transposed very accurately in her model. Robert drew a very simple person (Figure 13.6) but then produced an intricate boy, wearing a cap, on a skateboard. This time he gave the model legs.

Figure 13.3 (a) Kay's first-visit sketch of *Little Dancer*

RETROSPECTIVE

Looking back on the work completed I found that the children had started to observe in far more detail than I had been aware of previously. By the second visit they were starting to look more closely at the pieces and to give their views and ideas of what the sculptures represented. During that visit they were encouraged to look at the pieces from different

Figure 13.3 (b) Kay's third-visit drawing of *Little Dancer*, showing more detail on dress and legs, arms placed behind back, and feet (after correction) positioned more accurately

directions, as suggested by Finn (1989). Background information was given about particular pieces, and connections began to be made between them. The use of books on the sculptors extended that process and the younger children in the class were drawn into the conversations. The older children gave them additional information which they had gained from the visit.

During the third visit the children responded differently to the pieces. I felt that the children had gradually begun to appreciate sculpture in complex ways. Some evidence showed that their knowledge of sculptors

Figure 13.4 (a) Kay's first-visit sketch of *Bucket Man*

Figure 13.4 (b) Kay's third-visit drawing of *Bucket Man* shows a greatly improved self-confidence and attention to detail in comparison to her first sketch

Figure 13.5 Kay's sketch of *Lady and Dog*. She carefully transferred details (bows on shoes, in hair) from this sketch to her model of a girl and dog

had increased and they were able to compare pieces of work by the same sculptor and talk about them with confidence. They had seen a sculptor at work and looked at some of the different materials that sculptors use. They had also begun to use different materials in school to produce 3D models and to appreciate the different properties of these materials,

Figure 13.6 Boy on a Skateboard. Robert's preparatory sketch was developed into a model of a boy with cap, detailed face and, on this occasion, legs

progressing from using Plasticine to clay, and realising that clay has to be kept damp to be workable. Emmalene observed that if the joins were not made correctly, 'bits fell off and we didn't know that to begin with'. They had also come to realise that in order to make models stand, they could use different solutions to the problem. Following the third visit they started to explore the use of Mod-Roc and wire, learning about their properties. It is too early to report on their results in this medium. They also began to realise that by planning their work they could sometimes achieve better results. They came to this conclusion on their own.

The children are now able to look at something afresh and to sketch and record what they see. They have begun to form judgements about what they have seen and to talk about their feelings about what they have observed. They have also had access to a variety of artists' work which has enabled them to compare techniques and materials, as well as styles. I now know that it is possible for young children to observe sculpture in great detail and that they are able to change their original observations. This can be achieved if they are given the time to look closely and sketch, and by using questioning techniques in the gallery which require them to look at the pieces more closely, asking for their judgements on different aspects of the sculptures. Receiving additional background information on the sculptor and his or her work can also add to their greater understanding, but the timing of this and the way in which the knowledge is imparted can be varied, both in and out of the gallery.

FURTHER READING

Department for Education (1995) *Art in the National Curriculum*, London: Her Majesty's Stationery Office.

Finn, D. (1989) *How to Look at Sculpture*, New York: Harry N. Abrams.

Marcousé, R. (1974) *Using Objects: Visual Learning and Visual Awareness in the Museum and Classroom*, London: Van Nostrand Reinhold.

—— (1983) *The Listening Eye*, London: Her Majesty's Stationery Office.

Schools Council (1978) *Art 7–11*, London: Schools Council.

Taylor, R. (1986) *Educating for Art: Critical Response and Development*, Harlow: Longman.

Chapter 14

American North West Coast art, story, and computer animation

Rachel Reed

My initial interest in using the device of story to interpret art began when teaching my class of Year 5 children about the works of some Victorian artists. This was part of a humanities project on the Victorians. It fascinated me that certain artists used very clear images in their work to convey a story with a message to the observer. I noticed that the children looked very closely at the paintings to try to fathom out the stories behind them. This device appeared to give the children the chance to interpret what they saw and make it part of their understanding of the Victorian period and some of its art. When I was planning the North West Coast project I wondered if, by using the same format with artefacts in the Sainsbury Collection, the children would offer the same kinds of response, as these are different kinds of objects, from a distinctly different culture. I realised that the Victorian painters wanted the observer to interpret their work in ways which were part of 'our' culture.

With the North West Coast artefacts the meanings which they might originally have been made to convey were not necessarily significant in our quite different cultural context. This factor made the idea of using objects from another culture as a stimulus for children's art even more interesting. Although the children could learn about the artists' original intentions, they could be free to make their own interpretations of the subjects, and to devise creative projects in other media, thus making art which is meaningful to them, in their own circumstances.

I wanted the project to be exciting and different from what they had done before. My class of twenty-three children were in their first year in middle school. The school serves a small market town, and its pupils represent a wide range of social backgrounds in an entirely monocultural, white community. Over a number of years older children in the school have been successful, locally and nationally, in writing and publishing poetry. I chose the American North West Pacific Coast objects partly for these reasons. I also chose to base part of the project on the computer program *Art and Time*, in an attempt to ensure that the children, in studying another culture, would not merely try to imitate its art when they made their own work. *Art and Time* is a program which enables *Paintspa* pictures drawn by the children to be animated. It was new to me and, I believed, new to the children, but I felt it would be a useful tool in handling and extending the notion of story, and in transforming ideas from one art form to another.

Taylor (1986) claims to have found storytelling a useful tool in helping children to interpret what they see in art objects. His general concern is with helping a child to look constructively and in a prolonged way at an object, rather than looking casually or instantly dismissing it. He found through his research that:

> children recall plenty of detail, but are certainly not restricted simply to listing objects, for they are equally sensitive to the mood and symbolism of the work. Of course, they had done extensive research and practical work of their own and discussed Winner's imagery with the artist, gallery staff and teachers, but four months later, it is the mood and atmosphere of the works which they so vividly recall.
>
> (Taylor 1986: 112)

He claims that storytelling and narrative work can advance his aim to develop this kind of attitude and information handling. The device of storytelling, he says, is a way of identifying with the personal ideas of children, and using it is a way of connecting prior interests with the study of works of art:

> Much research in art education has ignored or denigrated the importance of initial storytelling and speculation in the child's development of a genuine understanding of a work of art. I think that when a child tells a story about a work – be it a Leonardo or a Lowry – this is the stage when he or she can hypothesise, can tentatively reach out to a work of art and invest it with personal meaning.
>
> (Taylor 1986: 261)

Deciding just what this notion of investment with personal meaning might imply in relation to objects from a different kind of art and distinct culture was a matter which I would need to explore. My teaching aims for the project were:

- To develop the children's knowledge and understanding of the North West Coast American people, through their art;
- To encourage the children to observe and interpret art objects through the use of characterisation;
- To extend the children's knowledge of North West Coast America art by using the device of story;
- To use all of the above as a basis for the children's construction of their own computer art.

Beyond the work in the gallery, which involved observing, sketching, and 'characterisation' of the art objects, the strategies I chose to use included:

- Adopting the genre of folk tales to encourage the children to write their own stories incorporating ideas based on some of the artefacts they saw;
- Encouraging the pupils to imagine personal characteristics for the displayed artefacts and develop them in their stories;
- Using books about the area to put their study of art objects and folk tales into context;
- Giving the opportunity for a range of interpretations, adaptations and personal ideas through the writing of their own stories;
- Using *Art and Time* to transform what they saw and their own stories into a different art form, set in their own contemporary context.

My research aims were to investigate how the teaching strategies based on the notion of story help children to interpret art objects. I also wanted to know how they would use them in their own artwork in ways which are transformed to their own situations and creative opportunities. I collected various forms of evidence during the project so that I could analyse whether, through my teaching strategies, my aims for the project had been achieved. I will describe how each aim was tackled and my judgement of the success of each strategy, based on the evidence. The evidence I chose to gather included:

- Children's drawings of the North West Coast region at the beginning and end of the project;
- Audio taped records of what the class deduced from selected objects by close observation;
- A written record of the folk tales made up by individuals in response to the art objects;
- Video records of computer animations devised as a result of the stories created;
- Questionnaire responses to find out what the children understood.

In planning the project, questions arose which I hoped to answer by collecting the following range of evidence:

Before and after pictures

- How much will the children learn about the culture during the project?

Sketches made and the transcribed tape

- How will the children respond to the tasks set?
- Will they be able to interpret what they see in a way which is meaningful to them?

Stories written in response to the visit

- By writing stories will the children be able to develop ideas around the character devised from the object they drew?
- Will this help them when transferring their ideas into *Art and Time*?

The questionnaire

- Did the children transfer their interpretation of the objects they saw into their work?
- Did the story help them in their interpretation?
- Did they work in the style of the North West Coast artists?
- Did their observations and characterisation influence their work?

The Art and Time *pictures and interviews with the children*

- Do the animations show interpretation or copying?
- Do they reflect what the children saw at the gallery?

PREPARATORY LESSONS

The preparation for the visit to the gallery consisted of two lessons. In one the children used maps to find out about the environment in which the people live(d). In the second they learned about some of the visual conventions in their art and painted an animal in the traditional style. I began by finding out what the children already knew about the North West Coast Americans. We looked for clues in maps of the area. Lists were written during a brainstorming session. For example, environment: lots of conifer trees, hardly any crops, mountains, a few silver mines, they eat fish, temperature in January −20°C and in July +20°C, oil fields, windy, hydroelectric power, copper and gold supplies, Alpine; names of places: Red Deer, Reindeer Lake, White Horse, Yellow Knife, Great Bear Lake, Old Crow, Swift Current.

After the brain-storming session the children worked on pictures of their images of North American native people. Their images were based on what they had learned by looking at the maps and their personal knowledge. They did not distinguish between the North West Coast people and the Plains Indians, so many of their images were based on films they had seen. Many referred to the Walt Disney film *Peter Pan* in which Indians frequently appeared. Over the next few days they brought in artefacts from home including moccasins, models, rugs, books and a complete set of Indian Playmobile.

In preparation for the gallery visit I wanted the children to be familiar with the traditional artistic style of the North West Coast Americans. I began by introducing the children to the basic shapes of their art:

the ovoid and the U-shape. I also explained how traditionally art forms flow to make one overall, unified shape. The children did a puzzle to see if these rules applied to examples found in books. They counted the ovoid and U-shapes and tried to distinguish what animals the art forms represented.

In the next lesson the children made templates of ovoids and U-shapes and used the templates to create their own animals. Once they had drawn their animals I explained to them about the traditional use of colour. For example, black is sometimes used for the outline of shapes, and as a dominant infill colour of shapes. White is also used, providing contrast. Red and green are commonly used for shapes or covering the surface of objects. I also explained that a gap is often left between the outline and the coloured shapes, or between the shapes themselves, revealing the natural colour of materials from which the objects are made. Examples of these traditional principles helped the children to design and paint their various animals accordingly.

THE VISIT

During the visit the children's tasks included making two sketches. They were able to choose from any of the North West Coast exhibits. They also had to answer three questions about their chosen objects: what is its appearance? (describe it); what personality might the figure have? (say why); what would he/she say if able to tell you a story?

The class was split into three groups, each with an adult guide. My group consisted of ten children, six boys and four girls, and it is the experience of these children which formed the focus of my research. We began by looking at a particular group of objects. The children commented that most of the exhibits were made mainly of wood. The shoulder blanket was a notable exception. They noticed the traditional shapes in the exhibits, the ovoid and the U-shapes. They chose the objects they were going to use for their drawings: a bird clapper, a bird rattle, a head-dress frontlet, and a seal. None of the group chose the shoulder blanket or the grease bowl, although children from the other groups did choose these items. Most of them wanted to tell me their observations and ideas about the 'personality' of their chosen object.

Tim chose the head-dress frontlet which he described as having a long nose and looking like a crow. He thought the object would try to get revenge on others and if it could speak would say 'Get lost!' Francis chose the bird clapper, and commented that it was like a mother with children. He thought she would be normal and caring and would say 'Hello, children'. Liam chose the seal, which he described as stupid-looking because of the expression on its face. He thought if it could speak it would say 'Please rescue me'. They all worked carefully on their sketches, noticing and recording small details and drawing the object from different angles of observation.

The group also looked at the North American exhibits in another section of the gallery. After looking at all the objects available the children each chose the exhibit they were going to observe closely and draw. Two children chose a head-dress frontlet. Neil quickly offered a suggestion about the purpose of the frontlet: 'It's like on the forehead of Tutankhamun, like a snake going up there.' Francis related to this as he had also seen the same image during the Egyptian project in the Autumn term. They decided this object represented a bear because of the teeth and the paws. Again they noticed the ovoid and U-shapes in the object. They commented that it had ovoids in the eyes and the eyebrows were U-shaped. They did not recognise the small pieces on the side of the head-dress as shell, but Neil commented that they looked like petrol in a puddle. I asked them what character the frontlet might have, and Francis said that he was like the Joker from Batman: 'He's got that little smile round his mouth and he's a bit bad tempered.'

Frances also chose the head-dress frontlet for her close observation and drawing. She thought that it was a bear who was evil because of the grin on its face. She commented that in her story she would write about him working for a witch trying to capture something. She also thought that if he could speak he would say 'I'll get them back for this'.

Towards the end of the session I thought that the children were becoming much more confident with the idea of making their own suggestions and interpretation of the personality of the objects. The following transcription of a discussion between seven children in the group, about three wooden knives, illustrates their understanding of the task and their own interpretations:

TIM   I think that middle one looks like an Egyptian Pharaoh.

FRANCIS   I reckon it looks like a billy goat.

FRANCES   It's quite nice, isn't it?

LIAM   Yeah, Billy goat, Billy Goat Gruff.

TIM   A lioness to me, lioness with a beard.

SARA   But a lioness is a girl.

R.R.   Why have they chosen that to go on a knife?

TIM   It gives him wisdom.

ANN   And it protects him when they fight.

TIM   Yeah, when they fight it gives him wisdom so they know what to do.

R.R.   You had that idea earlier about him being a god.

FRANCIS   It looks like a god, don't it?

ANN   Yeah, he protects them.

R.R.   What did you want to say?

SARA   It looks like a bear. They kill bears and use it like that and use the idea of a bear.

TIM   [*interrupts*] Maybe it is a little bit like a bear and the bear scares the enemies away from them.

SARA   Like a special bear hunt.

R.R.   Do you think that the people show respect for animals?

ANN   Yeah, yeah. 'Cos that's why they live in the country – in the rain forest they respect the wildlife.

FRANCES   Respects his god. When he fights he can remind him of when he fights.

TIM   He can give him confidence when he fights.

SARA   It has got a little face that the owl is sitting on.

R.R.   What is the owl sitting on?

SARA   It looks like a snake.

NEIL   It looks like another bird.

SARA   Hang on, that's got arms there. It's got arms going up and then . . .

TIM   [*interrupts*] That's what I am trying to tell you. It's clinging on to a little animal.

SARA   That's its prey.

NEIL   When they go hunting they use it as a club and then they're meant to be like an owl when they catch their prey.

R.R.   Any ideas what the owl might say?

TIM   It's quite wise and doesn't speak very much. It might tell you to take care and watch out really slowly. It cares about people. It's like the leader of the town. It tells people what to do.

FRANCIS   Yeah, like take care on your journey. When they've got problems he cheers them up.

FOLLOW-UP WORK

The follow-up to the visit began with the children listening to a number of folk tales from a tape called *The Keeper of the Earth – Native American Indian Stories*. We discussed why the people tell folk tales. The children decided that it showed their understanding of how things happen. They had been particularly impressed by the legend called *How The Sea Came To Be* in which a young girl loses her fingers, which become the whales and seals of the sea. We discussed how the sketches could be used to write their own story. They selected and looked at one of their sketches, deciding on a 'personality characteristic' of the artefact which they had previously noted and which could be extended. They imagined how the animal obtained this trait, as a basis for their story, and created working titles. Some examples of the children's ideas included: How The

Crab Got His Shell, How The Walrus Got His Teeth, How The Whale Became So Shy, How the Raven Became So Cheeky.

Throughout the project, fiction and non-fiction books about the North American native people were available to the children. During this time they worked on a task called 'fact or fiction'. The children wrote down as many statements as they could from what they knew of the people. A list compiled as part of the fact or fiction lesson said that:

- They live in wigwams;
- They carve on bits of wood called totem poles;
- They eat lots of fish;
- They name lots of places by the names of animals;
- They wear very bright clothes;
- They fight with the cowboys;
- They cook on camp fires;
- They live out in the open;
- They kill animals for their food;
- They love art.

They chose some of their statements to investigate, using books to find out if the statements were fact or fiction, and they wrote down and drew what they discovered. They tackled as many statements as they could. Towards the end of the project I felt that, although the children had gained greater knowledge of the people and their art, many of their preconceived ideas towards the culture still existed. After the visit and the completion of their stories the children worked on their *Art and Time* animations. They worked in pairs, each pair given two hours of teacher supervised computer time. During this time the children were expected to become familiar with the program and to produce an animation based upon a character they had devised. Their sketches and stories were available to help them to achieve this.

In becoming familiar with the program most children needed to revise their understanding of *Paintspa*, a basic art program. Most were familiar with changing colours, filling in shapes and drawing their picture. Few had ever experimented with the different brushes available or used the zoom facility when adding detail. I began my teaching of the program by making each group aware of what was available to them in *Paintspa*. After allowing some time to explore the facilities we moved on to the storing of the picture.

The *Art and Time* program differs from *Paintspa* in that after storing a number of pictures, which are basically the same but with slight alterations, it plays them in sequence, so that the picture appears to move. Whilst showing the program to the children I also emphasised the importance of making a gradual change to each picture, otherwise the animation would not flow and could appear disjointed. The children began by discussing with their partner whose drawing and/or story they were going to base the animation on. Once they decided this, they discussed with me how they intended to show the personality of the character in the animation.

Neil and John chose one of the wooden knives which Neil had drawn. They thought the sketch looked like a pig and Neil had described it as 'cheeky and funny'. They decided to draw a pig's head with a funny and cheeky face. As the animation progressed they moved the pig's mouth and rolled its eyes. They also changed the colour of the pig's mouth and included a rising sun in the background. Sara and Claire chose a comb which Sara had sketched. Sara also based her story 'How The Crab Got His Shell' on the comb, which she thought was like a crab. In the story the crab hid away from others because it was always frightened. In their animation they drew the crab moving from side to side and moving its eyes, creating a nervous impression. In the background they drew a fishing boat which is also mentioned in the story.

LOOKING AT THE DATA

The data which I gathered were used to search for evidence which could help me to answer the questions I had in mind at the start of the research. It is only possible here to record a summary of what I deduced from each of the kinds of data.

Pictures

The children drew two pictures during the project, the first during the maps lesson and the other at the end of the project. Both pictures were drawn under the same instruction: the children could choose any aspect of Indian life to base their picture on; in both pictures they had to base their work on what they knew about North American Indians; while working on the pictures they could not refer to any information other than their own thoughts and understanding.

The power of their preconceived ideas at the beginning of the project surprised me. In spite of guidance towards various books and the visit to the gallery, these strong stereotype images remained. By the end of the project the Indians still said 'How' and fought cowboys. The children also had difficulty in separating the past from the present. I assumed that the pictures would drastically change over the project time, and that the children's preconceived ideas would be more malleable. The project did not dispel their basic views.

Sketches

The children drew two sketches. From these I wanted to know, first, how children responded to the task and, second, if the children were able in their drawing to interpret what they saw in a way meaningful to them. All the sketches were drawn under the same conditions: the children first looked at all the exhibits; next they chose one exhibit that appealed to them; then, when sketching it, they had three questions to answer about its appearance, its personality, and what it would say if it could speak. They sketched it in as much detail as they could and drew it from different angles.

When listening to the children in the gallery and analysing the sketches it seemed clear that they enjoyed imagining that the exhibit was a real live personality. They observed closely and drew in great detail because they were looking for any evidence that would tell them the personality of the exhibit. As the day progressed the children became more confident in their verbal expression of ideas. For example, the transcribed conversation shows the children discussing the purpose and personality of each of the knives in turn. By the end of the conversation the characters appeared to have come alive to them, and to have active roles in their original social contexts. The children responded in the way that I had hoped they would, by constructing their own stories based on what they observed.

Stories

From reading the finished stories I wanted to find out if the children had developed the character and its story, derived from the object they had drawn. I also wondered if the finished story would influence their animation work. All the stories were written in response to the same task: they included at least one of the artefacts sketched, and they were written in the genre of a folk tale explaining how something came to be. The trait 'that came to be' in the story had to be based on something that the children noticed when observing the artefact.

All but two out of twenty-three stories included one of the characters that the children had sketched, and all the children did develop the character of their chosen artefact by adding their own ideas to what they had recorded at the time of the visit.

Questionnaire

The children completed a questionnaire at the end of the project, devised to establish if they believed that they had worked in the style of North West Coast art, and that their sketches and stories had influenced their animation work. Twenty-three pupils completed it. All the children said they found the task of making two detailed sketches attainable. When asked about their story all except two said they based the character in their story on at least one of the artefacts they had drawn. When asked about their familiarity with *Art and Time* only seven said they knew how to use the program at the beginning. By the end of the project all the children could use it.

Animations

When asked about what they had based their animation on the majority answered that they based their animation only on their sketches. They also said that they used their story as a basis for their animation. (Since the story itself was based on the observations, sketching, and characterisation, and on the folk tale lesson, my questionnaire clearly needed rethinking! I had not distinguished between the animation character and the story/setting, but seemingly the children had.) I wanted to find out the extent to which the animations showed evidence of the direct use of the images of the artefacts, interpretation close to it, or transformation in the children's own terms. When I looked at their finished animations it appeared that they were influenced by the background and follow-up work. The red raven of Sue and Frances was made up of ovoid and U-shapes as well as being backed by snow-capped mountains. Frank and Ben's wolf was accompanied by a native person in costume, a teepee, a red sun, and a tree. The 'personality' of the artefact could be seen clearly in some of the animations: Sara and Claire's frightened crab jumping from side to side and moving its eyes in a frightened way; Matthew and Michael's cheeky raven stealing a worm. In terms of how far the children had copied, interpreted, or transformed what they had seen, the animations included drawings which appeared very close in style to the original object; some in which the main character appeared to be a mixture of influences; and some which were completely in the children's own style.

CONCLUSIONS

The conclusions I drew from the preparatory work, the gallery visit and the follow-up work, bearing in mind my original aims for the project, can be summarised as follows. The preparatory lessons were useful for the children because they put the children's study and interpretations of the art objects into context. When the children visited the gallery many knew which works were from the North West Pacific Coast because they had learned about traditional art forms before the visit. They were able to place their stories and animations in the context of the place and culture, because of the preparatory work. The before and after pictures showed that the children's knowledge of the North West Coast native Americans had greatly increased in its detail. However, the pictures also showed that the children had very strong images in their minds of what the people were like. These basic images did not alter. They were simply embellished with that detail.

The notion of story seemed to work well in the context of the gallery visit. It directed the children's focus when observing the objects. The sketches showed the attention to detail that they gave when drawing what they saw. It also provided a theme for developing the characterisation of the objects so that the children were very clear about their character when they came to write their stories.

The writing of stories and the creation of animations based on the genre of the folk tale constrained the children in their written interpretation of what they saw, as they were obliged to work with such a highly structured format. It would be interesting in the future to see if they could use other formats to generate their interpretations of art objects, and how they would respond to them.

The stories were generally not used in the animation quite as I had anticipated. In writing their stories the children interpreted what they saw by bringing to their work prior knowledge and understanding, including some individual idiosyncrasies. On reflection, the sequence of tasks was very complex. I expected the children to make shifts from reading, listening, receiving instructions, observing, and imagining, to the technical construction of characterisations and stories, in two media of expression. The animation work proved to be much more demanding than I had envisaged. The two hours of teaching time each child received was largely spent becoming familiar with the program. The nature of the task required the children to use their original sketch and the extent to which the products were based on copying, interpretation, and transformation varied among the children. In spite of these unforeseen outcomes the children completed the tasks involved and produced some interesting work of their own. The children's enthusiasm for, and experience of, the computer program has meant that they will also be able to use it as a means of interpretation in the future, drawing from other sources.

The teaching strategies used fulfilled the original aims of the project to a large extent. The North West Coast American culture and art objects proved to be of great interest to the children throughout the whole project. Most children learned how to use the computer program. Most importantly, the project showed another possibility for using the device of story as a means of interpreting art objects and creating one's own art via this device. However there were some constraints on the children's ideas which I should want to vary in the future. To achieve that, new strategies would be used for other projects which include the teaching of interpretation involving the notion of story in art. These would include:

- Allowing the children more freedom in their storytelling to interpret what they see;
- Giving children the opportunity to research into a culture more fully as part of looking at artefacts;
- Setting tasks which encourage children to use ideas derived from more extensive knowledge of original art objects, but with more time to devise and develop their own ideas in contemporary media.

FURTHER READING

Barnes, R. (1989) *Art, Design, And Topic Work 8–13*, London: Routledge.
Hitchcock, G. and Hughes, D. (1989) *Research and the Teacher*, London: Routledge.
Hopkins, D. (1985) *A Teacher's Guide to Classroom Research*, Milton Keynes: Open University Press.
Taylor, R. (1986) *Educating for Art: Critical Response and Development*, Harlow: Longman.

Chapter 15

In search of Mundesley totems

Jeny Walding

Mundesley First School is on the North Norfolk coast, about half a mile from the sea. There are 128 children in the school between the ages of four and eight. My class consists of twenty-four Year 2 and Year 3 children. This project was done by the whole class, but to make the research manageable I decided to base it on six Year 3 children, Sarah, Isobel, Stuart, Neville, Alex and Tony. I chose them because they showed particular curiosity in the research project, they are articulate, are not shy to express an opinion, and are all in my judgement imaginative and creative.

When I first saw the exhibits in the Sainsbury Collection, I was especially attracted to the work of the North West Pacific Coast of America – by the abundance of design even on the most ordinary article such as a comb or a spoon, by the designs themselves, and by the social significance of the exhibits, such as the ceremonies where the grease bowl (Plate 15.1), the rattle and the head-dress frontlet would be used. I also thought it would be appropriate to study this coastal culture, because Mundesley is also on the coast at approximately the same latitude, and the people in both places relied on the sea for much of their livelihood in the past.

Because I was enthusiastic and wanted to know more about the culture, I thought my class would feel the same. The idea of researching totems came later when I was thinking about the aspect on which I was going to concentrate. As my knowledge of the Pacific North West Coast of America, and totems in particular, was initially almost non-existent, I realised that I would have to do a lot of research into the subject before I could pass on the relevant information to my class.

My teaching aims were:

- To give the children opportunities for sketching as a means of recording what they observe;
- To give them an opportunity to see the original work of artists and sculptors;
- To teach them about the art of a different culture;

Plate 15.1 Grease bowl (wood) North West Coast of America (Robert and Lisa Sainsbury Collection; photograph: James Austin)

- To encourage the children to plan their work and then to try to work from their plan;
- To extend the experience of using a variety of materials;
- To teach the meaning of totems, and the nature and purpose of totem poles.

The strategies I used to fulfil these aims are reported in this chapter. They were the main focus of the research, the aims of which were:

- To record the pupils' responses to the art objects of the Pacific North West Coast;
- To seek evidence of their understanding of aspects of that culture;
- To see how far they could relate ideas from one culture to their own community.

I hoped to achieve my teaching aims by studying the art objects and by placing these in context through telling legends from the native people, by showing photographs and slides, and by telling the pupils about totem designs and totem poles. The practical artwork was intended to reinforce their understanding at each stage.

As this would be the first time that any of the children had visited an art gallery, I wanted to prepare them for recording some of what they would see, and so I decided to spend some time on an observational drawing of a familiar object. The children were asked to take off one shoe and make a very careful drawing of it. They had a variety of media which they could use: pencil crayon, wax crayons, felt tips and some new pastel crayons in black, sienna and white. They could also use paper in differing colours and sizes and shapes. They were very amused by the exercise and after drawing the shoe on the table in front of them, they had to put it on the floor and make a second drawing looking at it from above. I displayed the drawings round the room and they tried to identify which drawing belonged to which shoe. The finished results were better than I had expected and several children were so intrigued by the effect created by pastels that they did several more drawings.

THE VISIT

I had told the class about the Sainsbury Centre in preparation for the visit. Initially the children were free to look round the Collection. I had also chosen some specific exhibits for them to look at and comment on. The children had sheets on which I had printed the things they had to search for and some questions for discussion with their group leaders. They had to look for objects from the North West Coast of America: an oolichan (eulachon) grease bowl; a head-dress frontlet; a raven rattle. These were to be the focus for my research topic.

The groups discussed these objects with their group leaders and the guides told them about some exhibits. I worked with my group of six and tape-recorded their responses. They were very inquisitive and were so interested in each object that we did not discuss everything on the sheet. They drew on their prior knowledge in seeking to understand the objects and I found their comparison of the head-dress frontlet to the mask of Tutankhamun an interesting idea. I also liked their guesses about the abalone shell which decorates the head-dress frontlet:

SARAH   It looks like a god.
ISOBEL   It could be an animal – like a lion. Bit like Tutankhamun.
SARAH   Where the jewels are, it looks like the sea because of all the colours.
J.W.   Are they jewels?
OTHERS   They are more like stones.
SARAH   Where the waves go over.
J.W.   What do you think it is? Look around it.
SEVERAL   It's a mask! There are holes.
SARAH   It could be an Indian mask to scare predators away.
ALEX   They might put it on the back of their heads [*he saw there were no eye holes*] to scare lions away.

[*Discussion about how the mask might be worn.*]

J.W.   When would you wear it?
TONY   When you're going out somewhere.

NEVILLE When you're going somewhere nice.
ALEX An emperor's party.

They were all very intrigued by the amount of design on the rattle and tried to work out what animals were represented and how many were portrayed:

SARAH It looks like a goblin.
NEVILLE He's putting his tongue out. It might be a devil because he's red.
SARAH I think it's a goblin because gods would have had posher clothes on – crowns.
ALEX Yes, but gods could have had armies of goblins and everything.
SARAH Yes, but gods can do stuff, stuff they can do on their own – they don't need armies because they are good.
J.W. How would you make it rattle?
NEVILLE Try to put your hand through and shake it.
TONY That piece of wood near the bottom, you could get your fingers in there.
J.W. What's this near the bottom?
ALEX It's like elastic stuff.
J.W. Yes, it's a sinew again for binding it round. What would happen if you took it off?
NEVILLE It might fall to bits because it's got a crack down there and that's holding it together.
J.W. If that's a rattle and that bit keeps it together, why might you want to take it apart?
SARAH You wouldn't take it apart.
ALEX You'd take it apart and put something in it to make it rattle.

Their thought about the oolichan (eulachon) grease bowl showed a similar depth of inquisitiveness, and a willingness to use the information which was available to them:

ISOBEL It's a bowl – it's a beaver from South Alaska.
SARAH It looks like you put the paints in there to mix them around.
ALEX No, you put grease in there!
J.W. What's it made from?
TONY Pottery.
ALEX Wood – it says wood. They must have been very clever.
J.W. Who made it?
ISOBEL The people from South Alaska Tlingit.

[*Discussion about pronunciation.*]

J.W.   What animal does this look like?

ALL   Beaver.

ALEX   It's probably chewing a baboon [bamboo] shoot!

J.W.   What do you think was put inside it?

ALL   Grease.

ALEX   Cooking oil – cooking oil, some sort of grease.

NEVILLE   It might be a cup.

J.W.   Can you see those little holes? What do you think those were for?

STUART   They could hang it round their neck.

SARAH   They could dip their hands in to pray for the gods.

[*They are told about the oolichan or candle fish.*]

TONY   It's gone all red.

SARAH   It's like varnish.

J.W.   Is it varnish?

ALEX   I don't think they'd have had varnish then.

J.W.   It looks just like varnish. What could it be?

SARAH   It could be dried grease. There might have been so much grease, that it came out of that hole and went all over there.

THE START OF FOLLOW-UP WORK

After the visit I told the children that we were going to find out more about the art of the native people of the North West Coast of America. We found the area on a globe and in an atlas. I told them something of the geography of the region and how the people had first populated America by crossing the Bering Strait, thousands of years ago. They were told about the richness of resources both in the sea and on land. From what they had seen at the gallery they guessed at some of the types of animals and fish living in the region.

Having discussed what animals would be important to the people, they thought about what animals were important in their own area. They suggested sheep, crabs, lobsters, fish of various kinds, and sea gulls. They were asked if they could see any similarities between local life and the life of the North West Coast people. They thought that both lived by the sea so the fishing was very important to both. They thought, from what they had been told about the art objects, that the people there probably had lots of parties, because they would dress up in the frontlet, use the raven rattle in their dances and pass round oil in bowls like the oolichan grease bowl. In storytime that day I told them the story of the raven opening the secret box and carrying out the light which broke into pieces – the largest becoming the sun and moon and the smaller pieces becoming the stars. I compared it with our story of the Creation in the Bible.

STUDYING DESIGN

Before we could begin a search for local comparisons equivalent to totems, I needed to learn more about the art of the North West Coast myself. We had talked about the importance of animals in both cultures and had seen some of the designs used on masks, spoons, head-dresses, combs, blankets and so on: work in three dimensional sculpture, in flat design, and in a variety of materials. Here we were looking at images and their meanings, coming to appreciate that the art has 'vitality and profound meaning for those of its culture . . . the social and spiritual order was visually confirmed through their art' (Stewart 1979). Many of the objects portrayed the crest of their owner, as well as declaring the owner's lineage, wealth and status. Some had mythical or spiritual meanings. These seemed to be crucial ideas to understand the art of the North West Coast, beyond the aesthetic appreciation with which I had begun. However, at this stage in my teaching I chose to familiarise the children with the motifs traditionally used by the people. Illustrations were used to identify and separate out the various motifs and designs based on the animals of the region – killer whale, raven, bear, dogfish, salmon, etc.

The children decided that fish were important to their own village and worked on a design using an outline of a fish shape, which they filled with three of the basic motifs. I limited the colours to red, black, blue-green and white as these colours were frequently used in the objects we had seen. The outline was filled using the characteristic design motifs of North West Coast images.

The study of totem poles was done from slides, books and photographs. The animal designs on the totems are symmetrical, so I decided to do some work on symmetry and mapping. I also told the story of the thunderbird. The thunderbird was a large mythical bird which could eat whales. Its wings made the sound of thunder. Lightning was produced when the bird threw a kind of snake, called a lightning snake, at a whale in order to kill it. One of the illustrations we had looked at showed a thunderbird carrying off a whale.

As so many thunderbirds feature on totem poles I wanted the children to be familiar with the story and to know what they looked like in carved form. I had prepared a worksheet on squared paper showing half of a canoe, so that the children would grasp the idea of symmetry using a simple shape, and also half of a thunderbird. The children were to mirror the other half. They coloured in the shapes using the same colours as for the fish designs, but now they had to remember to make sure they coloured in the bird symmetrically.

The introduction to these design principles seemed to be necessary preparation for a planned extension to the project – the construction of large totem sculptures. Through the initial restrictions of, and practice with, the motifs, the colours, the layouts, and now the symmetrical use of these, my intention was to prepare the children to be able to apply these ideas in combination, to their versions of this significant art form. I thought the children would find it easier to plan the symmetrical creatures on their totem poles after these exercises.

A SEARCH FOR UNDERSTANDING

I wanted to know how much knowledge my group had so far acquired about the North West Coast people and their art. I asked them to try to remember as much as they could from the project. They could remember about the designs and colours they used, that the people had ceremonies and used special objects at these ceremonies. They discussed the raven rattle, head-dress frontlet and grease bowls. They remembered some of the legends, and the animals who were important to the people, and that these featured on totems, as decoration on houses, and in objects used in the houses.

Alex and Sarah tried to imagine what it must have been like living there in the past. Their considerations were extensive and provided source material for later discussion in the class. A short extract illustrates this:

> It was probably scary to live there, especially at night for the kids, because animals could come at night into their camp. You'd have to be there to really understand it. You'd have to train to make totem poles – practise making them until they are really good. The girls would probably cook and fetch water and the boys would probably make things, do carving and go hunting. They must have had their own sort of fighting. People came and built on their land. They would need a sort of council – a president, head people. The Indians were having a happy time until the Europeans came.

We discussed what they had said, and I helped the children to understand those things that they were confused about, as well as picking up points for discussion. Their understanding of the culture seemed sufficient to extend work on the meaning of totems and totemism. Totem is said to come from the Cree word 'opotema', which means 'one's relations'. I said to the children that I found it hard to understand what a totem was and that we would try to find out what it meant before we started to design our own totem poles. Kirsty suggested looking in our school library, and came back and told us what she had found:

> The word totem comes from the language of the Ojibways. A totem is usually some kind of animal. People treat it in special ways, the animal totem is supposed to be an ancestor of the tribe. The people in the tribe are not allowed to eat or touch that animal except on special

days. They think it will give them strength. Some of the animals are the bear, the wolf, the turtle, the deer and the eagle. Sometimes the pole tells the family history in pictures.

(*Children's Encyclopaedia Britannica*)

We talked about these ideas, and that in some ways totem designs were like a family badge or crest. If a stranger came to the village, he might know which house would be friendly to him by the totem pole or design painted on each house. Originally, house posts were decorated with the family totem and these developed into tall totem poles. I showed the children several photographs of totem poles, and some colour slides which included people standing near to them (Plate 15.2). It was the first time that they had been able to see them in proportion to people and they were very surprised at the height. They wondered whether they were carved in a standing position or whether the people laid the tree trunk down, carved it and then stood it up again. Alex said that they would not be able to do the sticking out bits properly while it was lying down. Their puzzling was resolved by further photographic evidence (Plate 15.3).

We tried to identify what animals were represented. They could see very clearly that the poles were symmetrical, what colours had been used and how every part is filled with motifs. They recognised that the size of the head of each creature is generally enlarged in proportion to the rest, and that the eyes, eyebrows, nose and mouth are given prominence. Illustrations of totem poles were used to get ideas for designing their own totems and to extend the opportunity for them to see the designs used in North West Coast art. I did not want them to copy the designs but hoped it would give them an increased awareness of the individuality of the designs. This was intended to show that each artist would make important decisions about their particular piece of work, within the traditions of the art forms.

A SEARCH FOR PERSONAL RELEVANCE

The North West Coast people had a high opinion of wildlife – their cunning, their hunting instinct, their swiftness of foot, and the fact that they never lacked food (Spence 1994). It is no wonder that they admired them and placed themselves under the protection of the bird or animal whose attribute was particularly respected. After a few generations, tribes would start to think of these animals as their ancestors.

I encouraged the children to think about animals that might be appropriate for their own family totems. Stuart said, 'My family was in the army, perhaps I would do a dragon!' We also had a discussion about where we might see evidence which could raise memories of our ancestors.

Plate 15.2 Recently carved totem pole in contemporary setting, Duncan, British Columbia, 1990 (photograph: Les Tickle)

Plate 15.3 Contemporary totem carving, Duncan, British Columbia, 1990 (photograph: Les Tickle)

Suggestions included: gravestones and old photographs; the idea that we could learn more about them from our parents and grandparents; and the possibility of owning things that they had given to us to remind us of them. I asked the children to draw an animal that was significant to them or their family and to do drawings for a totem pole design if they wanted to.

Sarah chose animal designs for her family but did not say why they were appropriate to each member (Figure 15.1). Tony, however, thought of an appropriate animal for everybody (Figure 15.2)

TONY   My Daddy is an owl because he is quite clever at making musical instruments. My Mum is a beaver because she has brown hair and brown skin. I am an eagle because I have sharp eyes. Georgina is a bear because she has sharp hands and sharp teeth. Jenny is a sloth because she doesn't like getting up in the morning.

Others described their designs for totem poles:

NEVILLE   On my totem I had an eagle because my dad has good eyesight.
STUART   I put a thunderbird at the top because that's what they often did (Figure 15.3). The fish was because my great-grandad worked in a fish shop. The snake was because my great, great grandad killed a snake in Africa, the books was because my grandad prints books. The bagpipes because the Firths were Scottish, the rhino was because my dad owns a rhino jeep. The shell was because my dad works on Shell gas rigs and because when the sand covers the shells, it makes oil and gas.

When totem-making day arrived, the children were very excited. Eight children decided to paint cardboard boxes and planned to put them on top of each other to make a tall totem pole. Some children made poles from large cardboard tubes, fixing three together with newspaper strips to make a column 30 cm in diameter and 1.5 m high. They tackled the task with enthusiasm! They knew what they wanted to put on their totems and tackled the main technical problem of fixing the beaks, wings, tails, and so on, which were made in a variety of media, to the support columns.

A SEARCH FOR EVIDENCE IN THE COMMUNITY

Many European and Asiatic people have held comparable ideas and we should be able to find examples in our history. Crests are family symbols which were inherited from the days when people painted them on their shields as a form of identification or protection. We have adapted over the centuries stylised and sometimes mythical emblems of lions, dragons, and unicorns, which feature on coats of arms, bank signs, banners, and

Figure 15.1 Sarah's animal symbols

so on. We visited the village church searching for examples of what the children might regard as being comparable to totems, and wrote about what was found. Many picked the royal coat of arms. Isobel said that this was the Queen's totem. The animals on her totem were the lion and the unicorn. Some of the children said that the Union Jack and the British Legion flags were like totems, even though they were not animals, because only certain people were entitled to display them. Sarah drew a dove from one of the kneelers as a totem, because the dove was a symbol for peace. Stuart said that the poppies on the war memorial were like totems because they represented the brave men who had died in the war. Some of the children said the cross was like a totem because, whenever we see it, it reminds us that Christ died on the cross for us. Many of the children said that the crests of two local families were like totems. Some references and meanings were national symbols of rather different kinds (e.g. the flags, the poppies, the royal coat of arms), rather than precise equivalents to totems pertinent to the local community or to individuals or families. There are interesting conceptual issues and problems to tackle here, in terms of identifying with smaller and larger groups, and the use of particular kinds of symbols and art objects in the locality.

Figure 15.2 Tony's animal symbols for his family

Figure 15.3 Stuart's totem pole

CONCLUSIONS

It was difficult to end our project. It had become the most important part of our term's work and whenever the children had a chance to draw, they often included a totem. A display was arranged in our classroom and we sent invitations to all the parents. The parents of 17 out of the 24 children in my class came to look round, and the children became the guides. I was amused by Neville who had adopted my way of questioning to draw answers from children, and used it with parents. I was able to tape-record some of his technique:

NEVILLE   Now look carefully at the picture. What does it tell you about the sort of country the North West Coast people lived in?

[*Various suggestions.*]

NEVILLE   Now look at this mask. Can you guess what it's made from?

[*All guess.*]

NEVILLE   No, it's a shell called an abalone shell. Can you say that, a-b-a-l-o-n-e [*slowly*]? Well done!

After we had finished the project, I looked back to see how many of my teaching and research aims I had achieved. The children had without doubt learnt a great deal about the art and culture of the North West Coast – the informed way they passed on information to their parents and to children from other classes demonstrated that. Some of them, at least, had shown an understanding of the meaning of totems and totemism and had been able to make connections between some of the things they saw in the church as pictorial representations of an idea, or as crests which could only be used by specific families. They had also:

- Experienced at first hand the works of artists and sculptors and had discussed and shown an appreciation of them;
- Had several chances to represent what they observed by sketches;
- Worked practically and imaginatively in three dimensional work on totems;
- Used a range of materials for their artwork.

FURTHER READING

Boas, F. (1955) *Primitive Art*, New York: Dover Publications.
Bruggmann, M. and Gerber, P. R. (1987) *Indians of the North West Coast*, New York: Facts on File.
Chaplin, S. (1975) *North American Indians: 5–13 Projects*, London: Macdonald Educational.
Gardner, H. (1980) *Artful Scribbles*, London: Jill Norman.

Spence, L. (1994) *North American Indians: Myths and Legends*, Washington DC: Senate.
Steltzer, U. (1984) *A Haida Potlatch*, Seattle: University of Washington Press.
Stewart, H. (1979) *Looking at Indian Art of the North West Coast*, Seattle: University of Washington Press.

Index

Abbs, P. 11, 33
action research 2–3, 64–6, 181, 200, 202
Adler, M. 11
aesthetics 8–9, 31
Alexander, K. 11
Andrews, G. 30, 32, 132
animation 247
Anning, A. 114, 129
Archer, H. 125, 126
Arnheim, R. 11, 207
art: abstract 84, 184; avant-garde 17; as communication 182, 189–90, 192; cross-curricular links 209–13; definitions 185, 196, 197, 213–14; emotion 73–4, 79; knowledge and understanding 11, 18–19, 62; making of 4–5, 16, 25, 29, 31, 34, 62–3, 97–106; and mimicry 18, 26, 34, 83, 103; National Curriculum 1, 4–5, 13, 23–6, 29, 33, 64; realism 63–4, 80, 173, 177, 179, 217; storytelling 185–6, 237, 238, 246, 254; study of 4–5, 16, 30–1, 109; traditional/innovative 18, 22–3, 28
art criticism 31–2
art education 11–12, 29
art experiences 1–2, 12, 34–5
art gallery visit: behaviour 68, 142–3, 202; evaluation 60–1, 79–81, 106, 109, 123, 125, 130–1, 142–3, 164–5, 179, 191–2, 213–14, 230–6, 247–9, 263; family involvement 221, 225; find-a-friend technique 135–6, 137, 191, 204–5; interviews 207–9, 215–18; as learning experience 121–3, 202–3; preconceptions 196, 220–1; preparations 133–6, 191, 240–1; response 4, 90, 135, 205–7, 221, 225;

sketches 45–51, 71, 165, 241; structured 68, 71–6; unstructured 78, 169, 221, 252
art history 31
art movements 17–18
art objects 5–10, 26, 44–5, 63–4, 79, 134–5; *see also* artefacts; Inuit cultural objects
Art Show 168, 197
Art and Time computer program 237–8, 239, 244–5, 247
art-specialist teachers 12
artefacts: everyday/works of art 188; materials 241; musical instruments 199, 201; personality 241–2, 243–4, 246, 247; *see also* art objects; Inuit cultural objects
artistic maturation 62–3, 144–5
artistic style 34, 177–8
artists 10, 119–20, 226; art explorations 19–23; factual information 9; imagination 187, 189; influences 19–20, 83, 98, 102, 109; intentions 163–4, 175; reference books 175–6, 225, 226; relationships 16–17, 23; *see also* paintings; sculpture
artists-in-residence 12
Arts Council 86
Arts PROPEL Project 35
Arts in Schools, The 30
Atkins, R. 17, 18
Avercamp, Hendrick 186

baby sculpture 80
Bacon, Francis 21
Badderley, G. 81
Barnes, R. 62
Bassili, J. 160